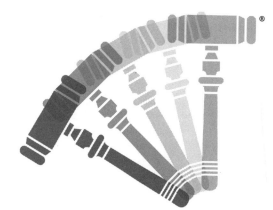

Casenote™ *Legal Briefs*

BUSINESS ORGANIZATIONS

Keyed to
Eisenberg's
Corporations and Other
Business Organizations

PUBLISHERS

1185 Avenue of the Americas, New York, NY 10036
www.aspenpublishers.com

This publication is designed to provide accurate and authoritative information in regard to the subject matter covered. It is sold with the understanding that the publisher is not engaged in rendering legal, accounting, or other professional services. If legal advice or other expert assistance is required, the services of a competent professional person should be sought.

— From a *Declaration of Principles* adopted jointly by
a Committee of the American Bar Association and a
Committee of Publishers and Associates

© 2002 Aspen Publishers, Inc.
A WoltersKluwer Company
www.aspenpublishers.com

Permissions
Aspen Publishers
1185 Avenue of the Americas
New York, NY 10036

Printed in the United States of America.

ISBN 0-7355-5176-6

2 3 4 5 6 7 8 9 0

About Aspen Publishers

Aspen Publishers, headquartered in New York City, is a leading information provider for attorneys, business professionals, and law students. Written by preeminent authorities, our products consist of analytical and practical information covering both U.S. and international topics. We publish in the full range of formats, including updated manuals, books, periodicals, CDs, and online products.

Our proprietary content is complemented by 2,500 legal databases, containing over 11 million documents, available through our Loislaw division. Aspen Publishers also offers a wide range of topical legal and business databases linked to Loislaw's primary material. Our mission is to provide accurate, timely, and authoritative content in easily accessible formats, supported by unmatched customer care.

To order any Aspen Publishers title, go to *www.aspenpublishers.com* or call 1-800-638-8437.

For more information on Loislaw products, go to *www.loislaw.com* or call 1-800-364-2512.

For Customer Care issues, e-mail CustomerCare@aspenpublishers.com; call 1-800-234-1660; or fax 1-800-901-9075.

Aspen Publishers
A Wolters Kluwer Company

FORMAT FOR THE CASENOTE LEGAL BRIEF

PARTY ID: Quick identification of the relationship between the parties.

NATURE OF CASE: This section identifies the form of action (e.g., breach of contract, negligence, battery), the type of proceeding (e.g., demurrer, appeal from trial court's jury instructions) or the relief sought (e.g., damages, injunction, criminal sanctions).

NATURE OF CASE: Appeal from judgment affirming verdict for plaintiff seeking damages for personal injury.

FACT SUMMARY: This is included to refresh the student's memory and can be used as a quick reminder of the facts.

FACT SUMMARY: Helen Palsgraf (P) was injured on R.R.'s (D) train platform when R.R.'s (D) guard helped a passenger aboard a moving train, causing his package to fall on the tracks. The package contained fireworks which exploded, creating a shock that tipped a scale onto Palsgraf (P).

CONCISE RULE OF LAW: Summarizes the general principle of law that the case illustrates. It may be used for instant recall of the court's holding and for classroom discussion or home review.

CONCISE RULE OF LAW: The risk reasonably to be perceived defines the duty to be obeyed.

FACTS: This section contains all relevant facts of the case, including the contentions of the parties and the lower court holdings. It is written in a logical order to give the student a clear understanding of the case. The plaintiff and defendant are identified by their proper names throughout and are always labeled with a (P) or (D).

FACTS: Helen Palsgraf (P) purchased a ticket to Rockaway Beach from R.R. (D) and was waiting on the train platform. As she waited, two men ran to catch a train that was pulling out from the platform. The first man jumped aboard, but the second man, who appeared as if he might fall, was helped aboard by the guard on the train who had kept the door open so they could jump aboard. A guard on the platform also helped by pushing him onto the train. The man was carrying a package wrapped in newspaper. In the process, the man dropped his package, which fell on the tracks. The package contained fireworks and exploded. The shock of the explosion was apparently of great enough strength to tip over some scales at the other end of the platform, which fell on Palsgraf (P) and injured her. A jury awarded her damages, and R.R. (D) appealed.

ISSUE: The issue is a concise question that brings out the essence of the opinion as it relates to the section of the casebook in which the case appears. Both substantive and procedural issues are included if relevant to the decision.

ISSUE: Does the risk reasonably to be perceived define the duty to be obeyed?

HOLDING AND DECISION: This section offers a clear and in-depth discussion of the rule of the case and the court's rationale. It is written in easy-to-understand language and answers the issue(s) presented by applying the law to the facts of the case. When relevant, it includes a thorough discussion of the exceptions to the case as listed by the court, any major cites to other cases on point, and the names of the judges who wrote the decisions.

HOLDING AND DECISION: (Cardozo, C.J.) Yes. The risk reasonably to be perceived defines the duty to be obeyed. If there is no foreseeable hazard to the injured party as the result of a seemingly innocent act, the act does not become a tort because it happened to be a wrong as to another. If the wrong was not willful, the plaintiff must show that the act as to her had such great and apparent possibilities of danger as to entitle her to protection. Negligence in the abstract is not enough upon which to base liability. Negligence is a relative concept, evolving out of the common law doctrine of trespass on the case. To establish liability, the defendant must owe a legal duty of reasonable care to the injured party. A cause of action in tort will lie where harm, though unintended, could have been averted or avoided by observance of such a duty. The scope of the duty is limited by the range of danger that a reasonable person could foresee. In this case, there was nothing to suggest from the appearance of the parcel or otherwise that the parcel contained fireworks. The guard could not reasonably have had any warning of a threat to Palsgraf (P), and R.R. (D) therefore cannot be held liable. Judgment is reversed in favor of R.R. (D).

CONCURRENCE / DISSENT: All concurrences and dissents are briefed whenever they are included by the casebook editor.

DISSENT: (Andrews, J.) The concept that there is no negligence unless R.R. (D) owes a legal duty to take care as to Palsgraf (P) herself is too narrow. Everyone owes to the world at large the duty of refraining from those acts that may unreasonably threaten the safety of others. If the guard's action was negligent as to those nearby, it was also negligent as to those outside what might be termed the "danger zone." For Palsgraf (P) to recover, R.R.'s (D) negligence must have been the proximate cause of her injury, a question of fact for the jury.

EDITOR'S ANALYSIS: This last paragraph gives the student a broad understanding of where the case "fits in" with other cases in the section of the book and with the entire course. It is a hornbook-style discussion indicating whether the case is a majority or minority opinion and comparing the principal case with other cases in the casebook. It may also provide analysis from restatements, uniform codes, and law review articles. The editor's analysis will prove to be invaluable to classroom discussion.

EDITOR'S ANALYSIS: The majority defined the limit of the defendant's liability in terms of the danger that a reasonable person in defendant's situation would have perceived. The dissent argued that the limitation should not be placed on liability, but rather on damages. Judge Andrews suggested that only injuries that would not have happened but for R.R.'s (D) negligence should be compensable. Both the majority and dissent recognized the policy-driven need to limit liability for negligent acts, seeking, in the words of Judge Andrews, to define a framework "that will be practical and in keeping with the general understanding of mankind." The Restatement (Second) of Torts has accepted Judge Cardozo's view.

QUICKNOTES

QUICKNOTES: Conveniently defines legal terms found in the case and summarizes the nature of any statutes, codes, or rules referred to in the text.

FORESEEABILITY – The reasonable anticipation that damage is a likely result from certain acts or omissions.

NEGLIGENCE - Failure to exercise that degree of care which a person of ordinary prudence would exercise under similar circumstances.

PROXIMATE CAUSE – Something which in natural and continuous sequence, unbroken by any new intervening cause, produces an event, and without which the injury would not have occurred.

NOTE TO STUDENTS

Aspen Publishers is proud to offer *Casenote Legal Briefs*—continuing thirty years of publishing America's best-selling legal briefs.

Casenote Legal Briefs are designed to help you save time when briefing assigned cases. Organized under convenient headings, they show you how to abstract the basic facts and holdings from the text of the actual opinions handed down by the courts. Used as part of a rigorous study regime, they can help you spend more time analyzing and critiquing points of law than on copying out bits and pieces of judicial opinions into your notebook or outline.

Casenote Legal Briefs should never be used as a substitute for assigned casebook readings. They work best when read as a follow-up to reviewing the underlying opinions themselves. Students who try to avoid reading and digesting the judicial opinions in their casebooks or on-line sources will end up shortchanging themselves in the long run. The ability to absorb, critique, and restate the dynamic and complex elements of case law decisions is crucial to your success in law school and beyond. It cannot be developed vicariously.

Casenote Legal Briefs represent but one of the many offerings in Aspen's Study Aid Timeline, which includes:

- Casenotes *Legal Briefs*
- Emanuel *Outlines*
- *Examples & Explanations* Series
- *Introduction to Law* Series
- Emanuel *Law in a Flash* Flashcards
- Emanuel *CrunchTime* Series

Each of these series is designed to provide you with easy-to-understand explanations of complex points of law. Each volume offers guidance on the principles of legal analysis and, consulted regularly, will hone your ability to spot relevant issues. We have titles that will help you prepare for class, prepare for your exams, and enhance your general comprehension of the law along the way.

To find out more about Aspen Study Aid publications, visit us on-line at www.aspenpublishers.com or e-mail us at legaledu@aspenpubl.com. We'll be happy to assist you.

Free access to Briefs on-line!

● Download the cases you want in your notes or outlines using the full cut-and-paste feature accompanying our on-line briefs. Please fill out this form for full access to this useful feature. No photocopies of this form will be accepted.

① **Name:** _____ **Phone:** (____) _____

Address: _____ **Apt.:** _____

City: _____ **State:** _____ **ZIP Code:** _____

Law School: _____ **Year (circle one):** 1st   2nd   3rd

② **Cut out the UPC found on the lower left-hand corner of the back cover of this book. Staple the UPC inside this box. Only the original UPC from the book cover will be accepted. (No photocopies or store stickers are allowed.)**

> **Attach UPC inside this box.**

③ **E-mail:** _____ (Print LEGIBLY or you may not get access!)

④ **Title (course subject) of this book** _____

⑤ **Used with which casebook (provide author's name):** _____

⑥ **Mail the completed form to:**   Aspen Publishers, Inc.
Legal Education Division
Casenote On-line Access
675 Massachusetts Ave., 11th floor
Cambridge, MA 02139

I understand that on-line access is granted solely to the purchaser of this book for the academic year in which it was purchased. Any other usage is not authorized and will result in immediate termination of access. Sharing of codes is strictly prohibited.

_____
Signature

● Upon receipt of this completed form, you will be e-mailed codes so that you may access the Briefs for this Casenote Legal Brief. On-line Briefs may not be available for all titles. For a full list of available titles please check www.aspenpublishers.com/casenotes.

HOW TO BRIEF A CASE

A. DECIDE ON A FORMAT AND STICK TO IT

Structure is essential to a good brief. It enables you to arrange systematically the related parts that are scattered throughout most cases, thus making manageable and understandable what might otherwise seem to be an endless and unfathomable sea of information. There are, of course, an unlimited number of formats that can be utilized. However, it is best to find one that suits your needs and stick to it. Consistency breeds both efficiency and the security that when called upon you will know where to look in your brief for the information you are asked to give.

Any format, as long as it presents the essential elements of a case in an organized fashion, can be used. Experience, however, has led *Casenotes* to develop and utilize the following format because of its logical flow and universal applicability.

NATURE OF CASE: This is a brief statement of the legal character and procedural status of the case (e.g., "Appeal of a burglary conviction").

There are many different alternatives open to a litigant dissatisfied with a court ruling. The key to determining which one has been used is to discover *who is asking this court for what.*

This first entry in the brief should be kept as *short as possible.* The student should use the court's terminology if the student understands it. But since jurisdictions vary as to the titles of pleadings, the best entry is the one that apprises the student of who wants what in this proceeding, not the one that sounds most like the court's language.

CONCISE RULE OF LAW: A statement of the general principle of law that the case illustrates (e.g., "An acceptance that varies any term of the offer is considered a rejection and counteroffer").

Determining the rule of law of a case is a procedure similar to determining the issue of the case. Avoid being fooled by red herrings; there may be a few rules of law mentioned in the case excerpt, but usually only one is *the* rule with which the casebook editor is concerned. The techniques used to locate the issue, described below, may also be utilized to find the rule of law. Generally, your best guide is simply the chapter heading. It is a clue to the point the casebook editor seeks to make and should be kept in mind when reading every case in the respective section.

FACTS: A synopsis of only the essential facts of the case, i.e., those bearing upon or leading up to the issue.

The facts entry should be a short statement of the events and transactions that led one party to initiate legal proceedings against another in the first place. While some cases conveniently state the salient facts at the beginning of the decision, in other instances they will have to be culled from hiding places throughout the text, even from concurring and dissenting opinions. Some of the "facts" will often be in dispute and should be so noted. Conflicting evidence may be briefly pointed up. "Hard" facts must be included. Both must be *relevant* in order to be listed in the facts entry. It is impossible to tell what is relevant until the entire case is read, as the ultimate determination of the rights and liabilities of the parties may turn on something buried deep in the opinion.

The facts entry should never be longer than one to three *short* sentences.

It is often helpful to identify the role played by a party in a given context. For example, in a construction contract case the identification of a party as the "contractor" or "builder" alleviates the need to tell that that party was the one who was supposed to have built the house.

It is always helpful, and a good general practice, to identify the "plaintiff" and the "defendant." This may seem elementary and uncomplicated, but, especially in view of the creative editing practiced by some casebook editors, it is sometimes a difficult or even impossible task. Bear in mind that the *party presently* seeking something from this court may not be the plaintiff, and that sometimes only the cross-claim of a defendant is treated in the excerpt. Confusing or misaligning the parties can ruin your analysis and understanding of the case.

ISSUE: A statement of the general legal question answered by or illustrated in the case. For clarity, the issue is best put in the form of a question capable of a "yes" or "no" answer. In reality, the issue is simply the Concise Rule of Law put in the form of a question (e.g., "May an offer be accepted by performance?").

The major problem presented in discerning what is *the* issue in the case is that an opinion usually purports to raise and answer several questions. However, except for rare cases, only one such question is really the issue in the case. Collateral issues not necessary to the resolution of the matter in controversy are handled by the court by language known as *"obiter dictum"* or merely *"dictum."* While dicta may be included later in the brief, it has no place under the issue heading.

To find the issue, the student again asks *who wants what* and then goes on to ask *why did that party succeed or fail in getting it.* Once this is determined, the "why" should be turned into a question.

The complexity of the issues in the cases will vary, but in all cases a single-sentence question should sum up the issue. *In a few cases,* there will be two, or even more rarely, three issues of equal importance to the resolution of the case. Each should be expressed in a single-sentence question.

Since many issues are resolved by a court in coming to a final disposition of a case, the casebook editor will reproduce the portion of the opinion containing the issue or issues most relevant to the area of law under scrutiny. A noted law professor gave this advice: "Close the book; look at the title on the cover." Chances are, if it is Property, the student need not concern himself with whether, for example, the federal government's treatment of the plaintiff's land really raises a federal question sufficient to support jurisdiction on this ground in federal court.

The same rule applies to chapter headings designating sub-areas within the subjects. They tip the student off as to what the text is designed to teach. The cases are arranged in a casebook to show a progression or development of the law, so that the preceding cases may also help.

It is also most important to remember to *read the notes and questions* at the end of a case to determine what the editors wanted the student to have gleaned from it.

HOLDING AND DECISION: This section should succinctly explain the rationale of the court in arriving at its decision. In capsulizing the "reasoning" of the court, it should always include an application of the general rule or rules of law to the specific facts of the case. Hidden justifications come to light in this entry; the reasons for the state of the law, the public policies, the biases and prejudices, those considerations that influence the justices' thinking and, ultimately, the outcome of the case. At the end, there should be a short indication of the disposition or procedural resolution of the case (e.g., "Decision of the trial court for Mr. Smith (P) reversed").

The foregoing format is designed to help you "digest" the reams of case material with which you will be faced in your law school career. Once mastered by practice, it will place at your fingertips the information the authors of your casebooks have sought to impart to you in case-by-case illustration and analysis.

B.   BE AS ECONOMICAL AS POSSIBLE IN BRIEFING CASES

Once armed with a format that encourages succinctness, it is as important to be economical with regard to the time spent on the actual reading of the case as it is to be economical in the writing of the brief itself. This does not mean "skimming" a case. Rather, it means reading the case with an "eye" trained to recognize into which "section" of your brief a particular passage or line fits and having a system for quickly and precisely marking the case so that the passages fitting any one particular part of the brief can be easily identified and brought together in a concise and accurate manner when the brief is actually written.

It is of no use to simply repeat everything in the opinion of the court; the student should only record enough information to trigger his or her recollection of what the court said. Nevertheless, an accurate statement of the "law of the case," i.e., the legal principle applied to the facts, is absolutely essential to class preparation and to learning the law under the case method.

To that end, it is important to develop a "shorthand" that you can use to make margin notations. These notations will tell you at a glance in which section of the brief you will be placing that particular passage or portion of the opinion.

Some students prefer to underline all the salient portions of the opinion (with a pencil or colored underliner marker), making marginal notations as they go along. Others prefer the color-coded method of underlining, utilizing different colors of markers to underline the salient portions of the case, each separate color being used to represent a different section of the brief. For example, blue underlining could be used for passages relating to the concise rule of law, yellow for those relating to the issue, and green for those relating to the holding and decision, etc. While it has its advocates, the color-coded method can be confusing and time-consuming (all that time spent on changing colored markers). Furthermore, it can interfere with the continuity and concentration many students deem essential to the reading of a case for maximum comprehension. In the end, however, it is a matter of personal preference and style. Just remember, whatever method you use, underlining must be used sparingly or its value is lost.

For those who take the marginal notation route, an efficient and easy method is to go along underlining the key portions of the case and placing in the margin alongside them the following "markers" to indicate where a particular passage or line "belongs" in the brief you will write:

N   (NATURE OF CASE)
CR   (CONCISE RULE OF LAW)
I   (ISSUE)
HC   (HOLDING AND DECISION, relates to the CONCISE RULE OF LAW behind the decision)
HR   (HOLDING AND DECISION, gives the RATIONALE or reasoning behind the decision)
HA   (HOLDING AND DECISION, APPLIES the general principle(s) of law to the facts of the case to arrive at the decision)

Remember that a particular passage may well contain information necessary to more than one part of your brief, in which case you simply note that in the margin. If you are using the color-coded underlining method instead of margin notation, simply make asterisks or checks in the margin next to the passage in question in the colors that indicate the additional sections of the brief where it might be utilized.

The economy of utilizing "shorthand" in marking cases for briefing can be maintained in the actual brief writing process itself by utilizing "law student shorthand" within the brief. There are many commonly used words and phrases for which abbreviations can be substituted in your briefs (and in your class notes also). You can develop abbreviations that are personal to you and which will save you a lot of time. A reference list of briefing abbreviations will be found elsewhere in this book.

C. USE BOTH THE BRIEFING PROCESS AND THE BRIEF AS A LEARNING TOOL

Now that you have a format and the tools for briefing cases efficiently, the most important thing is to make the time spent in briefing profitable to you and to make the most advantageous use of the briefs you create. Of course, the briefs are invaluable for classroom reference when you are called upon to explain or analyze a particular case. However, they are also useful in reviewing for exams. A quick glance at the fact summary should bring the case to mind, and a rereading of the concise rule of law should enable you to go over the underlying legal concept in your mind, how it was applied in that particular case, and how it might apply in other factual settings.

As to the value to be derived from engaging in the briefing process itself, there is an immediate benefit that arises from being forced to sift through the essential facts and reasoning from the court's opinion and to succinctly express them in your own words in your brief. The process ensures that you understand the case and the point that it illustrates, and that means you will be ready to absorb further analysis and information brought forth in class. It also ensures you will have something to say when called upon in class. The briefing process helps develop a mental agility for getting to the *gist* of a case and for identifying, expounding on, and applying the legal concepts and issues found there. Of most immediate concern, that is the mental process on which you must rely in taking law school examinations. Of more lasting concern, it is also the mental process upon which a lawyer relies in serving his clients and in making his living.

ABBREVIATIONS FOR BRIEFING

acceptance	acp
affirmed	aff
answer	ans
assumption of risk	a/r
attorney	atty
beyond a reasonable doubt	b/r/d
bona fide purchaser	BFP
breach of contract	br/k
cause of action	c/a
common law	c/l
Constitution	Con
constitutional	con
contract	K
contributory negligence	c/n
cross	x
cross-complaint	x/c
cross-examination	x/ex
cruel and unusual punishment	c/u/p
defendant	D
dismissed	dis
double jeopardy	d/j
due process	d/p
equal protection	e/p
equity	eq
evidence	ev
exclude	exc
exclusionary rule	exc/r
felony	f/n
freedom of speech	f/s
good faith	g/f
habeas corpus	h/c
hearsay	hr
husband	H
in loco parentis	ILP
injunction	inj
inter vivos	I/v
joint tenancy	j/t
judgment	judgt
jurisdiction	jur
last clear chance	LCC
long-arm statute	LAS
majority view	maj
meeting of minds	MOM
minority view	min
Miranda warnings	Mir/w
Miranda rule	Mir/r
negligence	neg
notice	ntc
nuisance	nus
obligation	ob
obscene	obs

offer	O
offeree	OE
offeror	OR
ordinance	ord
pain and suffering	p/s
parol evidence	p/e
plaintiff	P
prima facie	p/f
probable cause	p/c
proximate cause	px/c
real property	r/p
reasonable doubt	r/d
reasonable man	r/m
rebuttable presumption	rb/p
remanded	rem
res ipsa loquitur	RIL
respondeat superior	r/s
Restatement	RS
reversed	rev
Rule Against Perpetuities	RAP
search and seizure	s/s
search warrant	s/w
self-defense	s/d
specific performance	s/p
statute of limitations	S/L
statute of frauds	S/F
statute	S
summary judgment	s/j
tenancy in common	t/c
tenancy at will	t/w
tenant	t
third party	TP
third party beneficiary	TPB
transferred intent	TI
unconscionable	uncon
unconstitutional	unconst
undue influence	u/e
Uniform Commercial Code	UCC
unilateral	uni
vendee	VE
vendor	VR
versus	v
void for vagueness	VFV
weight of the evidence	w/e
weight of authority	w/a
wife	W
with	w/
within	w/i
without prejudice	w/o/p
without	w/o
wrongful death	wr/d

TABLE OF CASES

Continued on next page.

TABLE OF CASES (Continued)

CHAPTER 1
AGENCY

QUICK REFERENCE RULES OF LAW

1. **Agent's duty of loyalty.** Fidelity in an agent is what is aimed at, and, as a means of securing it, the law will not permit him to place himself in a position in which he may be tempted by his own private interests to disregard those of the principal. (Tarnowski v. Resop)

   [For more information on agency, see Casenote Law Outline on Corporations, Chapter 1, § I, The Partnership.]

2. **Authority.** An incorporator may be held personally liable for the debts of a corporation if he or she acts on behalf of the company knowing that no valid incorporation took place. (Morris Oil Co. v. Rainbow Oilfield Trucking, Inc.)

TARNOWSKI v. RESOP

Buyer (P) v. Agent (D)

Minn. Sup. Ct., 51 N.W.2d 801 (1952).

NATURE OF CASE: Appeal from grant of rescission of sales contract.

FACT SUMMARY: Tarnowski (P) contended that Resop (D), while acting as agent for him, collected a secret commission, for consummating a sale, and that the representations about the business made by Resop (D) were fraudulent.

CONCISE RULE OF LAW: Fidelity in an agent is what is aimed at, and, as a means of securing it, the law will not permit him to place himself in a position in which he may be tempted by his own private interests to disregard those of the principal.

FACTS: Tarnowski (P) hired Resop (D) as his agent to investigate and negotiate for the purchase of a coin-operated machine route. Relying on the advice of Resop (D) and the investigation he had made, Tarnowski (P) bought such a business from Loechler and Mayer. Tarnowski (P) contended that Resop (D) represented that he had done a thorough investigation of the route. As a matter of fact, Resop (D) had made only a superficial investigation and had adopted false representations of Loechler and Mayer as to the health of the business and had passed them on to Tarnowski (P) as his own. Tarnowski (P) also contended that Resop (D) collected a secret commission from Loechler and Mayer for consummating the sale. Tarnowski (P) then sued Resop (D), pleading rescission of the contract and demanding that his sales investment be returned. The jury returned a verdict for Tarnowski (P), and Resop (D) appealed.

ISSUE: Is fidelity in an agent what is aimed at, and, as a means of securing it, will the law not permit him to place himself in a position in which he may be tempted by his own private interests to disregard those of the principal?

HOLDING AND DECISION: (Knutson, J.) Yes. Fidelity in an agent is what is aimed at, and, as a means of securing it, the law will not permit him to place himself in a position in which he may be tempted by his own private interests to disregard those of the principal. It is not material that no actual injury to the principal resulted, or that the policy recommended may have been for its best interest. It is enough to know that the agent in fact placed himself in such relations that he might be tempted by his own interests to disregard those of his principal. Here, Resop (D) received a secret commission of $2,000 from Loechler and Mayer, for making false representations regarding the health of the subject business to Tarnowski (P). Thus, Tarnowski (P) has the absolute right to recover the money that he invested in the business as Resop (D) accepted a secret commission to perform his duties and, in doing so, placed his interests above those of Tarnowski (P). Affirmed.

EDITOR'S ANALYSIS: Usually, an agent's primary duty is to make profits for the principal. His duty to account includes accounting for any unexpected and incidental accretions whether or not received in violation of duty. Thus, an agent who, without the principal's knowledge, receives something in connection with a transaction conducted for the principal, has a duty to pay this to the principal.

[For more information on agency, see Casenote Law Outline on Corporations, Chapter 1, § I, The Partnership.]

QUICKNOTES

RESCIND - To cancel an agreement restoring the parties to their original positions prior to the formation of the contract.

RESCISSION - The canceling of an agreement and the return of the parties to their positions prior to the formation of the contract.

RESTATEMENT, AGENCY § 407(2) - If an agent has violated a duty of loyalty to the principal, a third party action does not prevent the principal from recovering profits from the agent.

RESTATEMENT, TORTS § 910 - A person injured by another's tort is entitled to recover all damages caused by the tort.

NOTES:

MORRIS OIL CO. v. RAINBOW OILFIELD TRUCKING, INC.
Oil company (P) v. Trucking company (D)
N.M. Ct. App., 106 N.M. 237 (1987).

NATURE OF CASE: Suit to recover monies owed.

FACT SUMMARY: Morris (P) sued to recover funds due for the delivery of diesel fuel from Dawn (D), who held receipts from a bankrupt Rainbow (D) operation.

CONCISE RULE OF LAW: An undisclosed principal is subject to liability to third parties with whom the agent contracts where such transactions are usual in the business conducted by the agent, even if the contract is contrary to the express direction of the principal.

FACTS: Dawn and Rainbow (D) entered into several contracts whereby Rainbow (D) was permitted to use Dawn's (D) certificate of public convenience and necessity in operating a trucking enterprise in Hobbs. The parties also entered into a terminal management agreement granting Dawn (D) complete control over Rainbow's (D) Hobbs operation. Rainbow (D) established a relationship with Morris (P) whereby Morris (P) installed a bulk dispenser at the Rainbow (D) terminal and periodically delivered diesel fuel. Rainbow (D) declared bankruptcy owing Morris (P) $25,000. When Rainbow (D) ceased operations, Dawn (D) was holding some $73,000 in receipts from the Hobbs (D) operation. Morris' (P) claim was never paid and it sought to garnish the $13,000 remaining in that account. The trial court entered a default judgment against Rainbow (D).

ISSUE: Is an undisclosed principal subject to liability to third parties with whom the agent contracts where such transactions are usual in the business conducted by the agent, even if the contract is contrary to the express direction of the principal?

HOLDING AND DECISION: (Garcia, J.) Yes. An undisclosed principal is subject to liability to third parties with whom the agent contracts where such transactions are usual in the business conducted by the agent, even if the contract is contrary to the express direction of the principal. Dawn (D) asserted one point of error on appeal, that the trial court erred in finding liability based on a principal-agent relationship between the defendants. Dawn (D) relies on two provisions from its terminal management agreement with Rainbow (D). Such reliance is misplaced. The agreement specifically states that Rainbow (D) may create liabilities for Dawn (D) in the ordinary course of business of operating the terminal. The liability to Morris (P) was thus created. Second, such language does not bind third parties who deal with one of them without knowledge of that provision. This case is governed by the principals of undisclosed agency. An agent for an undisclosed principal subjects the principal to liability for acts done on his account if they are usual or necessary in such transactions. This is true even if the principal has previously forbidden the agent to incur debts so long as the transaction is in the usual course of business engaged in by the agent. Here there was no evidence that Morris (P) had any actual knowledge of the existence of the Rainbow-Dawn (D) agency or any limitations by Dawn (D) on Rainbow's (D) authority. To the contrary, Morris (P) thought it was dealing solely with Rainbow (D) when it sold it fuel. Affirmed.

EDITOR'S ANALYSIS: The court notes that "secret instructions or limitations placed upon the authority of an agent must be known to the [third] party dealing with agent, or the principal is bound as if the limitation had not been made." Chevron Oil Co. v. Sutton, 85 N.M. 679 (1973). In addition, Dawn (D) later ratified the transaction, also giving rise to its liability.

NOTES:

CHAPTER 2
PARTNERSHIP

QUICK REFERENCE RULES OF LAW

1. **Revised uniform partnership act 101(6), 202.** While words are not determinative, where a transaction bears all of the aspects of a loan, no partnership arrangement will be found. (Martin v. Peyton)

   [For more information on Agency, see Casenote Law Outline on Corporations, Chapter 1, § I, The Partnership.]

2. **Partnership formation.** A partnership is an association of two or more persons to carry on as co-owners a business for profit. (Lupien v. Malsbenden)

   [For more information on partnership formation, see Casenote Law Outline on Corporations, Chapter 1, § I, The Partnership.]

3. **The Ongoing Operation of Partnerships.** Business differences in a partnership must be decided by a majority of the partners provided no other agreement between the partners speaks to the issues. (Summers v. Dooley)

   [For more information on Partnership, see Casenote Law Outline on Corporations, Chapter 1, § I, The Partnership.]

4. **Partnership Interests and Partnership Property.** Under New York Partnership Law, unless the parties have agreed otherwise, a person cannot become a member of a partnership without consent of all the partners, but the assignee of a partnership interest is entitled only to receive the profits of the assigning partner. (Rapoport v. 55 Perry Co.)

   [For more information on Partnership Formation, see Casenote Law Outline on Corporations, Chapter 1, Unincorporated Associations, § I, The Partnership.]

5. **The Partnership's Duty of Loyalty.** Joint adventurers owe to one another, the duty of finest loyalty, a standard of behavior most sensitive. (Meinhard v. Salmon)

   [For more information on Joint Ventures, see Casenote Law Outline on Corporations, Chapter 1, § II, The Joint Venture.]

6. **Dissolution by rightful election.** A partnership at will is a partnership which has no definite term or particular undertaking and can rightfully be dissolved by the express will of any partners. (Dreifuerst v.Dreifuerst)

   [For more information on Partnership Structure, see Casenote Law Outline on Corporations, Chapter 1, § I, The Partnership.]

7. **Dissolution by rightful election.** A partnership may be dissolved by the express will of any partner when no definite term or particular undertaking is specified. (Page v. Page)

   [For more information on Partnership Dissolution, see Casenote Law Outline on Corporations, Chapter 1, § I, The Partnership.]

8. **Dissolution by Judicial Decree and wrongful dissolution.** A partner causes dissolution of a partnership wrongfully by willfully and persistently committing a breach of the partnership agreement and by conducting himself in matters relating to partnership business so as to render impracticable the carrying on of the business in partnership with him. (Drashner v. Sorenson)

    [For more information on Partnership Dissolution, see Casenote Law Outline on Corporations, Chapter 1, § I, The Partnership.]

MARTIN v. PEYTON
Creditor (P) v. Alleged partner (D)
246 N.Y. 213 (1927).

NATURE OF CASE: Action to hold parties as partners in an existing firm.

FACT SUMMARY: Peyton (D) and others (D) loaned a partnership money so that it could carry on its brokerage business.

CONCISE RULE OF LAW: While words are not determinative, where a transaction bears all of the aspects of a loan, no partnership arrangement will be found.

FACTS: The partnership of Knauth (D), Nachod (D) and Kuhne (D) was in financial difficulty. Hall (D), one of the partners, arranged a loan from Peyton (D) and other friends (D). In exchange for the loan of $2,500,000 in liquid securities, Peyton (D) and the others were to receive a percentage of the profits until the loan was repaid. Peyton (D) was to have a veto over speculative investments; an insurance policy was to be taken out on Hall's (D) life; the securities could be pledged as a loan; Peyton (D) and the others were to receive dividends from the securities; plus many other controls and provisions. Peyton (D) could not bind the partnership, nor could he initiate any action on his own. The agreement specifically stated that it was a loan and not a partnership arrangement. It stated that no liability was to accrue to Peyton (D) and the others (D) for partnership debts. Martin (P), a creditor of the partnership, brought suit against it, plus Peyton (D) and the others (D). Martin (P) alleged that a partnership interest had been formed by the agreement. The court found for Peyton (D).

ISSUE: Where the only control exerted or sharing of profits occurs to protect and pay off a loan, will a partnership arrangement be found?

HOLDING AND DECISION: (Andrews, J.) No. Words alone are not determinative of a relationship. Merely declaring that no partnership is intended will not be dispositive of the issue. If the words, acts, and agreements establish the existence of a partnership arrangement, the parties will be liable as partners. Nothing in Peyton's (D) words or actions establishes a partnership. Therefore, we must look to the contract alone. Nothing in it is other than what were necessary precautions to protect the loan. Any control was negative in nature and was to prevent any misuse of the funds. Peyton (D) had no right to control or initiate policy or to bind the contract. This was a loan and Peyton (D) and the others are not liable. Judgment affirmed.

EDITOR'S ANALYSIS: A partnership results from either express or implied contracts. An arrangement for the sharing of profits is often an important factor in determining the existence of a partnership. Of equal importance is the right to share in the decision-making function of the partnership and/or to bind the partnership to contractual obligations.

[For more information on Agency, see Casenote Law Outline on Corporations, Chapter 1, § I, The Partnership.]

QUICKNOTES

PARTNERSHIP - A voluntary agreement entered into by two or more parties to engage in business and to share any attendant profits and losses.

NOTES:

LUPIEN v. MALSBENDEN
Auto buyer (P) v. Auto maker (D)
Me. Sup. Ct., 477 A.2d 746 (1984).

NATURE OF CASE: Appeal from a judgment holding the defendant to partnership liability in an action for breach of contract.

FACT SUMMARY: Although Malsbenden (D) insisted his interest in a portion of Cragin's business was that of a banker, Lupien (P) insisted that Malsbenden (D) and Cragin were partners, and therefore, Malsbenden (D) had partnership liability for Cragin's breach of his contract to build Lupien (P) a Bradley automobile.

CONCISE RULE OF LAW: A partnership is an association of two or more persons to carry on as co-owners a business for profit.

FACTS: Lupien (P) signed a contract with Cragin, doing business as York Motor Mart, for the construction of a Bradley automobile. Although Cragin signed the bill of sale, it identified the seller as York. However, when Lupien (P) visited York every week to see how his car was progressing, he generally dealt with Malsbenden (D). When Cragin later disappeared, Malsbenden (D) had physical control of York's premises and continued to dispose of assets there for over three years. Because Cragin never finished Lupien's (P) car, Lupien (P) filed suit against Malsbenden (D) for breach of contract. Malsbenden (D) testified that his interest in the Bradley operation of York was only that of a banker, since he had lent Cragin the money, without interest, to finance that portion of the business. The trial court, finding that Malsbenden (D) and Cragin were partners in the Bradley portion of York's business, held Malsbenden (D) to partnership liability on Lupien's (P) contract. Malsbenden (D) appealed.

ISSUE: Is a partnership an association of two or more persons to carry on as co-owners a business for profit?

HOLDING AND DECISION: (McKusick, C.J.) Yes. A partnership is an association of two or more persons to carry on as co-owners a business for profit. The testimony at trial, respecting Malsbenden's (D) financial interest in the enterprise and his involvement in day-to-day business operations, amply supported the trial court's conclusion. Unlike a banker, Malsbenden (D) had the right to participate in control of the business and in fact did so on a day-to-day basis. Although Malsbenden (D) characterized his investment as a loan, the "loan" carried no interest. Furthermore, the "loan" was not to be repaid in fixed amounts or at fixed times, but rather only upon the sale of Bradley automobiles. Thus, whatever the intent of these two men as to their respective involvements in the making and selling of Bradley cars, as a matter of law, that arrangement amounted to a partnership. Affirmed.

EDITOR'S ANALYSIS: A finding that the relationship between two persons constitutes a partnership may be based upon evidence of an agreement, express or implied, to pool their money, effects, labor, and skill, or some or all of them, in business with the understanding that any profits will be shared. No one factor alone determines the existence of a partnership. If the arrangement between the parties otherwise qualifies as a partnership, it does not matter that they did not expressly agree, or even intend, to form one.

[For more information on partnership formation, see Casenote Law Outline on Corporations, Chapter 1, § I, The Partnership.]

QUICKNOTES
PARTNERSHIP - A voluntary agreement entered into by two or more parties to engage in business and to share any attendant profits and losses.

NOTES:

SUMMERS v. DOOLEY
Partner (P) v. Partner (D)
Idaho Sup. Ct., 94 Idaho 87 (1971).

NATURE OF CASE: Claim for reimbursement of partnership funds.

FACT SUMMARY: In Summers' (P) suit against his partner Dooley (D) for reimbursement of his expenditure of $11,000 for the purpose of hiring an employee, Dooley (D) contended that because he did not approve of hiring the additional employee, the majority of partners did not consent to his hiring, and that Summers (P) should not be reimbursed for his unilateral hiring decision.

CONCISE RULE OF LAW: Business differences in a partnership must be decided by a majority of the partners provided no other agreement between the partners speaks to the issues.

FACTS: Summers (P) and Dooley (D) entered into a partnership for the purpose of operating a trash collection business. The business was operated by the two men and when either of them was unable to work, the non-working partner provided a replacement at his own expense. Dooley (D) became unable to work, and Summers (P), at his own expense, hired an employee to take Dooley's (D) place. Four years later, Summers (P) approached Dooley (D) regarding the hiring of an additional employee, but Dooley (D) refused. Summers (P), on his own, then hired another person and paid him out of his own pocket. Dooley (D) objected and refused to pay for the new person out of partnership funds. Summers (P) kept the man employed, but filed an action against Dooley (D) for reimbursement of Summers' (P) expenditures of $11,000 in hiring the extra employee. Dooley (D) argued that the majority of partners had not approved of the hiring, and that Summers (P) should not be reimbursed for his unilateral hiring decision. The trial court denied Summers (P) relief, and he appealed.

ISSUE: Must business differences in a partnership be decided by a majority of the partners provided no other agreement between the partners speaks to the issues?

HOLDING AND DECISION: (Donaldson, J.) Yes. Business differences in a partnership must be decided by a majority of the partners provided no other agreement between the partners speaks to the issues. Here, the record shows that although Summers (P) requested Dooley's (D) acquiescence in the hiring of the extra employee, such requests were not honored. In fact, Dooley (D) made it clear that he was "voting no" with regard to the hiring of an additional employee. An application of Idaho law to the factual situation presented here indicates that the trial court was correct in its disposal of the issue since a majority of the partners did not consent to the hiring of the extra man. Dooley (D)

continually voiced objection to the hiring. He did not sit idly by and acquiesce in Summers' (P) actions. Thus, it would be unfair to permit Summers (P) to recover for an expense which was incurred individually, not for the benefit of the partnership, but rather for the benefit of one partner. Affirmed.

EDITOR'S ANALYSIS: The rule that any difference arising as to ordinary matters connected with the partnership business may be decided by a majority of the partners, is subject to any agreement between them. Partnership agreements often contain provisions vesting management in a managing partner or management committee. The same result, however, may be reached without explicit agreement on the basis of course of conduct.

[For more information on Partnership, see Casenote Law Outline on Corporations, Chapter 1, § I, The Partnership.]

QUICKNOTES
L.C. § 53-318(8) - Any difference as to ordinary partnership matters may be decided by a majority of the partners.

NOTES:

RAPOPORT v. 55 PERRY CO.
Partner (P) v. Partnership (D)
N.Y. Sup. Ct., 50 A.D.2d 54 (1975).

NATURE OF CASE: Appeal from denial of summary judgment motion.

FACT SUMMARY: In the Rapoport's (P) action against 55 Perry Co. (D), seeking a declaration that they had an absolute right to assign their interests in 55 Perry (D) to their adult children without consent of the other partners of 55 Perry (D), the other partners of 55 Perry (D) argued that according to the partnership agreement, there could be no admission of additional partners to the partnership without the consent of all the existing partners.

CONCISE RULE OF LAW: Under New York Partnership Law, unless the parties have agreed otherwise, a person cannot become a member of a partnership without consent of all the partners, but the assignee of a partnership interest is entitled only to receive the profits of the assigning partner.

FACTS: The Rapoports (P) entered into a partnership agreement with the Parneses, forming a partnership, 55 Perry Co. (D). The Rapoports (P) then decided to assign a 10% interest of their shares in the partnership to their two adult children. The Rapoports (P) then requested the Parneses to execute an amended partnership agreement to reflect the changes in the partnership. The Parneses refused and the Rapoports (P) brought a declaratory action against 55 Perry (D) seeking a declaration that they had an absolute right to assign their interests in the partnership to their children without consent of the other partners. The Parneses and 55 Perry (D) contended that according to the partnership agreement, there could be no admission of additional partners to the partnership without the consent of all the existing partners. At trial, the Rapoports (P) moved for summary judgment. The trial court denied the motion, stating that the partnership agreement was ambiguous and that there was a triable issue regarding the intent of the parties. The Rapoports (P) appealed.

ISSUE: Under New York Partnership Law, unless the parties have agreed otherwise, can a person become a member of a partnership without consent of all the partners whereas an assignment may be made without consent, but the assignee is entitled only to receive the profits of the assigning partner?

HOLDING AND DECISION: (Tilzer, J.) No. Under New York Partnership Law, unless the parties have agreed otherwise, a person cannot become a member of a partnership without consent of all the partners whereas an assignment may be made without consent, but the assignee is entitled only to receive the profits of the assigning partner. Here, the partnership agreement clearly took cognizance of the differences between an assignment of interest in the partnership as compared to the full rights of a partner. Contrary to the Rapoports' (P) contentions, that the agreement intended to give the parties the right to transfer a full partnership interest to adult children without consent of all other partners, the agreement was instead intended to limit a partner with respect to his right to assign a partnership interest to the extent of prohibiting such assignments without consent of other partners except to children of existing partners who have reached majority. Thus, it must be decided that the Rapoports (P) could not transfer a full partnership interest to their children, and that the children only have rights as assignees to receive a share of the partnership income. Reversed.

DISSENT: (Nunez, J.) Here, the partnership agreement being ambiguous, construction is a mixed question of law and fact, and resolution thereof to determine the parties' intent should await a trial.

EDITOR'S ANALYSIS: As a business matter, there will usually be a separation between the property of a partnership and the property of the individual partners. Under the Uniform Partnership Act, individual partners own the partnership property in theory, but all the incidents of ownership are vested in the partnership. The result of this scheme is a functional two-level ownership structure somewhat comparable to the legal two-level ownership structure in a corporation. That is, a partnership is the functional owner of partnership property, and a partner is the owner of an interest in the partnership.

[For more information on Partnership Formation, see Casenote Law Outline on Corporations, Chapter 1, Unincorporated Associations, § I, The Partnership.]

QUICKNOTES
PARTNERSHIP LAW, § 40 - No person can become a member without consent of all the partners.

PARTNERSHIP LAW, § 53 - An assignee of a partnership interest is entitled to profits but may not interfere with management.

NOTES:

MEINHARD v. SALMON
Partner (P) v. Partnership (D)
N.Y. Ct. of App., 249 N.Y. 458, 164 N.E. 545 (1928).

NATURE OF CASE: Award of an interest in a lease.

FACT SUMMARY: Meinhard (P) and Salmon (D) were coadventurers in a lease on a hotel, but prior to the expiration of that lease, Salmon (D) alone, without Meinhard's (P) knowledge, agreed to lease the same and adjacent property.

CONCISE RULE OF LAW: Joint adventurers owe to one another, the duty of finest loyalty, a standard of behavior most sensitive.

FACTS: Salmon (D) leased from Gerry a New York hotel on Fifth Avenue for a period of 20 years. Later, Salmon (D) entered into a joint adventure with Meinhard (P) who contributed money while Salmon (D) was to manage the enterprise. Near the end of the lease, Gerry, who owned adjacent property as well as the hotel, desired to raze those buildings and construct one large building. Gerry, unable to find a new lessee to carry out his intentions, approached Salmon (D) with the idea when there was less than four months to run on his and Meinhard's (D) lease. The result was a 20-year lease to Midpoint Realty Company, wholly owned and controlled by Salmon (D). Meinhard (P) was never informed of the planned project or the negotiations for a new lease. After he learned of it, he made demand on Salmon (D) that the lease be held in trust as an asset of the venture, which was refused. This suit followed with an award to Meinhard (P) of a 25% interest in the lease, one-half of his value in the hotel lease proportionate to the new lease, while on appeal it was increased to 50%. Salmon (D) appealed arguing that he breached no duty to Meinhard (P).

ISSUE: Do joint adventurers owe to one another, while their enterprise continues, the duty of finest loyalty?

HOLDING AND DECISION: (Cardozo, C.J.) Yes. Joint adventurers owe to one another, while their enterprise continues, the duty of finest loyalty, a standard of behavior most sensitive. Many forms of conduct permissible in a workday world, for those acting at arm's length, are forbidden to those bound by fiduciary ties. Here, Salmon (D) excluded his coadventurer from any chance to compete, from any chance to enjoy the opportunity for benefit that had come to him alone by virtue of his agency. It was likely that Salmon (D) thought that with the approaching end of the lease he owed no duty to Meinhard (P), but, here, the subject-matter of the new lease was an extension and enlargement of the subject-matter of the old one. As for Meinhard's (P) remedy, he should have been awarded one share less than half of the shares in Midpoint Realty Company. As modified, affirmed.

DISSENT: (Andrews, J.) This was not a general partnership.

Rather, Meinhard (P) and Salmon (D) entered into a venture for a limited purpose. The interest terminated when the joint adventure expired. There was no intent to renew the joint adventure after its expiration.

EDITOR'S ANALYSIS: One of the most important aspects of the partnership relation is the broad fiduciary duty between partners. "The unique feature is their symmetry; each partner is, roughly speaking, both a principal and an agent, both a trustee and a beneficiary, for he has the property, authority, and confidence of his co-partners, as they do of him. He shares their profits and losses, and is bound by their actions. Without this protection of fiduciary duties, each is at the other's mercy." J. Crane.

[For more information on Joint Ventures, see Casenote Law Outline on Corporations, Chapter 1, § II, The Joint Venture.]

QUICKNOTES

DUTY OF LOYALTY - A director's duty to refrain from self-dealing or to take a position that is adverse to the corporation's best interests.

NOTES:

DREIFUERST v. DREIFUERST
Partner (P) v. Partner (D)
Wis. Ct. of App., 90 Wis.2d 566 (1979).

NATURE OF CASE: Appeal from decision dissolving a partnership.

FACT SUMMARY: In the Dreifuersts' (P) case against their brother, Dreifuerst (D), to dissolve a partnership in which they were all partners, Dreifuerst (D) contended that under Wisconsin law, he had a right to force a sale of partnership assets in order to obtain his fair share of the assets in cash upon dissolution.

CONCISE RULE OF LAW: A partnership at will is a partnership which has no definite term or particular undertaking and can rightfully be dissolved by the express will of any partners.

FACTS: The Dreifuersts (P) and their brother, Dreifuerst (D), formed a partnership operating two feed mills. There were no written articles of partnership governing the partnership. The Dreifuersts (P) served Dreifuerst (D) with a notice of dissolution and wind-up of the partnership. The dissolution complaint alleged that the Dreifuersts (P) elected to dissolve the partnership and there were no allegations of fault, expulsion, or contravention of an alleged agreement as grounds for dissolution. The partners were not, however, able to agree to a winding-up of the partnership. Hearings on dissolution were held, and Dreifuerst (D) requested that the partnership be sold and that the court allow a sale, at which time the partners would bid on the entire property. By such sale, Dreifuerst (D) argued that he could obtain his fair share of the assets in cash upon dissolution while the Dreifuersts (P) could continue to run the business under a new partnership. The trial court denied Dreifuerst's (D) request and divided the partnership assets in-kind according to the valuation presented by the Dreifuersts (P). Dreifuerst (D) appealed.

ISSUE: Is a partnership at will a partnership which has no definite term or particular undertaking and can be rightfully dissolved by the express will of any partner?

HOLDING AND DECISION: (Brown, J.) Yes. A partnership at will is a partnership which has no definite term or particular undertaking and can be rightfully dissolved by the express will of any partner. In the present case, the Dreifuersts (P) wanted to dissolve the partnership. This being a partnership at will, they could rightfully dissolve it with or without the consent of Dreifuerst (D). Here, the Dreifuersts (P) never claimed that Dreifuerst (D) violated any partnership agreement and, therefore, there has been no wrongful dissolution of the partnership. Partners who have not wrongfully dissolved a partnership have a right to wind up the partnership. Lawful dissolution gives each partner the right to have the business liquidated and his share of the surplus paid in cash. Thus, the trial court erred in ordering an in-kind distribution of the assets of the partnership. A sale is the best means of determining the true fair market value of the assets. Reversed and remanded.

EDITOR'S ANALYSIS: "Dissolution" sometimes designates the completion of the winding-up of partnership affairs. This, the end of the association, should be called termination of the partnership. Again, the term is sometimes used in referring to the process of liquidation or winding up. Lastly, the term may be used to designate a change in the relation of partners caused by any partner ceasing to be associated in carrying on the business.

[For more information on Partnership Structure, see Casenote Law Outline on Corporations, Chapter 1, § I, The Partnership.]

QUICKNOTES

§ 178.25(1) - A partnership is dissolved when any partner ceases to be involved.

§ 178.33 - When dissolution is caused in any way, each partner may have partnership property applied and discharge liabilities.

PARTNERSHIP-AT-WILL - A voluntary agreement entered into by two or more parties to engage in business and to share any attendant profits and losses, which lasts for an unspecified time period and may be terminated by either of the parties at any time and for any reason.

§ 178.32 - Partners who have not wrongfully terminated have the right to wind up or liquidate the partnership.

NOTES:

PAGE v. PAGE
Partner (P) v. Partner (D)
55 Cal. 2d 192, 359 P.2d 41 (1961).

NATURE OF CASE: Action for a declaratory judgment.

FACT SUMMARY: Page (P) sought a declaratory judgment that the partnership he had with Page (D) was a partnership at will which he could dissolve.

CONCISE RULE OF LAW: A partnership may be dissolved by the express will of any partner when no definite term or particular undertaking is specified.

FACTS: Page (P) and Page (D) were partners in a linen supply business they had entered into in 1949, pursuant to an oral agreement. Each had contributed about $43,000 to purchase linen, equipment, and land. It was not until 1958 that business began to show a profit. Page (P) was the sole owner of the corporation which was the partnership's major creditor, holding a $47,000 demand note, and in 1959, he sought a declaratory judgment that it was a partnership at will which he could terminate. The trial court found the partnership to be for a term, namely such reasonable time as was necessary to repay from profits the original outlays of Page (P) and Page (D) for equipment, etc.

ISSUE: Can a partnership be dissolved by the express will of any partner when no definite term or particular undertaking is specified?

HOLDING AND DECISION: (Traynor, J.) Yes. When no definite term or particular undertaking is specified, a partnership may be dissolved by the express will of any partner. Partners may impliedly agree to continue in business until certain debts are paid, until one or more partners recoup their investments, etc., but there is no evidence in this case to support any implied agreement of that nature. All partnerships are ordinarily entered into with the hope they will be profitable, but that alone does not make them all partnerships for a term and obligate the partners to continue in the partnerships until all of the losses over a period of many years have been recovered or original investments recouped. In holding that this is a partnership terminable at will, it is noted that the power to dissolve it must be exercised in good faith and not to "freeze out" a co-partner. Reversed.

EDITOR'S ANALYSIS: An important aspect of this leading case is the introduction of the concept that a partner holds his dissolution power as a fiduciary. That means he owes his partners fraternal duties of good faith and fair dealing in exercising his dissolution rights.

[For more information on Partnership Dissolution, see Casenote Law Outline on Corporations, Chapter 1, § I, The Partnership.]

QUICKNOTES
CAL. CORP. CODE § 15031 - Partnership may be dissolved by the express will of any partner when no definite term is specified.

NOTES:

DRASHNER v. SORENSON
Partner (P) v. Partner (D)
S.D. Sup. Ct., 75 S.D. 247 (1954).

NATURE OF CASE: Appeal from order dissolving a partnership.

FACT SUMMARY: In Drashner's (P) action against Sorenson (D) seeking an accounting, dissolution, and winding up of the partnership in which Drashner (P) was associated with Sorenson (D), Sorenson (D) contended that Drashner (P) caused dissolution of the partnership wrongfully and was, therefore, not entitled to receive any partnership property upon dissolution.

CONCISE RULE OF LAW: A partner causes dissolution of a partnership wrongfully by willfully and persistently committing a breach of the partnership agreement and by conducting himself in matters relating to partnership business so as to render impracticable the carrying on of the business in partnership with him.

FACTS: Drashner (P) and Sorenson (D) entered into a partnership with each other. They purchased a real estate and insurance agency with money advanced by Sorenson (D), a sum of $7,500. Differences arose among the partners when Drashner (P) drew out money for his own personal use from funds held in escrow by the partnership. Drashner (P) then requested that Sorenson (D) advance Drashner $100 personally. When Sorenson (D) refused, Drashner (P) brought an action to dissolve the partnership. At trial, Sorenson (D) contended that Drashner (P) caused the dissolution of the partnership wrongfully and was, therefore, not entitled to receive any partnership property upon dissolution. The court found that Drashner (P) had violated the terms of the partnership agreement in that he had demanded a larger share of the income of the partnership than he was entitled to receive under the terms of the agreement. The court also valued the partnership property at $4,498.90, and that this belonged to Sorenson (D) because he had not yet been reimbursed for his investment in the partnership. Drashner (P) appealed.

ISSUE: Does a partner cause dissolution of a partnership wrongfully by willfully and persistently committing a breach of the partnership agreement and by conducting himself in matters relating to the partnership business so as to render impracticable the carrying on of the business in partnership with him?

HOLDING AND DECISION: (Smith, J.) Yes. A partner causes dissolution of a partnership wrongfully by willfully and persistently committing a breach of the partnership agreement and by conducting himself in matters relating to partnership business so as to render impracticable the carrying on of the business in partnership with him. Here, evidence presented tends to show that Drashner (P) neglected the business and spent too much time in a nearby bar during business hours. At a time when Drashner (P) had overdrawn his partner and was also indebted to Sorenson (D) for personal advances, he requested $100, and his request was refused. Drashner (P) then threatened to dissolve the partnership and brought this action to do just that. It cannot be said that the trial court acted unreasonably in concluding that the insistent and continuing demands of Drashner (P) and his attendant conduct rendered it reasonably impracticable to carry on the business in partnership with him. It follows, then, that Drashner (P) caused the dissolution wrongfully. Affirmed.

EDITOR'S ANALYSIS: When a partnership dissolution is caused by the wrongful act of a partner, the innocent partners have an election of remedies. They may wind up the partnership business and seek damages from the wrongful partner. They may continue the business in the same name, either by themselves or jointly with others. Finally, they may continue the business and seek damages.

[For more information on Partnership Dissolution, see Casenote Law Outline on Corporations, Chapter 1, § I, The Partnership.]

QUICKNOTES

DISSOLUTION - The termination of a marriage.

NOTES:

3

CHAPTER 3
THE CORPORATE FORM

QUICK REFERENCE RULES OF LAW

1. **Consequences of Defective Incorporation.** One who deals with a de facto corporation as a corporation is estopped to deny its existence in an attempt to hold those with whom he dealt personally liable on its contracts. (Cantor v. Sunshine Greenery Inc.)

2. **Consequences of Defective Incorporation.** An incorporator may be held personally liable for the debts of a corporation if he or she acts on behalf of the company knowing that no valid incorporation took place. (Harris v. Looney)

3. **The Classical Ultra Vires Doctrine.** Where a corporation is contemplated but has not yet been organized at the time when a promoter makes a contract for the benefit of the contemplated corporation, the promoter is personally liable on it even though the contract will also benefit the future corporation. (Goodman v. Ladd Estate Co.)

   [For more information on preincorporation transactions, see Casenote Law Outline on Corporations, Chapter 2, § I, Formation Accomplished Under Law of State of Incorporation.]

4. **The Objective and Conduct of the Corporation.** Under New Jersey law, a corporate contribution to an educational institution is authorized if the donee institution does not own more than 10% of the voting stock of the donor and that the contribution shall not exceed 1% of capital and surplus unless authorized by the stockholders. (A.P. Smith Mfg. Co. v. Barlow)

CANTOR v. SUNSHINE GREENERY, INC.
Lessor (P) v. Lessee (D)
N.J. Sup. Ct., 165 N.J. Sup. 411, 398 A.2d 571 (1979).

NATURE OF CASE: Appeal from judgment for damages for breach of a lease.

FACT SUMMARY: Brunetti (D) disclaimed that any personal liability arose when he signed a lease with Cantor (P) in his capacity as president of a de facto corporation, Sunshine Greenery (D).

CONCISE RULE OF LAW: One who deals with a de facto corporation as a corporation is estopped to deny its existence in an attempt to hold those with whom he dealt personally liable on its contracts.

FACTS: When Cantor (P) leased his building to Sunshine Greenery (D), Brunetti (D) signed the document as president of Sunshine (D). At the time, Sunshine Greenery (D) was not a de jure corporation inasmuch as the certificate of incorporation that had been forwarded to the Secretary of State was not officially filed until two days after the lease was executed. Counsel for Sunshine Greenery (D) thereafter repudiated the lease agreement, and Brunetti (D) put a stop payment on the check supposedly covering the first month's rent and security deposit. Cantor (P) sued both Sunshine Greenery (D) and Brunetti (D). In appealing the personal judgment rendered against him, Brunetti (D) argued that a de facto corporation was in existence when the lease was signed, that Cantor (P) dealt with the corporation as such, and that he was thus estopped to deny its corporate existence so as to hold Brunetti (D) personally liable.

ISSUE: If one contracts with a de facto corporation as such, can he thereafter deny its corporate existence so as to hold those with whom he dealt personally liable on the contract?

HOLDING AND DECISION: (Larner, J.) No. A party who deals with a de facto corporation as if it is a corporation is estopped to deny its corporate existence so as to hold the individuals with whom he dealt personally liable on any contracts thus entered into. In this case, a de facto corporation clearly existed because the three necessary elements were present: (1) the existence of a law authorizing incorporation, (2) actual exercise of corporate powers, and (3) a bona fide (good faith) effort to satisfy all conditions precedent to incorporation under the existing law. Since Cantor (P) dealt with Sunshine Greenery (D) as if it were in fact a corporation, he is now estopped from denying its corporate existence so that he might hold Brunetti (D) personally liable on the lease contract. Reversed.

EDITOR'S ANALYSIS: Although "corporate" officers can escape personal liability by use of both theories, there is a difference between corporation by estoppel and corporation de facto. A de

facto corporation is considered a corporation as against all parties except the state (in a quo warranto proceeding to declare the corporation invalid). A corporation by estoppel, however, is given corporate status only as against the particular person in the particular proceeding before the court.

QUICKNOTES
DE FACTO CORPORATION - A corporation arising from the good faith attempt to comply with the statutory requirements of establishing a corporation.

ESTOPPEL - An equitable doctrine precluding a party from asserting a right to the detriment of another who justifiably relied on the conduct.

NOTES:

HARRIS v. LOONEY
Business Owner (P) v. Incorporators (D)
43 Ark.App. 127 (1993)

NATURE OF THE CASE: Appeal from order awarding judgment against defendant in strict liability action.

FACT SUMMARY: After a corporation defaulted on its promissory note for the purchase of the plaintiff's business, plaintiff sued defendant incorporators jointly and severally instead of the corporation, based on a delay between the time when the incorporators signed the articles of incorporation and when the articles were submitted to the Secretary of State.

CONCISE RULE OF LAW: An incorporator may be held personally liable for the debts of a corporation if he or she acts on behalf of the company knowing that no valid incorporation took place.

FACTS: Harris (P) sold his business to J & R Construction, a corporation incorporated by Looney (D) and others. The incorporators and Looney (D) signed the articles of incorporation but did not file them with the Secretary of State until several days later. J & R Construction subsequently defaulted on its promissory note, and Harris (P) filed against Looney (D) and the other incorporators as jointly and severally liable for the debts of the corporation, based on the fact that one incorporator, Joe Alexander, had entered into a contract with Harris (P) on behalf of the corporation before the corporation had been duly registered. The trial court awarded judgment against Alexander, but not Looney (D) and the other incorporators. Harris (P) appealed, amending his complaint and contending that the trial court erred by not including Looney (D) and the other incorporators as jointly and severally liable along with Alexander.

ISSUE: May an incorporator be held personally liable for the debts of a corporation if he or she acts on behalf of the company knowing that no valid incorporation took place?

HOLDING: (Pittman, J.) Yes. An incorporator may be held personally liable for the debts of a corporation if he or she acts on behalf of the company knowing that no valid incorporation took place. All persons purporting to act on behalf of a corporation, knowing that there is no valid incorporation under the applicable state law, are jointly and severally liable for all liabilities created while so acting. However, many states have statutes expressly providing that a person who acts prematurely on behalf of a corporation may be held personally liable. The legislature has adopted a heightened standard for imposing personal liability on persons entering into pre-incorporation transactions, requiring a finding that such persons: 1) acted on behalf of the corporation; and 2) knew there was no incorporation under the applicable incorporation laws. The evidence here shows that only Alexander signed the promissory note to Harris (P) and that Looney (D) and the other incorporators were not present when the transaction took place. The trial court did not commit error in so ruling. Affirmed.

EDITOR'S ANALYSIS: In its opinion, the appellate court analogized the limitation created by restricting liability to the "knowledge" of the individual incorporator to the standards of liability governing limited partnerships. In these cases, a limited liability partner is protected if he or she contributes capital to the partnership in the erroneous belief that a limited partnership certificate has been filed.

QUICKNOTES
LIMITED PARTNERSHIP - A voluntary agreement entered into by two or more parties whereby one or more general partners are responsible for the enterprise's liabilities and management and the other partners are only liable to the extent of their investment.

GOODMAN v. DARDEN, DOMAN & STAFFORD ASSOCIATES

Real estate agent (D) v. General partnership (P)

Wash. Sup. Ct., 100 Wash.2d 476, 670 P.2d 648 (1983).

NATURE OF CASE: Appeal from decision finding defendant a party to arbitration of a preincorporation contract.

FACT SUMMARY: Goodman (D) argued that his corporation, not he, should be liable under a preincorporation contract with Darden, Doman & Stafford Associates (DDS) (P) because DDS (P) had agreed not to hold him individually liable.

CONCISE RULE OF LAW: Where a corporation is contemplated but has not yet been organized at the time when a promoter makes a contract for the benefit of the contemplated corporation, the promoter is personally liable on it even though the contract will also benefit the future corporation.

FACTS: Goodman (D), a real estate agent, agreed to renovate an apartment building he had sold to DDS (P), a general partnership. Goodman (D) informed DDS (P) that he would be forming a corporation to limit his personal liability. When the renovation contract was executed between DDS (P) and Goodman (D), DDS (P) knew that Goodman's (D) corporation was not yet in existence. Goodman (D) subcontracted the work, which was not completed within the required time and was allegedly of poor quality. Not until after this apparent default did Goodman (D) file articles of incorporation and receive his corporate license. DDS (P) made five progress payments on the contract, making out the checks to both Goodman (D) and the corporation. After the default, DDS (P) served Goodman (D) with a demand for arbitration pursuant to the contract, naming both Goodman (D) and his corporation. Goodman (D) moved for a stay of arbitration and an order dismissing him as an individual from the arbitration, which the trial court granted. DDS (P) appealed and the court of appeals reversed. Goodman (D) appealed.

ISSUE: Where a corporation is contemplated but has not yet been organized at the time when a promoter makes a contract for the benefit of the contemplated corporation, is the promoter personally liable on it, even though the contract will also benefit the future corporation?

HOLDING AND DECISION: (Dimmick, J.) Yes. Where a corporation has not yet been organized at the time when a promoter makes a contract for the benefit of the contemplated corporation, the promoter is personally liable on it even though the contract will also benefit the future corporation. An exception to the general rule is that if the contracting party knew that the corporation was not in existence at the time of the contracting but nevertheless agreed to look solely to the corporation for performance, the promoter will not be held a party to the contract.

Goodman (D) has the burden of proving that such an agreement existed with DDS (P). Goodman (D) argues that the contractual language indicating that the corporation was "in formation" was an expression by the parties of their intent to make the corporation alone a party to the contract. Here, the trial court relied on three considerations to show that the parties agreed to release Goodman (D) from the contract: (1) DDS (P) knew of the corporation's existence; (2) Goodman (D) told DDS (P) that he was forming the corporation to limit his personal liability; and (3) the progress payments were made to the corporation. But the fact that a contracting party knows that a corporation is nonexistent does not indicate any agreement to release the promoter. To the contrary, such knowledge alone would seem to show that DDS (P) intended to make Goodman (D) a party to the contract. Goodman's (D) assertions that he was incorporating to limit his liability also is not dispositive of DDS's (P) intentions. DDS (P) had no duty to correct or even perceive Goodman's (D) mistaken interpretation of the promoter liability rules in his belief that incorporation would limit his liability. Also, the progress payment checks were written to the corporation only after Goodman (D) expressly instructed them to be made, and this evidence does not show with reasonable certainty that DDS (P) intended to contract only with the corporation. The trial court erred in dismissing Goodman (D) from arbitration proceedings. Remanded.

DISSENT: (Dore, J.) The trial court found that DDS (P) intended to look only to the corporation. There is substantial evidence in the record to support this finding. DDS (P) had no objection to issuing checks in the name of Goodman's (D) corporation. The corporation was fully capitalized and operating while DDS (P) continued to make progress payments, and Goodman (D) had the corporation ratify the contract as an action of incorporation.

EDITOR'S ANALYSIS: As Justice Rugg observed in *Old Dominion Copper Mining & Smelting Co. v. Bigelow*, 89 N.E. 193, (1909), the promoter of a corporation is one who takes the responsibility to form the corporation, procure for the corporation the rights, instrumentalities and capital by which it is to carry out the purposes set forth in its charter, and to establish it as fully able to do business. The promoter's work in seeking the opening for the venture and projecting a plan for its development begins long before organization of the corporation; this work may continue after incorporation by attracting the investment capital in its securities and providing it with the commercial breath of life.

[For more information on preincorporation transactions, see Casenote Law Outline on Corporations, Chapter 2, § I, Formation Accomplished Under Law of State of Incorporation.]

QUICKNOTES

PROMOTER - A person who initiates the formation of a corporation.

A.P. SMITH MFG. CO. v. BARLOW
Corporation (P) v. Shareholder (D)
N.J. Sup. Ct., 13 N.J. 145 (1953).

NATURE OF CASE: Appeal from judgment upholding a corporate donation.

FACT SUMMARY: Barlow (D), a Smith (P) stockholder, questioned whether a contribution made by Smith (P) to Princeton University was authorized under New Jersey corporate law.

CONCISE RULE OF LAW: Under New Jersey law, a corporate contribution to an educational institution is authorized if the donee institution does not own more than 10% of the voting stock of the donor and that the contribution shall not exceed 1% of capital and surplus unless authorized by the stockholders.

FACTS: A.P. Smith Mfg. Co. (P), pursuant to a resolution adopted by its board of directors, donated $1,500 to Princeton University as a contribution toward its maintenance. Barlow (D), a stockholder of Smith (P), questioned the donation and whether such a contribution was authorized under New Jersey corporate law. Smith (P) then instituted a declaratory judgment action to decide the legitimacy of the contribution. The trial court found that Smith's (P) contribution was intra vires, and Barlow (D) appealed.

ISSUE: Under New Jersey law, is a corporate contribution to an educational institution authorized if the donee institution does not own more than 10% of the voting stock of the donor and that the contribution shall not exceed 1% of the capital and surplus unless authorized by the stockholders?

HOLDING AND DECISION: (Jacobs, J.) Yes. Under New Jersey law, a corporate contribution to an educational institution is authorized provided the donee institution does not own more than 10% of the voting stock of the donor and that the contribution shall not exceed 1% of the capital and surplus unless so authorized by the stockholders. In 1950, the New Jersey legislature declared that it would be the public policy of the state and in furtherance of the public interest and welfare that encouragement be given to the creation and maintenance of institutions engaged in philanthropic, education, scientific, or benevolent activities. It expressly empowered corporations to contribute reasonable sums to such institutions. In light of this legislation and this court's view that corporate power to make reasonable charitable contributions exists under modern conditions, even apart from express statutory provision, Smith's (P) donation to Princeton must be held valid. Affirmed.

EDITOR'S ANALYSIS: Virtually all states have adopted statutory provisions relating to corporate contributions. These provisions usually do not incorporate a limit of reasonableness regarding donations, but it is generally agreed that such limit is to be implied. Donations should be reasonable in amount and in light of the corporation's financial condition and bear some reasonable relation to the corporation's interest.

NOTES:

4

CHAPTER 4
CORPORATE STRUCTURE

QUICK REFERENCE RULES OF LAW

1. **Allocation of Legal Power Between Management and Shareholder.** The business of a corporation, as defined and limited in its bylaws, is to be managed by its directors, and by such officers and agents under their direction as the directors shall appoint. (Charleston Boot and Shoe v. Dunsmore)

   [For more information on Management, see Casenote Law Outline on Corporations, Chapter 2, § II, Viewing the Corporation from Within.]

2. **Allocation of Legal Power Between Management and Shareholder.** Inequitable action does not become permissible simply because it is legally permissible. (Schnell v. Chris-Craft Industries, Inc.)

   [For more information on duty of loyalty, see Casenote Law Outline on Corporations, Chapter 8, § IV, Fiduciary Duties of Care and Loyalty.]

3. **Allocation of Legal Power Between Management and Shareholder.** A board of directors may not enlarge the size of the board for the purpose of preventing a majority of shareholders from voting to expand the board to give control to an insurgent group. (Blasius Industries, Inc. v. Atlas Corp.)

   [For more information on elections of directors, see Casenote Law Outline on Corporations, Chapter 2, § II, Viewing the Corporation from Within.]

4. **Allocation of Legal Power Between Management and Shareholder.** Provisions in corporate charters and bylaws relating to directorial elections approved by shareholders are presumptively valid. (Stroud v. Grace)

5. **Allocation of Legal Power Between Management and Shareholder.** A certification of incorporation which is silent with regard to shareholder rights plans does not preclude shareholder enacted bylaws regarding the implementation of rights plans. (International Brotherhood of Teamsters v. Fleming Co.)

6. **Allocation of Legal Power Between Management and Shareholder.** Unripe claims raising issues novel and important to Delaware corporate law should be dismissed. (General Datacom Industries v. Wisconson Investment Board)

7. **Limited Liability.** Under applicable state law, the court may pierce the corporate veil of a company and hold its shareholders personally liable only in cases involving fraud, or where the company is a mere instrumentality or alter ego of its parent company. (Fletcher v. Atex)

   [For more information on piercing the corporate veil, see Casenote Law Outline on Corporations, Chapter 2, III, Viewing the Corporation from Without.]

8. **Limited Liability.** Whenever anyone uses control of a corporation to further his own rather than the corporation's business, he will be liable for the corporation's acts. However, where a corporation is a fragment of a larger corporate combine which actually conducts the business, a court will not "pierce the corporate veil" to hold individual shareholders liable. (Walkovszky v. Carlton)

   [For more information on piercing the corporate veil, see Casenote Law Outline on Corporations, Chapter 2, § III, Viewing the Corporation from Without.]

9. **Limited Liability.** Where a person actively participates in corporate affairs of a company inadequately capitalized, and the person is an equitable owner in that corporation, he will be held personally liable for any corporate debts. (Minton v. Cavaney)

   [For more information on "Piercing the Corporate Veil", see Casenote Law Outline on Corporations, Chapter 2, § III, Viewing the Corporation from Without.]

10. **Limited Liability**. A corporate entity will be disregarded and the veil of limited liability pierced when there is such unity of interest and ownership that the separate personalities of the corporation and the individual no longer exist and when adherence to the fiction of separate corporate existence would sanction a fraud or promote injustice. (Sea-Land Services, Inc. v. Pepper Source)

    [For more information on limitations on limited liability, see Casenote Law Outline on Corporations, Chapter 2, § III, Viewing the Corporation from Without.]

11. **Limited Liability.** The corporate veil may be pierced on the basis of unjust enrichment where the owner, with knowledge of a debt to a creditor, uses corporate funds to pay personal expenses. (Sea-Land Services, Inc. v. Pepper Source)

    [For more information on limitations on limited liability, see Casenote Law Outline on Corporations, Chapter 2, § III, Viewing the Corporation from Without.]

CHARLESTOWN BOOT & SHOE CO. v. DUNSMORE

Corporation (P) v. Director (D)

N.H. Sup. Ct., 60 N.H. 85 (1980).

NATURE OF CASE: Action for damages against directors of a corporation.

FACT SUMMARY: In Charlestown Boot & Shoe Co.'s (P) suit against Dunsmore (D), a director of that corporation, for depreciation of the asset of the corporation, Dunsmore (D) contended that he used ordinary care and diligence in the care and management of the business and thus was not answerable for losses incurred by the corporation.

CONCISE RULE OF LAW: The business of a corporation, as defined and limited in its bylaws, is to be managed by its directors, and by such officers and agents under their direction as the directors shall appoint.

FACTS: Dunsmore (D) was elected an officer in Charlestown Boot & Shoe Co. (P). When Charlestown (P) chose to wind up its affairs, a committee was chosen by the shareholders to act with the directors to help in winding up. Osgood was chosen to head the committee, but Dunsmore (D) refused to act with Osgood. Osgood urged that Dunsmore (D) and the other directors dispose of certain goods of the corporation, but Dunsmore (D) refused and, as a result, corporate assets were depreciated. Charlestown (P) then brought suit against Dunsmore (D) for damages sustained. Dunsmore(D) contended that he used ordinary care and diligence in the care and management of the business and thus was not answerable for losses incurred by the corporation.

ISSUE: Is the business of a corporation, as defined and limited in its bylaws, to be managed by its directors and by such officers and agents under their direction as the directors shall appoint?

HOLDING AND DECISION: (Smith, J.) Yes. The business of a corporation, as defined and limited in its bylaws, is to be managed by its directors, and by such officers and agents under their direction as the directors shall appoint. The provision of the New Hampshire statute is that the business of a dividend-paying corporation shall be managed by the directors. The statute does not authorize a corporation to join another officer with the directors, nor compel the directors to act with one who is not a director. The statute does provide that powers granted to a corporation shall be exercised by any set of officers or any particular agents. Such powers can be exercised only by such officers or agents, although they are required to be chosen by the whole corporation; and if the whole corporation attempts to exercise powers which by the charter are lodged elsewhere, its action upon the subject is void. The vote choosing Osgood to head a committee to act with the directors in closing up the affairs of Charlestown (P) was thus inoperative and void. Judgment for Dunsmore (D).

EDITOR'S ANALYSIS: Shareholders of a corporation can remove a director for cause. Shareholders cannot remove a director without cause, absent specific authority in the certificate of incorporation or bylaws. However, a certificate of incorporation or by law provision can permit removal without cause of directors elected after the provision has been adopted.

[For more information on Management, see Casenote Law Outline on Corporations, Chapter 2, § II, Viewing the Corporation from Within.]

QUICKNOTES

N.H. G.L., C. 148 - Business of every corporation shall be managed by directors subject to the by-laws and carried out by officers appointed by the directors.

BYLAWS - Rules promulgated by a corporation regulating its governance.

NOTES:

SCHNELL v. CHRIS-CRAFT INDUSTRIES, INC.

Shareholder (P) v. Corporation (D)

Del. Sup. Ct., 285 A.2d 437 (1971).

NATURE OF CASE: Appeal from the denial of a petition by dissident stockholders for injunctive relief.

FACT SUMMARY: Chris-Craft's (D) managing directors amended the bylaws in accordance with the new Delaware Corporation Law, advancing the date of the annual stockholders' meeting.

CONCISE RULE OF LAW: Inequitable action does not become permissible simply because it is legally permissible.

FACTS: When the managing directors of Chris-Craft (D) met on October 18, 1971 to advance the date of the annual stockholders' meeting from January 11, 1971 to December 8, 1971 by amending the corporate bylaws, Schnell (P) and other dissident stockholders applied to the Delaware Court of Chancery for injunctive relief. Schnell (P) learned of management's action unofficially on October 27, 1971 and filed this action on November 1, 1971. The managing directors of Chris-Craft (D) contended that they complied strictly with the provisions of the new Delaware Corporation Law in changing the bylaw date. Schnell (P) contended that Chris-Craft's (D) management was attempting to impede Schnell's (P) efforts to solicit votes in favor of a rival slate of directors. The Chancery Court ruled that Schnell's (P) application for injunctive relief was tardy. Schnell (P) appealed.

ISSUE: Does inequitable action become permissible simply because it is legally permissible?

HOLDING AND DECISION: (Hermann, J.) No. Inequitable action does not become permissible simply because it is legally permissible. There is no indication of any prior warning of management's intent to amend the bylaws to change the annual stockholders' meeting date. Rather, it appears that management attempted to conceal its action as long as possible. Stockholders may not be charged with the duty of anticipating inequitable action by management and of seeking anticipatory injunctive relief to foreclose such action. Until management changed the date of the meeting, the stockholders had no need of judicial assistance. Accordingly, the judgment of the Chancery Court must be reversed and the case remanded with instructions to reinstate January 11, 1972 as the date for the next annual stockholders' meeting.

DISSENT: (Wolcott, C.J.) In view of the length of time leading up to the immediate events that caused the filing of this action, I agree with the lower court that the application for injunctive relief came too late.

EDITOR'S ANALYSIS: The Delaware Supreme Court declared that when the bylaws of a corporation designate the date of the annual meeting of stockholders, it is to be expected that those who intend to contest the reelection of incumbent management will gear their campaign to the bylaw date. It is not to be expected that management will attempt to advance that date in order to obtain an inequitable advantage in the contest. The advancement by directors of the bylaw date of a stockholders' meeting for such purposes may not be permitted to stand.

[For more information on duty of loyalty, see Casenote Law Outline on Corporations, Chapter 8, § IV, Fiduciary Duties of Care and Loyalty.]

QUICKNOTES

BYLAWS - Rules promulgated by a corporation regulating its governance.

NOTES:

BLASIUS INDUSTRIES, INC. v. ATLAS CORP.

Corporation (P) v. Takeover target (D)

Del Chancery Ct. 564 A.2d 651 (1988).

NATURE OF CASE: Action seeking to invalidate action by corporate directors.

FACT SUMMARY: The Board of Directors of Atlas Corp. (D) sought to prevent Blasius Corp. (P) from obtaining shareholder approval of its plan to enlarge the Board (D) by voting to expand the Board (D), and placing persons of its own choosing in the new seats.

CONCISE RULE OF LAW: A board of directors may not enlarge the size of the board for the purpose of preventing a majority of shareholders from voting to expand the board to give control to an insurgent group.

FACTS: Blasius Industries (P) acquired roughly 9% of the voting stock of Atlas Corp. (D). Blasius (P) presented the Board of Directors of Atlas (D) with a restructuring proposal that would have left Atlas (D) highly leveraged. The Directors (D) did not approve the proposal, considering it potentially damaging to the company. At this point, Blasius (P) began soliciting shareholders for approval of a proposal to expand the Board (D) from seven to fifteen members and to fill the eight new seats with persons of its choosing. This would have given control to Blasius (P). The Board (D) responded by voting to enlarge the board to nine members and choosing the persons to fill the new seats. Blasius (P) filed a lawsuit to invalidate the Board's (D) action, alleging breach of fiduciary duty.

ISSUE: May a board of directors enlarge the size of the board for the purpose of preventing a majority of shareholders from voting to expand the board to give control to an insurgent group?

HOLDING AND DECISION: (Allen, Chancellor) No. A board of directors may not enlarge the size of the board for the purpose of preventing a majority of shareholders from voting to expand the board to give control to an insurgent group. Shareholder franchise is the ideological basis for directorial power. The only legitimate reason why a select group of persons can control assets not belonging to them is a mandate from those who do control the assets. Consequently, any effort by the directors to frustrate the will of the majority, even if taken for the most unselfish of reasons, must fail. Directors are agents of shareholders, not their philosopher-kings. The business judgement rule simply does not apply in this context. Any attempt to frustrate shareholder voting cannot stand up to a challenge. Here, the Board (D) clearly based its action on a desire to prevent shareholder approval of a plan to give control to an insurgent group. Even though it was apparently taken by the Board (D) out of concerns for the welfare of the corporation, it was an invalid attempt to thwart shareholder voting power, and the action must therefore be voided. So ordered.

EDITOR'S ANALYSIS: Corporate directors, by virtue of their position, have a decided advantage with respect to corporate control. They have the power to set the corporate agenda and to time shareholder meetings. As the present case shows, however, this power is not unlimited. Courts will restrain overreaching by directors.

[For more information on elections of directors, see Casenote Law Outline on Corporations, Chapter 2, § II, Viewing the Corporation from Within.]

QUICKNOTES

RECAPITALIZATION - The restructuring of the capital of a corporation.

BUSINESS JUDGMENT RULE - Doctrine relieving corporate directors and/or officers from liability for decisions honestly and rationally made in the corporation's best interests.

NOTES:

STROUD v. GRACE

Subsidiary of Milliken family (P) v. Corporation (D) (Grace not identified.)

Del. Sup. Ct. 606 A.2d 75 (1992).

NATURE OF CASE: Cross-appeals from injunction striking down portions of corporate rules.

FACT SUMMARY: The Strouds (P) challenged provisions in the charter and bylaws of Milliken Enterprises (D) which related to directorial elections and had been approved by shareholders.

CONCISE RULE OF LAW: Provisions in corporate charters and bylaws relating to directorial elections approved by shareholders are presumptively valid.

FACTS: Milliken Enterprises (D) was controlled by the Milliken family, with family members having well over 50% of the voting stock. At a shareholder's meeting, certain amendments to the corporate charter and bylaws were approved. The amendments provided that Milliken family members were to have a right of first refusal when shares were sold. Also, provision was made that shareholders provide notice of their candidates for directorial positions well in advance of shareholder meetings so that the directors could review their qualifications as against those specified for corporate directors in the charter. The Strouds (P), a splinter group of the Milliken family, challenged these amendments as a breach of the directors' fiduciary duties. The chancery court upheld most of the amendments but struck down the notice bylaw. Both parties appealed.

ISSUE: Are provisions in corporate charters and bylaws relating to directorial elections approved by shareholders presumptively valid?

HOLDING AND DECISION: (Moore, J.) Yes. Provisions in corporate charter and bylaws relating to directorial elections approved by shareholders are presumptively valid. In the absence of fraud, a fully informed shareholder vote in favor of even a voidable transaction ratifies board action and places the burden of proof on the challenger. The challenger must then demonstrate that the challenged action was undertaken with some illegitimate purpose in mind, and such demonstration must be done with facts, not hypothetical arguments. Here, no such showing has been made with respect to any of the amendments. The Milliken (D) board did not face any threat to its control, as it constituted an effective majority of shareholders. Consequently, the amendments were not control-perpetuating devices. Nothing in the first-refusal provision or the notice provision approaches a breach of fiduciary duty, and consequently both are valid. Affirmed in part, reversed in part.

EDITOR'S ANALYSIS: The trial court in this instance found the notice provision to be facially invalid. Such a finding is inconsistent with a matter approved by shareholders. When shareholders approve a rule, legitimacy is presumed. The one claiming invalidity must then point to specific applications of the rule that are invalid. A facial challenge is inappropriate.

QUICKNOTES

DUTY OF CARE - A principal of negligence requiring an individual to act in such a manner as to avoid injury to a person to whom he or she owes an obligatory duty.

VOIDABLE TRANSACTION - A valid transaction that may later be avoided due to some defect, but that is binding until repudiated.

FIDUCIARY DUTY - A legal obligation to act for the benefit of another, including subordinating one's personal interests to that of the other person.

INTRINSIC FAIRNESS TEST - A defense to a claim that a director engaged in an interested director transaction by showing the transaction's fairness to the corporation.

NOTES:

INTERNATIONAL BROTHERHOOD OF TEAMSTERS v. FLEMING COMPANIES, INC.

Shareholder (P) v. Corporation(D)

Okla. Sup. Ct., ___ P.2d ___, 1999 WL 35227 (1999).

NATURE OF CASE: Certification to state supreme court by federal court of appeals to answer a question of law.

FACT SUMMARY: The Teamsters (P), shareholders in the Fleming Companies (D), proposed a proxy statement for the next annual shareholders meeting which included an amendment of the bylaws requiring ratification by shareholders of poison pill rights plans implemented by the company's board of directors.

CONCISE RULE OF LAW: A certification of incorporation which is silent with regard to shareholder rights plans does not preclude shareholder enacted bylaws regarding the implementation of rights plans.

FACTS: The International Brotherhood of Teamsters General Fund (P) owned sixty-five shares of Fleming Companies (D). Fleming (D) implemented a shareholders rights plan with an anti-takeover mechanism, also known as a "poison pill." The Teamsters (P), concerned that corporate authority regarding share marketability was being removed from the shareholders and vested exclusively in a board of directors, introduced a resolution at the annual shareholders meeting calling on the board to redeem the existing rights plan. Although the resolution was approved by a majority of the shareholders, the board refused to honor it. The next year, the Teamsters (P) proposed an amendment to the company's bylaws which would require any rights plan implemented by the board of directors to be put to the shareholders for a majority vote. This amendment was part of a proxy statement prepared for inclusion in the 1997 proxy materials. Fleming (D) refused to include the resolution in its 1997 proxy statement, declaring that the proposal was not a subject for shareholder action under state law. The Teamsters (P) then brought an action in the federal district court, which found in their favor that shareholders, through the device of bylaws, have a right of review. Fleming (D) appealed, and the 10th Circuit Court of Appeals submitted the certified question to the Oklahoma Supreme Court.

ISSUE: Does a certification of incorporation which is silent with regard to shareholder rights plans preclude shareholder enacted bylaws regarding the implementation of rights plans?

HOLDING AND DECISION: (Simms, J.) No. A certification of incorporation which is silent with regard to shareholder rights plans does not preclude shareholder enacted bylaws regarding the implementation of rights plans. A shareholders rights plan is essentially a variety of stock option plan. Its use as an anti-takeover mechanism does not change its essential character.

Stock option plans are not exempt from shareholders approval or ratification. Oklahoma has not passed a shareholders rights plan endorsement statute which would give explicit authority to directors of corporations. Without the authority granted in such an endorsement statute, the board may well be subject to the general procedures of corporate governance, including the enactment of bylaws which the limit the board's authority to implement shareholders rights plans.

EDITOR'S ANALYSIS: The court in this case discussed share rights plan endorsement statutes. At least twenty-four states have such laws. These statutes ensure that corporations are able to implement shareholders rights plans to protect the company from takeover. Such rights plans may serve to entrench the existing management and have the ability to strip shareholders of financial benefit which might normally be associated with a takeover.

QUICKNOTES

POISON PILL - A tactic employed by a company, which is the target of a takeover attempt, to make the purchase of its shares less attractive to a potential buyer by requiring the issuance of a new series of shares to be redeemed at a substantial premium over their stated value if a party purchases a specified percentage of voting shares of the corporation.

GENERAL DATACOMM INDUSTRIES, INC. v. WISCONSIN INVESTMENT BOARD

Corporation (P) v. State board (D)

Del. Ch., 1999 WL 66533 (1999).

NATURE OF CASE: Motion to expedite proceedings for declaratory and injunctive relief regarding the validity of a proposed bylaw.

FACT SUMMARY: General Datacomm Industries (GDC) (P) contended that a proposed repricing bylaw unlawfully restricted the directors' statutory power and authority.

CONCISE RULE OF LAW: Unripe claims raising issues novel and important to Delaware corporate law should be dismissed.

FACTS: GDC (P) alleged that a bylaw proposed by the State of Wisconsin Investment Board (SWIB)(D) for consideration at the upcoming annual shareholders meeting was invalid. The proposed repricing bylaw required shareholders' approval of any decision to reprice stock options already issued and outstanding to a lower strike price. The Securities and Exchange Commission (SEC) advised GDC (P) that it could not exclude the repricing bylaw proposal from its proxy materials. GDC (P) then sought declaratory and injunctive relief and moved to expedite proceedings one week before its annual meeting was scheduled to begin.

ISSUE: Should unripe claims raising issues novel and important to Delaware corporate law be dismissed?

HOLDING AND DECISION: (Stevens, J.) Yes. Unripe claims raising issues novel and important to Delaware corporate law should be dismissed. GDC (P) seeks to have this court determine the validity of a yet to be adopted bylaw. No irreparable harm is threatened and post-meeting adjudication would not unduly disrupt the corporation's affairs. This lack of urgency cuts against the need to determine a potentially important issue of Delaware law in haste. Absent an imminent threat of irreparable injury, there is no need for this court to step into the void when the SEC concludes that state law is not clear. The issues raised in GDC's (P) complaint are not yet ripe for judicial resolution. Motion denied.

EDITOR'S ANALYSIS: The court in this case refused to render an advisory opinion. It had to balance the reasons for not rendering a hypothetical opinion against the benefits to be derived from the rendering of a declaratory judgment. In the event the repricing bylaw was actually adopted by the GDC (P) stockholders, the court said it would consider a renewed application for expedited proceedings.

QUICKNOTES

EQUITY - Fairness; justice; the determination of a matter consistent with principles of fairness and not in strict compliance with rules of law.

RIPENESS - A doctrine precluding a federal court from hearing or determining a matter, unless it constitutes an actual and present controversy warranting a determination by the court.

PROXY - A person authorized to act for another.

FLETCHER v. ATEX, INC.
Keyboard user (P) v. Keyboard maker (D)
68 F.3d 1451 (2d Cir. 1995).

NATURE OF CASE: Appeal from summary judgment dismissing defendant in design defect case.

FACT SUMMARY: Fletcher (P) brought suit against Atex (D) and Eastman Kodak (D), its parent company, to recover for injuries incurred from the utilization of computer keyboards produced by Atex (D).

CONCISE RULE OF LAW: Under applicable state law, the court may pierce the corporate veil of a company and hold its shareholders personally liable only in cases involving fraud, or where the company is a mere instrumentality or alter ego of its parent company.

FACTS: Atex (D) was a wholly owned subsidiary of Kodak (D) until 1992, when Atex (D) sold substantially all of its assets to another party. Atex (D) then changed its name to 805 Middlesex Corp. Kodak (D) continued as the sole shareholder of Middlesex. Fletcher (P) and other claimants (P) brought suit against Atex (D) and Kodak (D) to recover for stress injuries they incurred from utilizing keyboards produced by Atex (D). Fletcher (P) argued that Kodak (D) exercised undue control over Atex (D) by using a cash management system, exerting control over Atex's (D) major expenditures, and by dominating Atex's (D) board of directors. The lower court dismissed Kodak (D) as a defendant on summary judgment. Fletcher et al. (P) appealed.

ISSUE: May the court pierce the corporate veil of a company and hold its shareholders personally liable only in cases involving fraud, or where the company is a mere instrumentality or alter ego of its parent company?

HOLDING AND DECISION: (Cabranes, J.) Yes. Under applicable state law, the court may pierce the corporate veil of a company and hold its shareholders individually liable only in cases involving fraud, or where the company is a mere instrumentality or alter ego of its parent company. New York state law looks to the law of the state of incorporation to determine whether the court will disregard the corporate form and hold shareholders individually liable for the actions of the corporation. Since Atex (D) is a Delaware corporation, the law of that forum applies. Under Delaware law, an alter ego claim is demonstrated by a showing that the parent and its subsidiary acted as a single economic entity, and it would be unjust or inequitable to treat them as distinct from one another. Factors the court may consider in making its determination include the adequacy of capitalization, the corporation's solvency, payment of dividends, observation of corporate formalities, and the intermingling of funds. Summary judgment may be granted for a defendant parent corporation where there has been an absence of sufficient evidence proffered to raise an issue of material fact as to the question of instrumentality. In this case, it would not be correct to disregard the corporate entity solely based on Kodak's (D) implementation of a cash management system. Such a system does not rise to the level of intermingling contemplated by the statute. Similarly, an overlap in the two companies' (D) boards of directors is not conclusive of Kodak's (D) domination over Atex (D). Fletcher (P) failed to demonstrate the degree of control necessary to pierce Atex's (D) corporate veil and hold Kodak (D) liable. Affirmed.

EDITOR'S ANALYSIS: It is not uncommon for publicly held corporations to own numerous subsidiaries. Subsidiaries are established in order to operate in areas that are either unrelated to the parent's main business, or that necessitate more centralized organization. Here Atex (D) was in the business of manufacturing keyboards, an enterprise unrelated to Kodak's (D) primary business. Although Atex (D) looked to Kodak (D) for support on significant transactions, it is not unusual for a parent corporation or a majority shareholder to participate in such transactions involving the subsidiary.

[For more information on piercing the corporate veil, see Casenote Law Outline on Corporations, Chapter 2, § III, Viewing the Corporation from Without.]

QUICKNOTES

ALTER EGO - Other self; under the "alter ego" doctrine, the court disregards the corporate entity and holds the individual shareholders liable for acts done knowingly and intentionally in the corporation's name.

CORPORATE VEIL - Refers to the shielding from personal liability of a corporation's officers, directors or shareholders for unlawful conduct engaged in by the corporation.

WALKOVSZKY v. CARLTON
Injured pedestrian (P) v. Cab company stockholder (D)
N.Y. Ct. App., 18 N.Y.2d 414, 276 N.Y.S.2d 585, 223 N.E.2d 6 (1966).

NATURE OF CASE: Action to recover damages for personal injury.

FACT SUMMARY: Walkovszky (P), run down by a taxicab owned by Seon Cab Corporation (D), sued Carlton (D), a stockholder of ten corporations, including Seon (D), each which had but two cabs registered in its name. Walkovszky (P) also sued each of the ten corporations (D), claiming that they operated as a single entity.

CONCISE RULE OF LAW: Whenever anyone uses control of a corporation to further his own rather than the corporation's business, he will be liable for the corporation's acts. However, where a corporation is a fragment of a larger corporate combine which actually conducts the business, a court will not "pierce the corporate veil" to hold individual shareholders liable.

FACTS: Walkovszky (P) was run down by a taxicab owned by Seon Cab Corporation (D). In his complaint, Walkovszky (P) alleged that Seon was one of ten cab companies of which Carlton (D) was a shareholder, and that each corporation had but two cabs registered in its name. The complaint, by this, implied that each cab corporation carried only the minimum automobile liability insurance required by law ($10,000). It was further alleged that these corporations were operated as a single entity with regards to financing, supplies, repairs, employees, and garaging. Each corporation and its shareholders were named as defendants because the multiple corporate structure, Walkovszky (P) claimed, constituted an unlawful attempt to "defraud members of the general public."

ISSUE: When ever anyone uses control of a corporation to further his own rather then the corporation's business, will he be liable for the corporation's acts?

HOLDING AND DECISION: (Fuld, J.) No. Whenever anyone uses control of a corporation to further his own rather than the corporation's business, he will be liable for the corporation's acts. Upon the principle of respondeat superior, the liability extends to negligent acts as well as commercial dealings. However, where a corporation is a fragment of a larger corporate combine which actually conducts the business, a court will not "pierce the corporate veil" to hold individual shareholders liable. While the law permits the incorporation of a business for the purpose of minimizing personal liability, this privilege can be abused. Courts will disregard the corporate form ("pierce the corporate veil") to prevent fraud or to achieve equity. General rules of agency — respondeat superior — will apply to hold an individual liable for a corporation's negligent acts. The court here had earlier invoked the doctrine in a case where the owner of several cab companies

(and whose name was prominently displayed on the cabs) actually serviced, inspected, repaired, and dispatched them. However, in such instances, it must be shown that the stockholder was conducting the business in his individual capacity. In this respect, Walkovszky's (D) complaint was deficient. The corporate form may not be disregarded simply because the assets of the corporation, together with liability insurance, are insufficient to assure recovery. If the insurance coverage is inadequate, the remedy lies with the legislature and not the courts. It is not fraudulent for the owner of a single cab corporation to take out no more than minimum insurance. Fraud goes to whether Carlton (D) and his associates (D) were shuttling their funds in and out of the corporations without regard to formality and to suit their own convenience.

DISSENT: (Keating, J.) The attempt to do corporate business without providing any sufficient basis of financial responsibility to creditors — here, through under-capitalization and minimum insurance liabilities — is an abuse of the corporate entity. Where the operation of the corporate enterprise yielded profits sufficient to purchase additional insurance, the legislature certainly did not intend to shield those individuals who organized these corporations to minimize their own personal liability.

EDITOR'S ANALYSIS: Courts, in justifying disregard of the corporate entity so as to pierce the corporate veil, advance an estoppel argument. If the entity is not respected by the shareholders, they cannot complain if the court, likewise, disregards the corporate arrangement page — this is to prevent abuse of the form. Since the corporate veil may be dismissed even in instances where there has been no reliance on a company's seeming healthiness — as in tort claims — whether or not creditors have been misled is not of primary importance. Rather, a court will look at the degree to which the corporate shell has been perfected and the corporation's use as a mere business conduit of its shareholders.

[For more information on piercing the corporate veil, see Casenote Law Outline on Corporations, Chapter 2, § III, Viewing the Corporation from Without.]

QUICKNOTES

RESPONDEAT SUPERIOR - Rule that the principal is responsible for tortious acts committed by its agents in the scope of their agency or authority.

CORPORATE VEIL - Refers to the shielding from personal liability of a corporation's officers, directors or shareholders for unlawful conduct engaged in by the corporation.

CAPITALIZATION - The aggregate value of all securities issued by a company.

MINTON v. CAVANEY
Deceased swimmer (P) v. Corporate director (D)
Cal. Sup. Ct. of Cal., 364 P.2d 473, 56 C.2d 576 (1961).

NATURE OF CASE: To recover on judgment for wrongful death of daughter.

FACT SUMMARY: Minton (P), unable to satisfy judgment obtained from Seminole for his daughter's drowning, sought to hold Cavaney (D) personally liable.

CONCISE RULE OF LAW: Where a person actively participates in corporate affairs of a company inadequately capitalized, and the person is an equitable owner in that corporation, he will be held personally liable for any corporate debts.

FACTS: Minton's (P) daughter drowned in a leased pool operated by Seminole Hot Springs Co. Minton (P) recovered a $10,000 judgment against Seminole for negligence, but when the judgment was not paid, he brought action against the estate of Cavaney (D), Seminole's attorney at the time of the accident. Cavaney (D) was a director, treasurer, and secretary of Seminole but only as a temporary accommodation to his corporate client. He also was to receive one share of Seminole's stock, and he did keep its records in his office. Before his death, Cavaney (D) stated that Seminole had no assets, and though duly organized, never functioned as a corporation. Minton (P) sought to hold Cavaney's (D) estate personally liable for the unsatisfied judgment against Seminole on the theory that Seminole was Cavaney's (D) "alter ego." Trial court gave judgment for Minton (P) and, on appeal, reversed on procedural grounds.

ISSUE: Where a person participates in a corporation's affairs and evidence shows him to be an equitable owner in such company, may that person be held personally liable for the corporation's debts where he knows it is undercapitalized?

HOLDING AND DECISION: (Traynor, J.) Yes. Seminole never had any substantial assets. Thus, there was no dispute as to its undercapitalization. Also, evidence established Cavaney (D) as equitable owner in Seminole since he acted as officer-director, kept its records for safekeeping, and was entitled to a share of stock. It is immaterial that he accepted the directorate as an accommodation. Once a person is named a corporate director, he may not divorce the responsibilities of that office from the statutory duties and powers imposed on the office. Thus, it does not matter that Cavaney (D) never performed directorial duties.

EDITOR'S ANALYSIS: Any attempt to do corporate business without providing sufficient assets to meet corporate responsibilities to creditors is an abuse of the corporate privilege. The law extends the corporate privilege so that corporate stockholders may not suffer personal liability inherent in partnerships. But if the capital supporting the corporation is illusory or small compared to anticipated risks, this is a fraud upon the public dealing with such corporation.

[For more information on "Piercing the Corporate Veil", see Casenote Law Outline on Corporations, Chapter 2, § III, Viewing the Corporation from Without.]

QUICKNOTES

CORPORATE VEIL - Refers to the shielding from personal liability of a corporation's officers, directors or shareholders for unlawful conduct engaged in by the corporation.

CAPITALIZATION - The aggregate value of all securities issued by a company.

ALTER EGO - Other self; under the "alter ego" doctrine, the court disregards the corporate entity and holds the individual shareholders liable for acts done knowingly and intentionally in the corporation's name.

NOTES:

SEA-LAND SERVICES, INC. v. PEPPER SOURCE
Shipper (P) v. Corporation owner (D)
941 F.2d 519 (7th Cir. 1991).

NATURE OF CASE: Appeal from summary judgment in favor of plaintiff in an action to collect monies owed.

FACT SUMMARY: Sea-Land Services (P) sued Marchese (D) individually and five business entities that he owned, including Pepper Source (PS) (D), on the grounds that all the corporations were alter egos of Marchese (D).

CONCISE RULE OF LAW: A corporate entity will be disregarded and the veil of limited liability pierced when there is such unity of interest and ownership that the separate personalities of the corporation and the individual no longer exist and when adherence to the fiction of separate corporate existence would sanction a fraud or promote injustice.

FACTS: Sea-Land (P), an ocean carrier, shipped Jamaican sweet peppers for PS (D), a corporation. When PS (D) did not pay its substantial freight bill, Sea-Land (P) sued. A default judgment was entered in Sea-Land's (P) favor for $86,767.70. PS (D), however, had been dissolved, and Sea-Land (P) could not recover. Sea-Land (P) then filed suit against Marchese (D) and five business entities he owned, including PS (D). Sea-Land (P) alleged that all the corporations were alter-egos of each other and of Marchese (D) and that they hid behind the veils of alleged separate corporate existence in order to defraud Sea-Land (P) and other creditors. An additional defendant corporation, Tie-Net (D), was not wholly owned by Marchese (D), but Sea-Land (P) argued that Tie-Net (D) was also Marchese's (D) alter ego and should be held liable for the judgment against PS (D). Sea-Land (P) then moved for summary judgment, which the trial court granted, and Marchese, et al. (D) were held jointly liable for the judgment and post-judgment interest. Marchese, et al. (D) appealed.

ISSUE: Will a corporate entity be disregarded and the veil of limited liability pierced when the unity of interest and ownership are such that the separate personalities of the corporation and the individual no longer exist and when adherence to the fiction of separate corporate existence would sanction a fraud or promote injustice?

HOLDING AND DECISION: (Bauer, C.J.) Yes. A corporate entity will be disregarded and the veil of limited liability pierced when the unity of interest and ownership are such that separate personalities of the corporation and the individual no longer exist and when adherence to the fiction of separate corporate existence would sanction a fraud or promote injustice. In this case, these corporate entities are little more than Marchese's (D) playthings. Marchese (D) is the sole shareholder of all the

corporations except Tie-Net (D), and none of the corporations have ever had a corporate meeting. Marchese (D) runs all of the corporations out of a single office with the same phone line, the same expense accounts, etc. He borrowed money from the corporate bank accounts to pay personal expenses. The first part of the Van Dorn test — unity of interest and ownership — has been met here. The second part of the test — corporate existence sanctioning a fraud or promoting injustice — is more problematic. To promote injustice, thus allowing the corporate veil to be pierced, some "wrong" must have been done by a defendant. Here, although Sea-Land (P) alleged intentional asset-and-liability-shifting akin to that in Van Dorn, it has yet to come forward with evidence akin to "wrongs" found in other cases. Its unsatisfied judgment is not enough. On remand, Sea-Land (P) should be required to produce evidence establishing wrongs such as unjust enrichment or an intent to hide assets. Reversed and remanded.

EDITOR'S ANALYSIS: Chief Justice Bauer noted in the Sea-Land case that the record established that Marchese (D) did not maintain corporate records and formalities. Marchese (D) commingled funds with abandon and Pepper Source (D), the offending corporation, as well as the other corporations owned by Marchese (D), had been undercapitalized; corporate assets had also been moved and tapped without regard to their source. This evidence was sufficient to satisfy the first half of the test articulated in Van Dorn Co. v. Future Chemical & Oil Corp., 753 F.2d 565 (7th Cir. 1985).

[For more information on limitations on limited liability, see Casenote Law Outline on Corporations, Chapter 2, § III, Viewing the Corporation from Without.]

QUICKNOTES
CORPORATE VEIL - Refers to the shielding from personal liability of a corporation's officers, directors or shareholders for unlawful conduct engaged in by the corporation.

LIMITED LIABILITY - An advantage of doing business in the corporate form by safeguarding shareholders from liability for the debts or obligations of the corporation.

CHAPTER 5
SHAREHOLDER INFORMATION RIGHTS AND PROXY VOTING

QUICK REFERENCE RULES OF LAW

1. **Shareholder Information Rights Under State Law.** A stockholder may demonstrate a proper demand for the production of corporate books and records upon a showing, by the preponderance of the evidence, that there exists a credible basis to find probable corporate wrongdoing. (Security First Corp.v. U.S. Die Casting and Development Co.)

2. **Private action under the Proxy rules.** Where a trial court makes a finding that a proxy solicitation contains a materially false or misleading statement under SEC 14(a), a stockholder seeking to establish a cause of action under such finding does not have to further prove that his reliance on the contents of the defects in the proxy solicitation caused him to vote for proposed transactions that later proved unfair to his interests in the corporation. (Mills v. Electric Auto-Lite Co.)

   [For more information on Regulation 14a, see Casenote Law Outline on Corporations, Chapter 6, § I, Regulation 14a of the SEC.]

3. **Private action under the Proxy rules.** Knowingly false or misleadingly incomplete statements of reasons made by corporate directors in a proxy solicitation may be actionable even though conclusory in form. (Virginia Bankshares, Inc. v. Sandberg)

   [For more information on private actions under the proxy rules, see Casenote Law Outline on Corporations, Chapter 6, § II, Implied Right of Action for Shareholders.]

4. **Shareholder Proposals.** Shareholder proposals that deal with ordinary business operations are not entitled to inclusion in proxy materials. (Roosevelt v. E.I. DuPont de Nemours & Co.)

   [For more information on shareholder proposals in proxy materials, see Casenote Law Outline on Corporations, Chapter 6, § I, Regulation 14a of the SEC.]

5. **Shareholder Proposals.** The promotion of corporate suffrage regarding a significant policy issue confers a substantial benefit regardless of the percentage of votes cast for or against the proposal at issue. (Amalagated Clothing and Textile Workers v. Walmart Stores)

   [For more information on shareholder right of participation, see Casenote Law Outline on Corporations, Chapter 3, § II, Structuring the Close Corporation.]

6. **Proxy Contests.** In policy contests, corporate funds may be used to pay reasonable and proper expenses incurred in a proxy fight (1) by incumbent directors acting in good faith in soliciting proxies and defending their corporate policies, and (2) by successful insurgent groups where, after gaining power, such groups receive ratification by stockholders for reimbursement of such expenses. (Rosenfeld v. Fairchild Engine and Airplane Corp.)

   [For more information on Proxy Contests, see Casenote Law Outline on Corporations, Chapter 6, § I, Regulation 14a of the SEC.]

SECURITY FIRST CORP. v. U.S. DIE CASTING AND DEVELOPMENT CO.

Corporation (D) v. Stockholder (P)

Del. Sup. Ct., 687 A.2d 563 (1997).

NATURE OF CASE: Appeal from court order granting demand for production of books and records.

FACT SUMMARY: U.S. Die (P), a stockholder, requested to inspect Security First's (D) corporate books and records to investigate possible mismanagement.

CONCISE RULE OF LAW: A stockholder may demonstrate a proper demand for the production of corporate books and records upon a showing, by the preponderance of the evidence, that there exists a credible basis to find probable corporate wrongdoing.

FACTS: Following the abrogation of a proposed merger of Security (D) and another corporation, Security (D) paid the other corporation a termination fee even though the events necessary for such payment had not occurred. The value of Security's (D) common stock then dropped significantly and did not rebound. Security (D) responded by increasing dividends. U.S. Die (P), a 5% owner of the common stock of Security (D), made a § 220 demand to inspect all of Security's (D) books and records related to the merger as provided in the Delaware General Corporation Law. Security refused to comply. The court of chancery granted U.S. Die's (P) request for inspection of Security's (D) books and records and its stockholder list. Security (D) appealed.

ISSUE: Does a stockholder demonstrate a proper demand for the production of corporate books and records upon a showing, by the preponderance of the evidence, that there exists a credible basis to find probable corporate wrongdoing?

HOLDING AND DECISION: (Veasey, C.J.) Yes. A stockholder may demonstrate a proper demand for the production of corporate books and records upon a showing, by the preponderance of the evidence, that there exists a credible basis to find probable corporate wrongdoing. The plaintiff must not only show a credible basis to find probable wrongdoing, but must justify each category of the requested production. By raising questions about Security's (D) payment of a termination fee, the drop in stock value, and increased dividends, U.S. Die (P) has produced evidence suggestive of misconduct. Therefore, U.S. Die (P) has established a proper purpose for its request to inspect books and records. However, the scope of the inspection is a separate issue on which U.S. Die (P) bears the burden of specific justification. U.S. Die (P) has not met its burden of proof to establish that each category of books and records requested is essential to the accomplishment of its stated purpose. In this case, the judgment of the trial court on the entitlement to books and records is affirmed, but the scope of the judgment is reversed

as overly broad. The proceeding is remanded for a determination of a properly tailored order of inspection. On the other hand, Security (D) has met its burden of proving that U.S. Die's (P) demand to inspect its stockholder list was not for a proper purpose. At trial, U.S. Die's (P) CEO admitted he had no idea what he would do with such a list. The court of chancery's decision to grant U.S. Die's (P) request to inspect Security's (D) stockholder list is reversed.

EDITOR'S ANALYSIS: The scope of an inspection under a § 220 proceeding must be tailored to its specific purpose. It is different from a comprehensive discovery order under local court rules. In the case above, the lower court's decision on the scope of the stockholder's inspection was reviewed for abuse of discretion; the stockholder's request to inspect a stockholder list was reviewed de novo.

QUICKNOTES

MERGER: The acquisition of one company by another, after which the acquired company ceases to exist as an independent entity.

COMMON STOCK: A class of stock representing the corporation's ownership, the holders of which are entitled to dividends only after the holders of preferred stock are paid.

DIVIDEND: The payment of earnings to a corporation's shareholders in proportion to the amount of shares held.

NOTES:

MILLS v. ELECTRIC AUTO-LITE COMPANY
Shareholder (P) v. Corporation (D)
396 U.S. 375 (1970).

NATURE OF CASE: Derivative suit and class action to set aside a merger.

FACT SUMMARY: Mills (P) brought a derivative suit and class action against the management of Auto-Lite (D) and other companies to set aside a merger obtained through allegedly misleading proxy solicitations.

CONCISE RULE OF LAW: Where a trial court makes a finding that a proxy solicitation contains a materially false or misleading statement under SEC 14(a), a stockholder seeking to establish a cause of action under such finding does not have to further prove that his reliance on the contents of the defects in the proxy solicitation caused him to vote for proposed transactions that later proved unfair to his interests in the corporation.

FACTS: In 1963, Electric Auto-Lite Co. (D) sought merger with Mergenthaler Linotype Co. The day before shareholders were to vote on the merger, Mills (P) and other shareholders of Auto-Lite (D) sought an injunction against Auto-Lite's (D) management to stop them from voting proxies obtained by means of an allegedly misleading proxy solicitation. The suit also named American Manufacturing Co., which owned about one-third of Mergenthaler's shares and had voting control of Mergenthaler. Mergenthaler owned about 50% of Auto-Lite's (D) common stock and had control of that company. But, since Mills (P) failed to seek a temporary restraining order, the voting on the merger proceeded and the merger was approved. Subsequently, Mills (P) amended his complaint, seeking to set aside the merger and to obtain other relief. The district court found that a two-thirds vote of Auto-Lite's (D) shares was required to approve the merger. Since Mergenthaler and American Manufacturing controlled about 54% of Auto-Lite's (D) shares, it was necessary to gain the approval of a substantial minority shareholder vote. At the stockholder's meeting, about 950,000 of 1,160,000 shares were voted in favor of the merger. 317,000 of these votes were obtained by the allegedly misleading proxy solicitation from minority shareholders. The district court found these votes necessary and indispensable to the approval of the merger, and granted an interlocutory judgment in favor of Mills (P) on grounds that a causal relationship had been shown between the solicitation and the injury. An interlocutory appeal was taken to the court of appeals. The court of appeals affirmed the district court's conclusion that the proxy statement was materially misleading, but reversed on the causation issue, holding that Mills (P) must further show that there was a causal connection between the injury suffered by Auto-Lite (D) stockholders and the misleading proxy solicitations. They held that the causation issue should be determined on the fairness of the terms of the merger. Mills (P) appealed from this reversal.

ISSUE: Where a trial court finds that a proxy solicitation contains materially false or misleading statements in violation of SEC 14(a), does a shareholder, in seeking to establish a cause of action for injury from such act, have to further prove that he relied on the contents of the defects in the proxy solicitation and such reliance caused him to vote for the proposed transaction?

HOLDING AND DECISION: (Harlan, J.) No. Where the misstatement or omission in a proxy statement is shown to be material, as is the case here, that determination alone embodies the conclusion that the defective statement was such that it might have been considered important enough by a shareholder to use it as a basis for deciding how to vote. Rule 14(a) contains the express requirement that the defect have a significant propensity to affect the voting process. There is no need to add to this requirement, as the court of appeals attempted to do, the further requirement of proof as to whether the defect did in fact have a decisive effect on voting. Where there has been a finding of materiality, a shareholder has made a sufficient showing of causal relationship between the violation of SEC 14(a) and the resulting injury, but only if there is proof by the plaintiff that the proxy solicitation and not the defect was the deciding link in causing such injury. The court of appeals "fairness test" as a defense to a violation of SEC 14(a) would confront small shareholders with an added obstacle to establishing a cause of action to a defective proxy statement. Whether or not the merger was fair has no bearing on establishing a cause of action under that section. As held in the Borak case, the purpose of 14(a) was stated to be the promotion of the free exercise of stockholder voting rights by requiring proxy solicitations contain explanations of the real nature of the questions for which authority to cast the proxies is sought. In the present case, once the causal relationship of the proxy material and the merger were established at trial — essentially questions of fact — the Supreme Court's only issue was whether the facts on which that conclusion was reached were sufficient at law to establish Mills' (P) cause of action under 14(a). The Court concluded they were. (III): This court held in Borak that on finding a violation of SEC 14(a), remedies must effect the congressional purpose behind the act. Such remedies are not limited to prospective relief, but may include retrospective relief based on factors governing relief in similar fraud cases. Possible terms of relief could be the setting aside of the merger or granting other equitable relief with fairness of the merger a contributing factor. But the courts are not required to unscramble a corporate transaction. A merger can't be set aside merely because the merger agreement is a void contract, compelling a conclusion that no enforceable rights are created even when a party is innocent of

Continued on next page.

the violation. But the guilty party is precluded from enforcing the contract against the unwilling innocent party. Thus, the contract becomes voidable at the option of the innocent party. As to monetary relief, if the defect in the proxy solicitations relates to specific terms of the merger, an accounting may be ordered; but if the misleading aspect does not relate to the merger terms, monetary relief is available to shareholders to the extent they can be shown. (IV): Concerning the awarding of the attorney fees and litigation expenses, although the general American rule does not allow for such recovery, one primary judge-made exception is to award such expenses where a plaintiff has successfully maintained a class action suit benefitting a group of others as he is benefitted. Mills (P) has rendered a substantial service to Auto-Lite (D) shareholders. The benefit furnished all the shareholders here is enforcement of the proxy statute.

DISSENT: (Black, J.) As to Part IV, stockholders who hire lawyers to prosecute their claims should not recover attorney fees in the absence of an agreement so providing or a statute creating such right of recovery.

EDITOR'S ANALYSIS: The rationale behind Rule 14(a) is to create an informed electorate of shareholders and, thus, further the ideal of corporate democracy. The court in the present case realized, however, that the purpose of the rule would be destroyed if oppressive burdens of proof of misuse of proxy statements were placed on shareholders in attempting to establish a cause of action against management. If stockholders in the present case were required to prove that they had actually relied on the false proxy statements, the burden of proof would be so heavy that many potentially valid causes of actions would be dropped before they were even started. This would give management an effective shield against shareholder action and prosecution for misuse of corporate proxy solicitations. The court in this case refused to encourage such wrongdoing.

[For more information on Regulation 14a, see Casenote Law Outline on Corporations, Chapter 6, § I, Regulation 14a of the SEC.]

QUICKNOTES

SECURITIES EXCHANGE ACT, § 14 (a) - Prevents management from obtaining illegal proxies.

MATERIALITY - Importance; the degree of relevance or necessity to the particular matter.

PROXY STATEMENT - A statement, containing specified information by the Securities and Exchange Commission, in order to provide shareholders with adequate information upon which to make an informed decision regarding the solicitation of their proxies.

SECURITIES EXCHANGE ACT, § 29(b) - Contracts made in violation of the Act are void.

VIRGINIA BANKSHARES, INC. v. SANDBERG

Corporation (D) v. Minority shareholder (P)

111 S. Ct. 2749 (1991).

NATURE OF CASE: Appeal from award of damages for violation of SEC Rule 14a-9 and breach of fiduciary duty.

FACT SUMMARY: After approval of a "freeze-out" merger at a shareholders' meeting, minority shareholder Sandberg (P) sought damages, alleging materially false and misleading statements in the proxy solicitations.

CONCISE RULE OF LAW: Knowingly false or misleadingly incomplete statements of reasons made by corporate directors in a proxy solicitation may be actionable even though conclusory in form.

FACTS: First American Bankshares, Inc., (FABI) (D) began a "freeze-out" merger in which the First American Bank of Virginia (Bank) (D) eventually merged into Virginia Bankshares, Inc. (VBI) (D), a wholly owned subsidiary of FABI (D). FABI (D) hired an investment banking firm to give an opinion on the appropriate price for shares of the minority holders, who would lose their interests in the Bank (D) as a result of the merger. After the investment bankers stated that $42 a share would be a fair price for the minority stock, the Bank's (D) executive committee approved the merger proposal at that price, and the full board followed suit. In their proxy solicitations, the board of directors urged adoption of the merger, stating they had approved the plan because of its opportunity for the minority shareholders to achieve a "high" value, which they elsewhere described as a "fair" price, for the stock. Sandberg (P) did not give the requested proxy, and, after approval of the merger, she sought damages in federal district court from VBI (D), FABI (D), and the directors of the Bank (D). The jury ruled for Sandberg (P), finding violations of Rule 14a-9 and a breach of fiduciary duties by the Bank's (D) directors, and awarding her $18 a share (based on a finding that she would have received $60 if her stock had been valued adequately). The court of appeals affirmed, holding that conclusory statements in the proxy solicitation were materially misleading under the rule, and that Sandberg (P) could maintain the action even though the minority shareholder votes had not been needed to approve the merger.

ISSUE: May knowingly false or misleadingly incomplete statements of reasons made by corporate directors in a proxy solicitation be actionable even though conclusory in form?

HOLDING AND DECISION: (Souter, J.) Yes. Knowingly false or misleadingly incomplete statements of reasons made by corporate directors in a proxy solicitation may be actionable even though conclusory in form. Whether $42 was "high," and the proposal "fair" to the minority shareholders depended on provable facts about the Bank's (D) assets. There was evidence

of a "going concern" value for the Bank in excess of $60 per share of common stock, a fact never disclosed. A statement of belief may be open to objection solely as a misstatement of the speaker's belief in what he says. The court of appeals observed that the jury was certainly justified in concluding that the directors did not believe a merger at $42 per share was in the minority stockholder's interest, but rather that they voted as they did for other reasons, e.g., retaining their seats on the board. Nevertheless, disbelief or undisclosed motivation, standing alone, without any demonstration that the proxy statement was false or misleading about its subject, is insufficient to satisfy the element of fact that must be established under § 14(a). However, recognition of any private right of action for violating a federal statute ultimately rests on congressional intent to so provide. The Act's text and legislative history reveal little that would help to understand the intended scope of any private right. Sandberg (P) failed to demonstrate the equitable basis required to extend the § 14(a) private action to shareholders whose initial authorization of the transaction prompting the proxy solicitation is unnecessary, when any indication of congressional intent to do so is lacking. She also failed the "essential link" test of causation of compensable damages for such shareholders. The theory of causation advanced by Sandberg (P) also rests upon the proposition that § 14(a) should provide a federal remedy whenever a false or misleading proxy statement results in the loss under state law of a shareholder plaintiff's state remedy for the enforcement of a state right. The law or facts of this case do not indicate that the proxy solicitation resulted in any such loss. Reversed.

CONCURRENCE: (Scalia, J.) The Court's disallowance of an action for misrepresentation of belief is entirely contrary to the modern law of torts.

CONCURRENCE AND DISSENT: (Stevens, J.) That the solicitation of proxies is not required by law or by the bylaws of a corporation does not authorize corporate officers, once they have decided for whatever reason to solicit proxies, to avoid the constraints of the statute. Thus, the judgment of the court of appeals should have been affirmed.

CONCURRENCE AND DISSENT: (Kennedy, J.) Where an implied right of action has become an established part of the securities laws, it should be enforced as a meaningful remedy unless it is to be eliminated altogether. If minority shareholders hold sufficient votes to defeat a management proposal and if the misstatement or omission is likely to be considered important in deciding how to vote, then there exists a likely causal link between the proxy violation and the enactment of the proposal justifying recovery by injured minority shareholders.

Continued on next page.

EDITOR'S ANALYSIS: It was not certain initially whether the broad prohibition against false or misleading material statements in a proxy solicitation could only be enforced by the Securities and Exchange Commission. Among many of its prior decisions cited by the Court, J.I. Case v. Borak, 377 U.S. 426 (1964), held that Rule 14a-9 did create an implied private right of action. Later, in Mills v. Electric Auto-Lite Co., 396 U.S. 375 (1970), the Court ruled that causation of damages by a material proxy misstatement could be demonstrated by showing that the proxy solicitation was an "essential link in the accomplishment of the transaction or merger." Finally, TSC Industries, Inc. v. Northway, Inc., 426 U.S. 438 (1976), held that a fact was materially significant "if there is a substantial likelihood that a reasonable shareholder would consider it important in deciding how to vote." Because Sandberg (P) was a minority shareholder whose vote was not necessary to the accomplishment of the merger, she could not satisfy the causation requirement of Mills.

[For more information on private actions under the proxy rules, see Casenote Law Outline on Corporations, Chapter 6, § II, Implied Right of Action for Shareholders.]

QUICKNOTES

SECURITIES EXCHANGE ACT, § 14 (a) - Prevents management from obtaining illegal proxies.

MATERIALITY - Importance; the degree of relevance or necessity to the particular matter.

RULE 14a-9 - Prohibits proxy solicitations containing false or misleading statements.

ROOSEVELT v. E.I. DU PONT DE NEMOURS & CO.
Shareholder (P) v. Corporation (D)
958 F.2d 416 (D.C. Cir. 1992).

NATURE OF CASE: Appeal of judgment excluding a shareholder proposal under Rule 14a-8.

FACT SUMMARY: Roosevelt (P) sought to have a shareholder proposal regarding the phaseout of chlorofluorocarbons production included in Du Pont's (D) proxy materials.

CONCISE RULE OF LAW: Shareholder proposals that deal with ordinary business operations are not entitled to inclusion in proxy materials.

FACTS: Roosevelt (P) sought to have two shareholder proposals included in Du Pont's (D) proxy materials sent to shareholders prior to the 1991 annual meeting. The proposals presented a timetable for the phaseout of production of chlorofluorocarbons (CFCs) and for a presentation of a report about environmentally safe substitutes. Du Pont (D) claimed that the matters dealt with ordinary business operations and that therefore, it was not required to include the proposals pursuant to § 14(a). Du Pont (D) notified the SEC of its intention to omit the proposals, and the SEC issued a "no action" letter which stated that the SEC would not recommend action against Du Pont (D) if the proposal were omitted. Roosevelt (P) filed an action to have the proposals included in the annual meeting proxy materials. The district court ruled for Du Pont, (D) and Roosevelt (P) appealed.

ISSUE: Must shareholder proposals which deal with matters of ordinary business operations be included in proxy materials for purposes of Rule 14a-8?

HOLDING AND DECISION: (Ginsburg, J.) No. Shareholder proposals regarding matters of ordinary business operations and do not have to be included in proxy materials pursuant to Rule 14a-8. The timing of production phaseouts is such a matter. Only shareholder proposals which have significant policy, or economic, implications must be included in proxy materials. The decision to phase out a major product may have important policy implications, but the timing of the phaseout is a matter of ordinary business operations unless there is a large time difference at stake. Roosevelt's (P) shareholder proposal presented a CFC phaseout timetable which differed from Du Pont's (D) plan by only a few years. Therefore, it is a matter of ordinary business operations and does not have to be included in proxy materials pursuant to Rule 14a-8. Affirmed.

EDITOR'S ANALYSIS: The implied right of action for shareholders under 14a-8 was first acknowledged in J.I. Case Co. v. Borak, 377 U.S. 426 (1964). Justice Ginsburg indicated in the decision that Borak's scope has been reduced over the years, but the core right of private action under Rule 14a-8 has remained.

[For more information on shareholder proposals in proxy materials, see Casenote Law Outline on Corporations, Chapter 6, § I, Regulation 14a of the SEC.]

QUICKNOTES

RULE 14(a)-8 (c) - Allows a corporation to omit a shareholder proposal because of certain enumerated circumstances.

AMALGAMATED CLOTHING AND TEXTILE WORKERS v. WAL-MART STORES
Shareholders (P) v. Corporation (D)
U.S. Ct. of App., 54 F.3d 69 (2d Cir. 1995).

NATURE OF CASE: Appeal from order of district court awarding attorney fees to plaintiffs for services rendered.

FACT SUMMARY: Amalgamated Clothing and Textile Workers (P), shareholders of Wal-Mart (D), sought an award of attorney fees for the costs of a suit to compel Wal-Mart (D) to include certain shareholder proposals in its proxy solicitation materials.

CONCISE RULE OF LAW: The promotion of corporate suffrage regarding a significant policy issue confers a substantial benefit regardless of the percentage of votes cast for or against the proposal at issue.

FACTS: Amalgamated Clothing and Textile Workers (P), shareholders of Wal-Mart (D), brought suit against Wal-Mart (D) claiming that Wal-mart (D) violated SEC Rule 14a-8 by refusing to include in its proxy solicitation materials a certain shareholder proposal to be voted upon at the annual meeting. The proposal required Wal-Mart's (D) directors to prepare and distribute reports about Wal-Mart's (D) equal opportunity and affirmative action policies. Wal-Mart (D) refused to include the proposal, claiming that it concerned a matter relating to the conduct of its ordinary business operations. The district court held that the proposal concerned significant policy issues, not day-to-day business operations, and must be included in the proxy materials. Wal-mart (D) included the proposal in its proxy materials the following year, and the proposal was defeated at the annual meeting by a wide margin. Subsequently, the shareholders (P) moved for an award of attorney fees, which the district court granted. On appeal, Wal-Mart (D) argued that because approximately ninety percent of the voting shares voted against the proposal, the shareholder (P) voting rights were not enhanced and they should therefore be unable to receive attorney fees.

ISSUE: Does the promotion of corporate suffrage regarding a significant policy issue confer a substantial benefit regardless of the percentage of votes cast for or against the proposal at issue?

HOLDING AND DECISION: (Miner, J.) Yes. The promotion of corporate suffrage regarding a significant policy issue confers a substantial benefit regardless of the percentage of votes cast for or against the proposal at issue. It is irrelevant that the shareholder (P) proposal was ultimately defeated or that the percentage that voted against it was very high. In itself, the right to cast an informed vote is a vital interest worthy of vindication. Therefore, the district court was correct in finding that the facilitation of communication between shareholders and management was a substantial interest vindicated by Amalgamated's (P) action. Affirmed.

EDITOR'S ANALYSIS: This was a very important holding for shareholders who challenge management decisions. If the court had not held that they were entitled to reimbursement, numerous other shareholders would undoubtedly think twice before they filed a similar suit. While the corporation would argue that it will encourage more suits, this does not necessarily follow because only plaintiffs whose interests are vindicated are entitled to reimbursement, not simply anyone who brings a suit.

[For more information on shareholder right of participation, see Casenote Law Outline on Corporations, Chapter 3, § II, Structuring the Close Corporation.]

NOTES:

ROSENFELD v. FAIRCHILD ENGINE & AIRPLANE
Shareholder (P) v. Corporation (D)
N.Y. Ct. of App., 128 N.E. 2d 291 (1955).

NATURE OF CASE: Stockholder derivative suit to recover misused corporate funds.

FACT SUMMARY: A proxy fight between incumbent management and insurgent group resulted in large expenses to the corporation in reimbursements to both sides.

CONCISE RULE OF LAW: In policy contests, corporate funds may be used to pay reasonable and proper expenses incurred in a proxy fight (1) by incumbent directors acting in good faith in soliciting proxies and defending their corporate policies, and (2) by successful insurgent groups where, after gaining power, such groups receive ratification by stockholders for reimbursement of such expenses.

FACTS: Rosenfeld (P) brought this derivative action against Fairchild Engine & Airplane Corp. (D) for the return to the corporation of reimbursements paid out of corporate funds to both sides in a proxy contest for their expenses. The proxy fight was between the incumbent board of directors and an insurgent group called the Fairchild group. The controversy centered around several issues, the most important of which was the compensation paid one director for his services. In defending their position, the incumbent directors spent $106,000 while still in office, and were reimbursed for an additional $28,000 by the Fairchild group once they took office. This $134,000 included expenses of sending out proxies, public relations, entertainment, chartered airplanes, and proxy solicitors. After the Fairchild group took office, they gained ratification by the stockholders, in a 16-1 vote, for reimbursement of their proxy-fight expenses amounting to $127,000, plus the $28,000 paid to the outgoing board of directors. All reimbursements were paid from corporate funds. An Official Referee dismissed Rosenfeld's (P) complaint, and the Appellate Division affirmed this decision.

ISSUE: Is it lawful for a corporation, on consent of a majority of its stockholders, to pay out of its funds the expenses of a proxy fight incurred by competing candidates for election as directors?

HOLDING AND DECISION: (Froessel, J.) Yes. If directors are not free to answer the challenges of outside groups trying to wrest control of the corporations for their own purposes, the corporation will be at the mercy of such insurgents, especially where they are adequately funded. Thus, in a proxy contest, directors may be forced to defend their actions with respect to corporate policy by sending out information to stockholders. Such expense, if incurred in good faith, is permissible. In addition, any insurgent group that wins the approval of stockholders in a proxy fight may, at the discretion of the stockholders, be reimbursed for bona fide and reasonable expenses incurred in such a contest. However,

corporate directors cannot engage in a proxy contest with the corporation's money to an unlimited extent. Where such corporate funds are spent for personal power, individual gain, or private advantage, and not in the best interests of the stockholders or corporation, or where the reasonableness of such amounts are challenged, the courts will disallow them.

CONCURRENCE: (Desmond, J.) Rosenfeld (P) failed to go forward with proof of his allegations that the directors, without unanimous stockholder approval, spent corporate funds in excess of the amounts necessary to give the stockholders bare notice of the election involving the contest between the incumbent directors and Fairchild group and the matters to be voted on. Rosenfeld (P) alleged this was illegal. This court recognizes that payment by a corporation of expenses of proceedings by one faction in its contest with another for control of the corporation is ultra vires expenditures. But since Rosenfeld (P) failed to do this, the complaint should have been dismissed, as it was. Also, the stockholders did not ratify reimbursement of the incumbent directors' expenses; they merely approved reimbursement of the Fairchild group.

EDITOR'S ANALYSIS: This case examines the problem of financing large-scale proxy contests. The rationale behind requiring stockholder approval of reimbursement is that the directors voting on it are apt to be interested. Since management has the advantage of corporate funds in a proxy fight, and the opposition does not, it is necessary to "equalize" the two factions. Otherwise, without the promise of indemnification of proxy expenses, new groups would never challenge incumbents.

[For more information on Proxy Contests, see Casenote Law Outline on Corporations, Chapter 6, § I, Regulation 14a of the SEC.]

QUICKNOTES
PROXY STATEMENT - A statement, containing specified information by the Securities and Exchange Commission, in order to provide shareholders with adequate information upon which to make an informed decision regarding the solicitation of their proxies.

NOTES:

CHAPTER 6
THE SPECIAL PROBLEMS OF CLOSE CORPORATION

QUICK REFERENCE RULES OF LAW

1. **An Introduction to to close Corporation.** When a close corporation repurchases stock from a member of the controlling group, it must offer each stockholder an equal opportunity to sell a ratable number of shares to the corporation at an identical price. (Donahue v. Rodd Electrotype Co.)

   [For more information on Close Corporation Minority shareholders, see Casenote Law Outline on Corporations, Chapter 3, § III, Viewing the Close Corporation from Within.]

2. **Voting Agreements.** An agreement among stockholders to cast their votes collectively in a certain way is not illegal and irrevocable under a statute prohibiting voting agreements by which the voting power of stock is irrevocably separated from the ownership of that stock. (Ringling Bros.-Barnum & Bailey Combined Shows v. Ringling)

   [For more information on Voting, see Casenote Law Outline on Corporations, Chapter 2, § II, Viewing the Corporation from Within.]

3. **Controlling Matters within the board's Discretion.** A contract among stockholders is illegal and void if it precludes the board of directors, at the risk of incurring legal liability, from changing officers, salaries, or policies, except by consent of the contracting parties. (McQuade v. Stoneham)

4. **Controlling Matters within the board's Discretion.** Close corporations will not be held to the same standards of corporate conduct as publicly held corporations in the absence of a showing of fraud or prejudice toward minority shareholders or creditors. (Galler v. Galler)

   [For more information on characteristics of a close corporation, see Casenote Law Outline on Corporations, Chapter 3, § I, Definition and Formation.]

5. **Supermajority voting and quorum requirement at the shareholder levels.** A court may not invalidate a provision in a certificate of incorporation requiring unanimous consent by shareholders where it is unambiguous. (Sutton v. Sutton)

6. **Fiduciary Obligations of Shareholders in close Corporation.** Stockholders in a close corporation are in a fiduciary relationship with each other. (Wilkes v. Springside Nursing Home, Inc.)

   [For more information on Close Corporation Shareholders Fiduciary Responsibility, see Casenote Law Outline on Corporations, Chapter 3, § III, Viewing the Close Corporation from Within.]

7. **Fiduciary Obligations of Shareholders in close Corporation.** Where a closed corporation's articles of incorporation include a provision designed to protect minority stockholders, the minority stockholders have a fiduciary duty to use the provision reasonably. (Smith v. Atlantic Properties, Inc.)

   [For more information on minority shareholders, Close Corporations, see Casenote Law Outline on Corporations, Chapter 3, § III, Viewing the Close Corporation from Within.]

8. **Fiduciary Obligations of Shareholders in close Corporation.** A closely held corporation will not have breached its fiduciary duty to an employee-minority shareholder when it terminates the employee without a legitimate business purpose, so long as the termination was not for the financial gain of majority shareholders or contrary to established public policy. (Merola v. Exergen Corp.)

[For more information on fiduciary duties in close, see Casenote Law Outline on Corporations, Chapter 3, § III, Viewing the Close Corporation from Within.]

9. **Valuation.** A judicial appraisal of stock requires a determination of the market value, the earnings value, and the net asset value of the stock, followed by an assignment of a percentage weight to each of the elements of value to come up with a resulting "fair value." (Piemont v. New Boston Garden Corp.)

[For more information on Appraisal Remedy, see Casenote Law Outline on Corporations, Chapter 8, § II, The Appraisal Remedy.]

10. **Restrictions on the Transferability.** Reasonable restrictions on the transferability of shares are valid and enforceable. (Allen v. Biltmore Tissue Corp.)

[For more information on Shares, see Casenote Law Outline on Corporations, Chapter 2, § I, Formation Accomplished Under Law of State of Incorporation.]

11. **Restrictions on the Transferability.** Employee shareholders may not complain about the terms of an otherwise enforceable buy-back provision. (Gallagher v. Lambert)

[For more information on structuring the close corporation, see Casenote Law Outline on Corporations, Chapter 3, § II, Structuring the Close Corporation.]

12. **Dissolution for Deadlock.** Irreconcilable differences, even among an unevenly divided board of directors, do not in all cases mandate dissolution of the corporation. (Wollman v. Littman)

[For more information on Corporate Dissolution, see Casenote Law Outline on Corporations, Chapter 2, § II, Viewing the Corporation from Within.]

13. **Dissolution of Oppression, and Mandatory Buy-Out.** Actions by majority shareholders to restrict distributions to the prejudice of minority shareholders may constitute oppression and justify dissolution. (Matter of Kemp and Beatley, Inc.)

[For more information on Controlling Shareholders, see Casenote Law Outline on Corporations, Chapter 4, § III, Controlling Shareholders.]

14. **Dissolution of Oppression, and Mandatory Buy-Out.** A minority shareholder is entitled to a buy-out of his interest when the directors or those in control of the corporation have acted in a manner unfairly prejudicial toward one or more shareholders in their capacities as shareholders or directors or as officers or employees of a closely held corporation. (McCallum v. Rosen's Diversified, Inc.)

15. **Dissolution of Oppression, and Mandatory Buy-Out.** When a corporation buys out a shareholder's stock in response to a dissolution petition, the shares may not be discounted solely because of their minority status or their lack of marketability. (Charland v. Country View Golf Club, Inc.)

[For more information on dissolution of the close corporation, see Casenote Law Outline on Corporations, Chapter 3, § III, Viewing the Close Corporation from Within.]

DONAHUE v. RODD ELECTROTYPE CO. OF NEW ENGLAND, INC.

Minority shareholder (P) v. Close corporation (D)

Mass. Sup. Jud. Ct., 367 Mass. 578, 328 N.E.2d 505 (1975).

NATURE OF CASE: Action to rescind a corporation's repurchase of shares.

FACT SUMMARY: Donahue (P), a minority shareholder in Rodd (D), complained that she was not offered the same deal to resell her shares to Rodd (D) as a majority shareholder in the close corporation.

CONCISE RULE OF LAW: When a close corporation repurchases stock from a member of the controlling group, it must offer each stockholder an equal opportunity to sell a ratable number of shares to the corporation at an identical price.

FACTS: Harry Rodd's two sons and a lawyer comprised the board of directors of Rodd Electrotype (D), a close corporation in which Donahue (P) was a minority stockholder. When Rodd Electrotype (D) repurchased shares from Harry Rodd after appropriate board action, Donahue (P) offered to sell her shares at the same price, but Rodd Electrotype (D) turned down the offer. Donahue (P) then brought an action to have the repurchase from Harry Rodd rescinded, charging the directors and controlling stockholders with violation of their fiduciary duty towards her as a minority shareholder. The trial court dismissed the bill of the merits, and Donahue (P) appealed.

ISSUE: When a Close Corporation repurchases stock from a member of the controlling group, must it offer each stockholder an equal opportunity to sell at a ratable number of his shares to the Corporation at an identical price?

HOLDING AND DECISION: (Tauro, J.) Yes. When a close corporation repurchases stock from a member of the controlling group, it must offer each stockholder an equal opportunity to sell a ratable number of his shares to the corporation at an identical price. Because a close corporation resembles a partnership, stockholders therein owe one another substantially the same fiduciary duty that partners owe one another, i.e. utmost good faith and loyalty. This means not giving a controlling shareholder the advantages of a corporate repurchase of his shares without offering those same advantages, by means of a similar repurchase, to other shareholders. Donahue (P) was denied the opportunity to sell her shares and is, therefore, entitled either to have the stock repurchase from Harry Rodd rescinded or sell 100% of her shares, as did Harry Rodd, to Rodd Electrotype (D) at the same price. She has asked for and will be granted the first form of relief.

CONCURRENCE: (Wilkins, J.) The rule herein announced does not necessarily apply to all operations of a close corporation affecting minority stockholders, e.g. salaries and dividend policy.

EDITOR'S ANALYSIS: There are two main benefits in a close corporation's repurchase of shares. First, the corporation is providing a ready market where none existed so that the shareholder can turn his liquid investment into ready cash. Second, the stockholder essentially receives a distribution of assets. This case simply holds the majority cannot reserve these benefits to themselves.

[For more information on Close Corporation Minority shareholders, see Casenote Law Outline on Corporations, Chapter 3, § III, Viewing the Close Corporation from Within.]

QUICKNOTES

MINORITY SHAREHOLDER - A stockholder in a corporation controlling such a small portion of those shares that are outstanding that its votes have no influence in the management of the corporation.

CONTROLLING SHAREHOLDER - A person who has power to vote a majority of the outstanding shares of a corporation, or who is able to direct the management of the corporation with a smaller block of stock because the remaining shares are scattered among small, disorganized holdings.

FIDUCIARY DUTY - A legal obligation to act for the benefit of another, including subordinating one's personal interests to that of the other person.

CLOSE CORPORATION - A corporation whose shares (or at least voting shares) are held by a closely knit group of shareholders or a single person.

FREEZE-OUT - Merger whereby the majority shareholder forces minority shareholders into the sale of their securities.

NOTES:

RINGLING BROS.-BARNUM & BAILEY
COMBINED SHOWS v. RINGLING
Corporation (D) v. Minority shareholder (P)
Del. Sup. Ct., 53 A.2d 441 (1947).

NATURE OF CASE: Appeal in a contest over disputed election of directors.

FACT SUMMARY: Edith Ringling (P) brought action to have the election of seven directors declared invalid on grounds the votes of Aubrey Haley (D) were cast in breach of a voting agreement.

CONCISE RULE OF LAW: An agreement among stockholders to cast their votes collectively in a certain way is not illegal and irrevocable under a statute prohibiting voting agreements by which the voting power of stock is irrevocably separated from the ownership of that stock.

FACTS: Edith Ringling (P) and Aubrey Haley (D) signed an agreement to pool their voting stock and vote jointly. The agreement provided for an arbitrator, Mr. Loos, to decide how the stock should be voted in case the parties were unable to agree. But when the election for the company directors was held in 1946, Aubrey Haley's (D) proxy, her husband James Haley, voted against the recommendations of Mr. Loos. Edith Ringling (P) brought an action to contest the validity of the election, and the Court of Chancery nullified the election, ordering a new one. This is an appeal by Ringling Bros.-Barnum & Bailey Combined Shows (D) from that decision on grounds that the agreement was illegal and irrevocable under Delaware law.

ISSUE: Is a voting agreement giving an arbitrator the power to make a binding decision as to how collective votes should be cast in case of a dispute an illegal and irrevocable agreement on grounds that the voting power of the stock has been irrevocably separated from its ownership?

HOLDING AND DECISION: (Pearson, J.) No. Such an agreement limits an arbitrator's role to situations where the parties fail to agree. No arbitrator can be given the power to vote shares or to compel another party to a voting agreement to vote in accordance with his directions. Here, the agreement did not contemplate transferring to Loos any such powers. The parties merely sought to bind each other, not to empower the arbitrator to enforce upon them decisions he might make. The control of the voting shares remained vested in the shareholders, Edith Ringling (P) and Aubrey Haley (D). Thus, the failure of Aubrey Haley (D) to exercise her voting rights in accordance with the decision of the arbitrator, Mr. Loos, was a breach of the voting agreement. However, this does not render the election null and void as was held by the lower court. It merely means that the votes representing Aubrey Haley's (D) shares should not be counted. The election of the six persons for whom Edith Ringling (P) voted

stands. This leaves one directorate vacant, to be filled at the next shareholders' meeting.

EDITOR'S ANALYSIS: The voting agreement, as typified in the Ringling case, has been held to be an alternative to the more formal voting trust. One advantage in this is to avoid possible invalidity of a voting agreement on grounds that it is a defective voting trust (i.e., a voting trust which does not comply with the formalities of statutes creating such trusts). The idea behind creating "irrevocable" voting agreements (or pooling agreements) is to make such agreements binding and enforceable. If they were "revocable," a shareholder entering an agreement could back out, that is, revoke their voting proxy and destroy the agreement. Such voting agreements can only be made irrevocable if they contemplate proxies coupled with an "interest." But what is meant by an "interest"? An interest in the stock or the corporation will suffice, or when the proxy holder has a charge, lien, or some other property interest in the shares, or a security interest given to protect the proxy holder for money advanced or obligations incurred. However, where there is only a voting agreement between shareholders, with no proxies given, the "interest" requirement is only an interest in the welfare of the corporation.

[For more information on Voting, see Casenote Law Outline on Corporations, Chapter 2, § II, Viewing the Corporation from Within.]

QUICKNOTES

VOTING TRUST - An agreement establishing a trust, whereby shareholders transfer their title to shares to a trustee who is authorized to exercise their voting powers.

CORPORATION LAW, REV. CODE § 18 - One or more stockholders may have a written agreement to deposit capital stock with a trustee for the purpose of voting as agreed for a period of time.

NOTES

McQUADE v. STONEHAM & McGRAW

Former officer (P) v. Corporate directors (D)

N.Y. Ct. of App., 189 N.E. 234 (1934).

NATURE OF CASE: To compel specific performance of a contract.

FACT SUMMARY: Stoneham (D) and McGraw (D) failed to uphold an agreement with McQuade (P) to use best efforts in maintaining him as an officer in NEC.

CONCISE RULE OF LAW: A contract among stockholders is illegal and void if it precludes the board of directors, at the risk of incurring legal liability, from changing officers, salaries, or policies, except by consent of the contracting parties.

FACTS: McQuade (P) bought 70 shares of a corporation called National Exhibition Co. (NEC), popularly known as the "Giants" baseball team. As part of that transaction, he entered into an agreement with co-stockholders Stoneham (D) and McGraw (D) providing that they would use their best efforts to continue each other as officers and directors of NEC. McGraw (D) and McQuade (P) bought about 3% each of NEC stock from Stoneham (D) who, after the sale, owned approximately 46% of NEC stock. McGraw (D) was elected vice president, Stoneham (D) president, and McQuade (P) treasurer. On May 2, 1928, McQuade (P) was voted out of office due to the failure of Stoneham (D) and McGraw (D) to vote. McQuade (P) brought this suit for specific performance of their agreement to use their best efforts to continue him as treasurer. Trial court awarded him damages but did not reinstate him.

ISSUE: May the stockholders of a corporation enter into an agreement that precludes their board of directors, at the risk of legal liability, from changing officers, salaries, or policies?

HOLDING AND DECISION: (Pound, C.J.) No. Shareholders may not enter into agreements to control directors in the exercise of their judgments. Stockholders may unite to elect directors, but this power is not extended to contracts that limit the director's power to manage the corporation. It is urged by McQuade (P) that the court should pay heed to the morals and manners of the marketplace to sustain this agreement. McQuade (P) contends that an agreement among directors to continue a man in office should not be broken as long as that man is a loyal officer to the interests of the corporation. However, as loyal as McQuade (P) was to the interests of the minority shareholders of NEC, his absence as treasurer does not injure the corporation. Stoneham (D) and McGraw (D) had no legal obligation to deal righteously with McQuade; their duty was to the corporation and its shareholders.

EDITOR'S ANALYSIS: Shareholders have no direct power in the management affairs of their corporation. Statutes require this in order to free the directors to manage the corporation's everyday affairs without annoying interference from stockholders as to minor or petty management decisions. Consequently, a court will not allow shareholders to contract away the inherent powers of a board of directors.

QUICKNOTES

MINORITY SHAREHOLDER - A stockholder in a corporation controlling such a small portion of those shares that are outstanding that its votes have no influence in the management of the corporation.

NOTES:

GALLER v. GALLER
Shareholder (P) v. Shareholder (D)
32 Ill. 2d 16, 203 N.E.2d 577 (1964).

NATURE OF CASE: Action for specific performance on a contract between shareholders in a close corporation.

FACT SUMMARY: Suit by Emma Galler (P) to compel specific performance of a shareholder agreement made between her deceased husband, Benjamin Galler, and Isadore Galler (D), his brother and business partner. The agreement bound the shareholders to vote for specific individuals and directors and called for mandatory dividends.

CONCISE RULE OF LAW: Close corporations will not be held to the same standards of corporate conduct as publicly held corporations in the absence of a showing of fraud or prejudice toward minority shareholders or creditors.

FACTS: Two brothers, Isadore (D) and Benjamin, incorporated their partnership in 1924 and operated as such for over 30 years. In 1955, the two brothers drew up a shareholders' agreement to provide for the financial security of their respective families in the event of either brother's death. The agreement provided for salary continuation payments to the surviving widow. It further allowed the surviving widow to remain on the board of directors and to name a successor to her husband. Specific dollar amounts of dividends were mandated by the agreement. However, these payments were qualified so as not to impair the capital of the corporation. After Benjamin's death, his wife Emma (P) sought enforcement of the agreement. Isadore (D) repudiated the agreement, claiming it violated the corporations code of Illinois and the public policy of that state.

ISSUE: Can shareholder agreements pertaining to dividend policy and selection of directors be enforced in the case of a close corporation when such agreements would not be permissible in a publicly held corporation?

HOLDING AND DECISION: (Underwood, J.) Yes. The unique nature of close corporations — close relationship of shareholders; lack of marketability of shares; and overlapping of shareholders and officers — creates a situation which should allow "slight deviations from corporate norms." These deviations should be permitted so long as they do not operate to defraud or prejudice the interests of minority shareholders or creditors. Since the principals in a close corporation usually have a close relationship, their agreements should be enforced where no clear statutory prohibitions are violated. Since the agreement did not imperil creditors and there were no minority shareholders' interests involved in this instance, the agreement was valid and enforceable.

EDITOR'S ANALYSIS: This case is representative of the growing acceptance by most jurisdictions of the basic differences between publicly held and closely held (close) corporations. There is a recognition that the parties in a close corporation regard themselves, in fact, as partners. This view allows for a latitude in enforcing shareholders' agreements that would be unacceptable in publicly held corporations. Many statutes regulating corporations are intended to protect the interests of the shareholders and creditors. Where the shareholders are few in number and operating, in essence, as partners, the need for such rigid protection is absent. As long as the rights of minority shareholders and creditors are not infringed, the close corporation can be given a relatively free reign as regards internal structure and operation.

[For more information on characteristics of a close corporation, see Casenote Law Outline on Corporations, Chapter 3, §I, Definition and Formation.]

QUICKNOTES

CLOSE CORPORATION - A corporation whose shares (or at least voting shares) are held by a closely knit group of shareholders or a single person.

ULTRA VIRES - An act undertaken by a corporation that is beyond the scope of its authority pursuant to law or its articles of incorporation.

NOTES:

SUTTON v. SUTTON
Shareholder (P) v. Director (D)
84 N.Y.2d 37 (1994).

NATURE OF THE CASE: Petition for declaration to amend certificate of incorporation.

FACT SUMMARY: A dispute arose between the shareholders of a corporation to strike out a provision in the certificate of incorporation requiring a unanimous vote by all of them to enter into business transactions or otherwise subsequently amend the certificate.

CONCISE RULE OF LAW: A court may not invalidate a provision in a certificate of incorporation requiring unanimous consent by shareholders where it is unambiguous.

FACTS: Prior to having any shareholders, the certificate of incorporation of Bag Bazaar, Ltd. was amended to provide that any business transaction, including the amendment of the certificate of incorporation, required the unanimous vote or consent of all common stock shareholders. David Sutton (D), nephew to the original shareholder Abraham Sutton, subsequently acquired shares of common stock, as did Solomon Sutton (P), who was the original shareholder's son. The two served as the only directors of Bag Bazaar. Disputes later arose between them regarding the management of the corporation. These disputes culminated in a shareholder's meeting where Solomon (P) and Abraham's widow voted to strike the unanimity provision, while David (D) voted against the resolution, preventing it from taking effect. Solomon (P) then commenced this proceeding, moving for a judgment to declare the resolution removing unanimity valid and enforceable, and compelling David (D) to sign. David (D) cross-moved to dismiss and to compel arbitration of the dispute.

ISSUE: May a court invalidate an unambiguous provision in a certificate of incorporation requiring unanimous consent by shareholders?

HOLDING: (Simons, J.) No. A court may not invalidate a provision in a certificate of incorporation requiring unanimous consent by shareholders where it is unambiguous. Solomon (P) submits that a statutory provision added the word "specifically" when discussing whether a certificate of incorporation may provide for a form of approval other than a two-thirds vote because the legislature recognized that unanimity provisions give minority shareholders the ability to deadlock corporate action. David (D) responds that the "specifically" was added to require that the certificate state exactly what specific circumstances were required, and what percentage vote was sufficient. We agree. A unanimous vote is an acceptable provision only where the certificate clearly calls for a unanimous vote. Nothing in the legislative history of the applicable statute suggests otherwise. Instead, the applicable case and statutory law reveal that an unambiguous provision in a certificate of incorporation requiring unanimous approval by shareholders may only be amended by unanimous consent. The provision in Bag Bazaar's certificate is likewise unambiguous, and there is nothing inherently unfair in the voluntary and consensual decision of an organization to impose such a requirement, leaving shareholders with sufficient deadlock remedies elsewhere. Affirmed with costs.

EDITOR'S ANALYSIS: Although the respondent submitted a specific statute for judicial consideration, the court instead chose to rely on the legislative history of a federal law, the Stock Corporation Law. In doing so, the court placed an implied limitation on its approval of unanimity provisions, by requiring adoption of the certificate of incorporation effective after 1951, the year this statute was amended to allow adoption for a supermajority provision by a two-thirds or greater shareholder vote.

WILKES v. SPRINGSIDE NURSING HOME, INC.
Director (P) v. Corporation (D)
353 N.E.2d 657.

NATURE OF CASE: Appeal from a ruling dismissing the complaint in an action for declaratory judgment.

FACT SUMMARY: Wilkes (P) was a director, employee, and shareholder in Springside Nursing Home, Inc., a close corporation. The other directors attempted to freeze him out of the corporation.

CONCISE RULE OF LAW: Stockholders in a close corporation are in a fiduciary relationship with each other.

FACTS: Wilkes (P), Quinn, Richie, and Conner formed a corporation to establish and operate a nursing home in 1951. Each of the men invested $1,000 and subscribed to 10 shares of $100 par value stock. Over the years the parties each bought more stock. At the time of incorporation it was understood that each would be a director of the corporation and participate in the management and operation thereof. It was further understood that each of the parties would receive money from the corporation in equal amounts for as long as they participated in the operation of the corporation. By 1955, each party was receiving $100 a week. In 1965, the relationship between the parties began to deteriorate. In February 1967, a directors' meeting was held, and a schedule of payments was set up in which Wilkes (P) was not included. In March 1967 the annual meeting was held. Wilkes (P) was not reelected a director and was not reemployed. Wilkes (P) brought suit arguing that the agreement of the parties was breached when he was forced out of the corporation. A master dismissed the complaint. Wilkes (P) appealed, contending that he was entitled to damages for breach of contract or breach of fiduciary duties owed to him.

ISSUE: May shareholders in a close corporation act, without a business purpose, to the detriment of other shareholders?

HOLDING AND DECISION: (Hennessey, C.J.) No. Stockholders in a close corporation are in a fiduciary relationship with each other. The standard of duty owed is one of utmost good faith and loyalty. The standard however, cannot be used to impose limitations on legitimate action by a controlling group. The majority has certain rights which must be balanced against the fiduciary obligation owed to the minority. Thus, where there is a legitimate business purpose for the action it may be valid. Here, it is apparent that the majority had no legitimate purpose for their action. There is no evidence of misconduct on the part of Wilkes (P) for the performance of his duties as a director or employee. The inescapable conclusion from this is that the action was designed to freeze Wilkes (P) out of the corporation in violation of the parties' original agreement. Reversed and remanded for further proceedings on the issue of damages.

EDITOR'S ANALYSIS: Controlling shareholders are given a large amount of discretion in establishing corporate policy. It is only where their actions cannot be justified by a business purpose and do injury to others, that the court will interfere. *Schwartz v. Marien,* 37 N.Y. 2d 487 (1975). In many older cases and in some jurisdictions, no business purpose is required so long as the majority acts within the permissible limits imposed by statute and their bylaws.

[For more information on Close Corporation Shareholders Fiduciary Responsibility, see Casenote Law Outline on Corporations, Chapter 3, § III, Viewing the Close Corporation from Within.]

QUICKNOTES

FIDUCIARY DUTY - A legal obligation to act for the benefit of another, including subordinating one's personal interests to that of the other person.

FREEZE-OUT - Merger whereby the majority shareholder forces minority shareholders into the sale of their securities.

MINORITY SHAREHOLDER - A stockholder in a corporation controlling such a small portion of those shares that are outstanding that its votes have no influence in the management of the corporation.

CLOSE CORPORATION - A corporation whose shares (or at least voting shares) are held by a closely knit group of shareholders or a single person.

NOTES:

SMITH v. ATLANTIC PROPERTIES, INC.

Shareholder (P) v. Corporation (D)

Mass. Ct. of App., 12 Mass. App. 201, 422 N.E. 2d 798 (1981).

NATURE OF CASE: Action for a determination of dividends, removal of a director, and a reimbursement order for penalty taxes.

FACT SUMMARY: Wolfson (D), a minority stockholder acting pursuant to a provision in the articles of incorporation, was able to prevent the distribution of dividends, as a result of which the corporation, Atlantic (D), had to pay a penalty tax for accumulated earnings.

CONCISE RULE OF LAW: Where a closed corporation's articles of incorporation include a provision designed to protect minority stockholders, the minority stockholders have a fiduciary duty to use the provision reasonably.

FACTS: Wolfson (D) purchased land in Norwood. Wolfson (D) then offered a quarter interest each in the land to Smith (P), Zimble (P), and Burke (P). Smith (P) then organized defendant corporation, Atlantic (D), to operate the real estate. Each of the four subscribers received 25 shares. At Wolfson's (D) request, the articles of incorporation included a provision that required an approval of 80% of the voting shares before any election, resolution, or action would be binding upon Atlantic (D). After 10 years of operation Atlantic (D) had accumulated $172,000 in earnings. Wolfson (D) wished to see the earnings devoted to repairs. Therefore he refused to vote for any dividends, and pursuant to the 80% provision Atlantic (D) was unable to declare any dividends. As a result, the Internal Revenue Service, pursuant to I.R.C. § 531 et seq., assessed and collected two penalty assessments for a total of approximately $45,000 for the unreasonable accumulation of earnings. Smith (P), Zimble (P), and Burke (P) then brought this action for determination of dividends, removal of Wolfson (D) from the Board of Directors, and a reimbursement of the penalty taxes from Wolfson (D). The trial court held for Smith (P), and Wolfson (D) appealed.

ISSUE: May a minority shareholder of a closed corporation use a provision in the articles of incorporation, which is designed to protect minority shareholders, in a manner that will unduly hamper the good-faith corporate interests of the majority stockholders?

HOLDING AND DECISION: (Cutter, J.) No. Where a closed corporation's articles of incorporation include a provision designed to protect minority stockholders, the minority stockholders have a fiduciary duty to use the provision reasonably so as not to unduly hamper the good-faith corporate interests of the majority stockholders. Here, the 80% provision in Atlantic's (D) articles of incorporation, which was designed to protect minority stockholders, was unreasonably used by

Wolfson (D). Wolfson (D) was warned of the penalty tax that could result from a failure to declare dividends. However, he refused to vote for any amount of dividends that would minimize the possibility of a penalty tax. Consequently, the trial judge was correct in protecting the majority stockholders by ordering Wolfson (D) to reimburse Atlantic (D) for the penalty taxes. In addition, the trial judge's order to Atlantic's (D) directors to declare a dividend is modified and affirmed.

EDITOR'S ANALYSIS: As this case illustrates, sometimes the articles of incorporation provide minority shareholders with an opportunity to obtain an ad hoc controlling interest. When this occurs, Heatherington, in the 1972 Duke L.J. at 944, states that the minority shareholder is bound by the same fiduciary standard imposed upon majority shareholders. In other words, both the majority shareholder and the ad hoc controlling minority shareholder should not exercise their corporate powers in a manner that is clearly adverse to the corporation's interest.

[For more information on minority shareholders, Close Corporations, see Casenote Law Outline on Corporations, Chapter 3, § III, Viewing the Close Corporation from Within.]

QUICKNOTES

FIDUCIARY DUTY - A legal obligation to act for the benefit of another, including subordinating one's personal interests to that of the other person.

MINORITY SHAREHOLDER - A stockholder in a corporation controlling such a small portion of those shares that are outstanding that its votes have no influence in the management of the corporation.

DIVIDEND - The payment of earnings to a corporation's shareholders in proportion to the amount of shares held.

NOTES:

MEROLA v. EXERGEN CORP.

Employee - minority shareholder (P) v. Corporation (D)

Mass. Sup. Jud. Ct., 423 Mass. 461, 668 N.E.2d 351 (1996).

NATURE OF CASE: Appeal from judgment in favor of a shareholder for breach of fiduciary duty.

FACT SUMMARY: Merola (P) came to work for Exergen (D), a closely held corporation, after he was told that he could become a major shareholder of Exergen (D) if he would work full-time and resign from his other job.

CONCISE RULE OF LAW: A closely held corporation will not have breached its fiduciary duty to an employee-minority shareholder when it terminates the employee without a legitimate business purpose, so long as the termination was not for the financial gain of majority shareholders or contrary to established public policy.

FACTS: Exergen (D) was a closely held corporation, with over 60% of shares owned by Pompei, the founder and president of Exergen (D). Merola (P) worked part-time for Exergen (D) and part-time for another company. Merola (P) was told by Pompei that if he came to work full-time for Exergen (D), he would have the chance to become a major shareholder of Exergen (D) and have continuing employment with Exergen (D). Merola (P) came to work full-time at Exergen (D), leaving his other job. Merola (P) purchased 5,300 shares of stock in Exergen (D). Merola (P) could have purchased the shares as a part-time employee. Exergen (D) had no general policy with regard to stock ownership and employment. Merola (P) was eventually fired. He then filed suit for breach of fiduciary duty and prevailed. Exergen (D) appealed.

ISSUE: If a closely held corporation terminates an employee-minority shareholder without a legitimate business purpose, does the termination prove a breach of fiduciary duty to the terminated employee?

HOLDING AND DECISION: (Lynch, J.) No. A closely held corporation will not have breached its fiduciary duty to an employee-minority shareholder when it terminates the employee without a legitimate business purpose, so long as the termination was not for the financial gain of majority shareholders or contrary to established public policy. If a closely held corporation terminates an employee who holds shares of stock and does so with the intent of increasing the value of remaining shares held by the majority shareholders, the majority stockholders have breached their fiduciary duty to the minority shareholder-employee. Here, there was no financial gain to Pompei in terminating Merola (P). Merola (P) was not required to buy stock to retain his job, and he could have bought the same shares while retaining both part-time jobs. Merola (P) was an at-will employee, and his termination, though for no legitimate business purpose, was in accordance with his employment contract. No basis for a

breach of fiduciary duty was established by Merola (P). Reversed.

EDITOR'S ANALYSIS: As this case demonstrates, when an employee of a close corporation is also a shareholder, termination of that employment can pose special problems. Normally, employment law permits termination at will, with or without cause. However, if the majority interest stands to gain financially by the termination, great care must be taken to demonstrate that financial gain to the majority interest was not the motivating factor. In such a situation, termination without cause is problematic at best, and effectively unavailable if the possibility of financial motivation cannot be disproven.

[For more information on fiduciary duties in close, see Casenote Law Outline on Corporations, Chapter 3, § III, Viewing the Close Corporation from Within.]

NOTES:

PIEMONTE v. NEW BOSTON GARDEN CORP.
Shareholder (P) v. Corporation (D)
Mass. Sup. Jud. Ct., 377 Mass. 719, 387 N.E.2d 1145 (1979).

NATURE OF CASE: Action seeking a judicial determination of the "fair value" of shares.

FACT SUMMARY: Piemonte (P) and others holding shares in the Boston Garden Arena Corporation were entitled to demand payment for their shares from the resulting corporation when Boston Garden merged with New Boston Garden (D), and they sought a judicial determination of the "fair value" of the shares.

CONCISE RULE OF LAW: A judicial appraisal of stock requires a determination of the market value, the earnings value, and the net asset value of the stock, followed by an assignment of a percentage weight to each of the elements of value to come up with a resulting "fair value."

FACTS: By statute, stockholders are entitled to demand payment for their shares from the surviving or resulting corporation when their corporation undergoes a merger. In pursuit of this right, Piemonte (P) and other shareholders in Boston Garden Arena Corporation sought a judicial determination of the "fair value" of their shares when their corporation decided to merge with New Boston Garden (P). The judge set about determining the "fair value" of their shares "as of the day preceding the date of the vote approving the proposed corporate action" (i.e., the merger). Both parties appealed from his judgment, voicing various objections to his method of determining value.

ISSUE: In making a judicial appraisal of the "fair value" of stock, should there be a determination of the market value, the earnings value, and the net asset value of the stock, followed by an assignment of a percentage weight to each of the elements of value?

HOLDING AND DECISION: (Wilkins, J.) Yes. The judge below adapted a general approach to the appraisal of stock known as the Delaware procedure or "Delaware block approach," which is quite appropriate. It calls for a determination of the market value, the earnings value, and the net asset value of the stock, followed by the assignment of a percentage weight to each of the elements of value. These factors are then used to compute the stock's "fair value." In making findings as to these various elements of value and the weight each should be given, the judge is not constrained to accept any particular party's valuation but is free to exercise his own discretion in the matter. As long as he does not abuse his discretion, the judge's valuations will be upheld. The record shows the judge may have felt bound by certain expert valuations, so the case is remanded for a clarification as to his own determinations of value in those instances.

EDITOR'S ANALYSIS: One of the primary problems in determining the earnings value of stock is deciding on the length of time over which a corporation's average earnings are to be computed. Delaware, where many of these appraisal rights cases have arisen, has adopted a five-year average as a general rule. However, some cases have used time spans of as little as two months where appropriate.

[For more information on Appraisal Remedy, see Casenote Law Outline on Corporations, Chapter 8, § II, The Appraisal Remedy.]

QUICKNOTES

MARKET VALUE - The price of particular property or goods that a buyer would offer and a seller accept in the open market, following full disclosure.

MERGER - The acquisition of one company by another, after which the acquired company ceases to exist as an independent entity.

G.L.C. 156 B., § 92 - Market value may be the dominant factor in determining the fair value of corporate shares.

NOTES:

ALLEN v. BILTMORE TISSUE CORP.

Estate executor (P) v. Corporation (D)

2 N.Y.2d 534, 161 N.Y.S.2d 418, 141 N.C.2d 812 (1957).

NATURE OF CASE: Action to compel issuance of new stock certificates to estate executors.

FACT SUMMARY: Biltmore (D) desired to exercise its option to repurchase the shares of a deceased stockholder, but Allen (P) and the other executors of the estate claimed the option constituted an unreasonable restraint on alienation and could not be enforced.

CONCISE RULE OF LAW: Reasonable restrictions on the transferability of shares are valid and enforceable.

FACTS: Kaplan had purchased Biltmore (D) shares that were subject to certain restrictions on alienation. One such restriction required that the stockholder wishing to sell give Biltmore (D) the opportunity to first purchase his shares at the same price for which he had purchased them from the corporation. Another provided that if a shareholder died, Biltmore (D) had the right to purchase his stock from the legal representative of the deceased for the original purchase price or to empower an existing stockholder to make such a purchase. If such action was not taken within 90 days, the legal representative had the right to dispose of the stock as she saw fit. Kaplan died, and Allen (P), an executor of his estate, refused to allow Biltmore (D) to purchase the shares as per the aforementioned option it enjoyed. Allen (P), who brought suit to compel Biltmore (D) to accept surrender of the old certificates and issue new ones to the executors, claimed the option constituted an unreasonable restraint on alienation and was therefore unenforceable. The Special Term held Biltmore (D) could enforce and exercise its repurchase option, but the appellate division reversed.

ISSUE: Are reasonable restraints on the transferability of shares valid and enforceable?

HOLDING AND DECISION: (Fuld, J.) Yes. Even if stock certificates are considered personal property rather than contractual choses in action, reasonable restraints on alienation are enforceable. Therefore, a restriction imposed on the transfer of stock is enforceable. It set forth a price formula agreed upon by the parties and did not attempt to preclude sale of the shares but only to postpone sale for a fixed time while Biltmore (D) decided whether to exercise its option. Reversed.

EDITOR'S ANALYSIS: There were earlier cases which characterized all stock transfer restrictions as illegal restraints on alienation. Even though some restrictions are now recognized as valid, the courts tend to interpret them strictly when faced with the task of ascertaining if a particular disposition fell within the scope of a particular restriction. In close corporations, first option restrictions are often used to give the partner-like stockholders the chance to "veto" the admission of a new participant.

[For more information on Shares, see Casenote Law Outline on Corporations, Chapter 2, § I, Formation Accomplished Under Law of State of Incorporation.]

QUICKNOTES

CAPITALIZATION - The aggregate value of all securities issued by a company.

UNIFORM STOCK TRANSFER ACT, § 15 - Provides that there shall be no restriction on the transfer of shares through by-laws unless the restriction is stated on the stock certificate.

CLOSE CORPORATION - A corporation whose shares (or at least voting shares) are held by a closely knit group of shareholders or a single person.

CHOSE IN ACTION - A right of bringing an action to procure payment of a sum of money or to recover a debt.

NOTES:

GALLAGHER v. LAMBERT
Director (P) v. Corporation owner (D)
N.Y. Ct. App., 74 N.Y.2d 562, 549 N.E.2d 136 (1989).

NATURE OF CASE: Appeal from a dismissal in an action alleging breach of fiduciary duty.

FACT SUMMARY: After Lambert (D) and Eastdil Realty (D) fired him twenty-one days before a higher valuation formula was to become effective, Gallagher (P) alleged breach of fiduciary duty of good faith and fair dealing and sought a higher repurchase price of his stock.

CONCISE RULE OF LAW: Employee shareholders may not complain about the terms of an otherwise enforceable buy-back provision.

FACTS: Gallagher (P) was employed by Lambert (D) and Eastdil Realty (D) as a mortgage broker. After leaving Eastdil (D), he later returned as a broker, officer and director, and, in addition, served as president and chief executive officer of Eastdil's (D) wholly owned subsidiary, Eastdil Advisors, Inc. Gallagher (P) was at all times an employee at will. Later, Eastdil (D) offered all its executive employees a chance to purchase stock subject to a mandatory buy-back provision, which provided that upon voluntary resignation or other termination prior to January 31, 1985, an employee would be required to return the stock for book value. After that date, the formula for the buy-back price would be keyed to Eastdil's (D) earnings. Gallagher (P) accepted the offer and its terms. On January 10, 1985, Gallagher (P) was fired by Eastdil (D). He didn't contest the firing but demanded payment for his stock shares calculated on the post-January 31, 1985 buy-back formula. Eastdil (D) refused, and Gallagher (P) sued, alleging breach of fiduciary duty of good faith and fair dealing. The trial court denied Eastdil's (D) motion for summary judgment, stating that factual issues had been raised regarding Eastdil's (D) motive in firing Gallagher (P). The appellate division reversed and dismissed Gallagher's (P) claims, ordering payment of the shares at book value. Gallagher (P) appealed.

ISSUE: May employee shareholders complain about the terms of an otherwise enforceable buy-back provision?

HOLDING AND DECISION: (Bellacosa, J.) No. Employee shareholders may not complain about the terms of an otherwise enforceable buy-back provision. Buy-back provisions, which require an employee shareholder to sell back stock upon severance from corporate employment, are designed to ensure that ownership of all stock, especially of a close corporation, stays within the control of the remaining corporate owner-employees, that is, those who will continue to contribute to its successes or failures. Here, the parties negotiated a written contract containing a common and plain buy-back provision. Gallagher (P) got what he bargained for — book value for his minority shares if his employment in the corporation ended before January 31, 1985. Gallagher (P) accepted the offer to become a minority shareholder, but only for the period during which he remained an employee. The buy-back price formula was designed for the benefit of both parties precisely so that they could

know their respective rights on certain dates and avoid costly and lengthy litigation on the "fair value" issue. Gallagher (P) not only agreed to the buy-back formula, he helped write it, and he reviewed it with his attorney during the negotiation process. Permitting Gallagher's (P) cause for breach of fiduciary duty of good faith and fair dealing would open the door to litigation on both the value of the stock and the date of termination, hindering the employer from fulfilling its contracted rights under the agreement. Affirmed.

CONCURRENCE: (Hancock, J.) I agree that the complaint should be dismissed. This court's holding in Ingle v. Glamore Motor Sales, 73 N.Y.2d 183, 535 N.E.2d 1311 (1989) and an analysis of the Ingle complaint, which this court dismissed, require dismissal of the claim asserted here.

DISSENT: (Kaye, J.) This case significantly differs from the Ingle case as it presents an alleged departure from a fiduciary duty of fair dealing existing independently of the employment which was not present in Ingle. Here, Gallagher (P) does question the duty Eastdil (D) owed him as a shareholder. He does contend that the corporation undervalued his shares and that it did not offer a fair price for his equity interest. Gallagher (P) alleges that Eastdil (D) and Lambert (D) had no bona fide business reason to terminate his employment when they did and charges that they fired him for the sole purpose of recapturing his shares at an unfairly low price and redistributing them themselves. Gallagher (P) claims that Eastdil (D) and Lambert (D), as holders of the majority of the corporate stock, breached distinctly different duties to him: (1) a duty of good faith in the performance of the shareholder's agreement; and (2) a fiduciary obligation owed to him as a minority shareholder by the controlling shareholders to refrain from purely self-aggrandizing conduct. Neither claim is foreclosed by Gallagher's (P) status as an at-will employee.

EDITOR'S ANALYSIS: In Gallagher, Justice Kaye, in a lengthy dissent, made the observation that if Gallagher had been a minority shareholder, but not an employee, Eastdil and Lambert would not have been able to act selfishly and opportunistically, as he claimed they did, for no corporate purpose. The controlling shareholders in a closely held corporation stand in relation to minority owners in the same fiduciary position as corporate directors generally and are held to the extreme measure of candor, unselfishness, and good faith. Directors and majority shareholders may not act for the aggrandizement or undue advantage of the fiduciary to the exclusion or detriment of the minority shareholders.

[For more information on structuring the close corporation, see Casenote Law Outline on Corporations, Chapter 3, § II, Structuring the Close Corporation.]

QUICKNOTES

MINORITY SHAREHOLDER - A stockholder in a corporation controlling such a small portion of those shares that are outstanding that its votes have no influence in the management of the corporation.

CLOSE CORPORATION - A corporation whose shares (or at least voting shares) are held by a closely knit group of shareholders or a single person.

WOLLMAN v. LITTMAN
Director (P) v. Director (D)
N.Y. Sup Ct., 35 A.D.2d 935, 316 N.Y.S.2d 526 (1970).

NATURE OF CASE: Action to dissolve a corporation.

FACT SUMMARY: Wollman (P) was part of one group, owning 50% of the stock in a corporation, that sought to dissolve the corporation because of irreconcilable differences with the Littman (D) group, which also owned 50% of the stock.

CONCISE RULE OF LAW: Irreconcilable differences, even among an unevenly divided board of directors, do not in all cases mandate dissolution of the corporation.

FACTS: Louis Nierenberg and her group, including Wollman (P), owned 50% of the stock in a corporation that was in the business of selling artificial fur fabrics to garment manufacturers. The Littmans (D), who also owned 50% of the corporation, claimed to have come up with the idea for such a business and to have developed a market for the fabrics among garment manufacturers. Each group had equal representation on the board of directors. The function of the Wollman (P) group was to procure the fabrics and then sell them to the corporation. The Littmans (D) were involved in the selling end. Eventually, the Littmans (D) brought an action claiming that Wollman (P) et al. were engaging in acts to adversely affect the corporation's business and were attempting to lure away customers to their own corporation. Wollman (P) et al. countered by filing an action for dissolution, claiming the management was at such odds among themselves that effective corporate management was impossible. The Special Term agreed.

ISSUE: Is corporate dissolution mandated in all cases of irreconcilable differences?

HOLDING AND DECISION: (Per Curiam) No. Dissolution of the corporation is not mandated in all cases of irreconcilable differences in management, even if such differences are among an evenly divided board of directors. This case is one requiring further exploration, so a receiver will be appointed. Since the functions of the two at odds are different, one selling and the other procuring, it is possible each can pursue its own without need for collaboration. Also, dissolution would accomplish a destruction of the business, which the Littmans (D) have charged, in another action, is precisely the improper goal of Wollman (P) et al.

EDITOR'S ANALYSIS: A number of states have laws permitting involuntary dissolution upon deadlock. Most are interpreted as making dissolution thereunder discretionary. Courts have proven most hesitant about exercising their discretion to order dissolution when a corporation is profit-making, but some reluctantly do so when it is deemed to be in the "best interests of the stockholders."

[For more information on Corporate Dissolution, see Casenote Law Outline on Corporations, Chapter 2, §II, Viewing the Corporation from Within.]

MATTER OF KEMP & BEATLEY, INC. (GARDSTEIN)
n/a
64 N.Y.2d 63, 484 N.Y.S.2d 799, 473 N.E.2d 1173 (1984).

NATURE OF CASE: Appeal from an order dissolving a corporation.

FACT SUMMARY: Gardstein (P) contended the corporation's refusal to make distributions to him in contrast to prior policy constituted oppressiveness justifying dissolution.

CONCISE RULE OF LAW: Actions by majority shareholders to restrict distributions to the prejudice of minority shareholders may constitute oppression and justify dissolution.

FACTS: Gardstein (P) and Dissin (P), two long-time employees of Kemp and Beatley (D), owned approximately 20% of the corporation's outstanding stock. While employed by the close corporation, they regularly received distributions as shareholders, yet after leaving the corporation's employ on less than friendly terms, they stopped receiving such distributions, while the other shareholders still did. They sued to dissolve the corporation, contending such action constituted oppression. The trial court ordered the dissolution, and Kemp and Beatley (D) appealed.

ISSUE: May actions by majority shareholders in close corporations to restrict distributions to minority shareholders constitute oppression and justify dissolution?

HOLDING AND DECISION: (Cooke, J.) Yes. Actions by majority shareholders of a close corporation to restrict distributions to the prejudice of minority shareholders may constitute oppression and justify dissolution. The action of the majority in this case defeated the expectation of the minority concerning the worth of their stock. Because this was a close corporation there was little hope of establishing a market for the stock. Thus, dissolution was the only viable remedy. Affirmed.

EDITOR'S ANALYSIS: Dissolution is an extraordinary remedy which is granted in very selective cases. Only where the actions constitute fraud, illegality, or oppression will dissolution be ordered. Oppression contemplates action significantly infringing on minority shareholder rights.

[For more information on Controlling Shareholders, see Casenote Law Outline on Corporations, Chapter 4, § III, Controlling Shareholders.]

QUICKNOTES

CLOSE CORPORATION - A corporation whose shares (or at least voting shares) are held by a closely knit group of shareholders or a single person.

DISSOLUTION - The termination of a marriage.

BUSINESS CORPORATION LAW, § 1104-a - Controls rules for involuntary dissolutions proscribes illegal, fraudulent and oppressive conduct.

McCALLUM v. ROSEN'S DIVERSIFIED, INC.

Former CEO and shareholder (P) v. Closely held corporation (D)

153 F.3d 701 (8th Cir. 1998).

NATURE OF CASE: Appeal from summary judgments for defendant.

FACT SUMMARY: McCallum (P) unsuccessfully sought to have his shares in Rosen's Diversified, Inc. (RDI) (D) redeemed for fair value pursuant to a court ordered buy-out.

CONCISE RULE OF LAW: A minority shareholder is entitled to a buy-out of his interest when the directors or those in control of the corporation have acted in a manner unfairly prejudicial toward one or more shareholders in their capacities as shareholders or directors or as officers or employees of a closely held corporation.

FACTS: RDI (D) was a closely held corporation which had hired McCallum (P) as Executive Vice President and Chief Executive Officer. When McCallum (P) was later terminated, he sought to redeem the shares of common stock he had been given as a bonus. The parties could not agree on a price, and McCallum (P) sued, alleging the company had engaged in self-dealing and undermined his authority as CEO. McCallum's (P) claims were dismissed as improperly pleaded derivative claims. The district court held that McCallum (P) failed to present evidence showing that RDI (D) acted unfairly prejudicial toward him and granted RDI's (D) motions for summary judgment. McCallum (P) appealed.

ISSUE: Is a minority shareholder entitled to a buy-out of his interest when the directors or those in control of the corporation have acted in a manner unfairly prejudicial toward one or more shareholders in their capacities as shareholders or directors or as officers or employees of a closely held corporation?

HOLDING AND DECISION: (Beam, J.) Yes. A minority shareholder is entitled to a buy-out of his interest when the directors or those in control of the corporation have acted in a manner unfairly prejudicial toward one or more shareholders in their capacities as shareholders or directors or as officers or employees of a closely held corporation. Since the Supreme Court of Minnesota has not decided the issue of when a minority shareholder is entitled to a court ordered buy-out, we must determine what that court would probably hold were it to decide the issue. The district court erred in dismissing certain of McCallum's (P) allegations as failing to observe the derivative pleading requirements for shareholder proceedings since McCallum (P) sought no relief on behalf of the corporation. In any event, McCallum (P) is entitled to equitable relief based on the uncontroverted assertions that were not dismissed as derivative claims. The phrase "unfairly prejudicial" is to be interpreted liberally. In deciding whether to order a buy-out, the court should consider the reasonable expectations of the shareholders with respect to each other and the corporation. The uncontested facts demonstrate that McCallum's (P) reasonable expectations were defeated. On his termination, McCallum (P) was divested of his primary expectations as a minority shareholder in RDI (D) - an active role in the management of the corporation and input as an employee. On remand, the district court shall determine the fair value of McCallum's shares in accordance with state law. Reversed and remanded.

EDITOR'S ANALYSIS: The holding in this case is from a Minnesota statute. The statute provides the courts with broad equitable authority to protect the interests of minority shareholders. The court held that terminating the CEO, and then offering to redeem his stock, which was partially issued to lure him to remain at the company, constituted conduct toward McCallum (P) as a shareholder sufficient to invoke the statute.

QUICKNOTES

MINN. STAT. § 302A.751 - provides for the buy-out of a minority shareholder's interest in a closely held corporation under certain circumstances.

CHARLAND v. COUNTRY VIEW GOLF CLUB, INC.
Minority shareholder (P) v. Corporation (D)
R.I. Sup. Ct., 588 A.2d 609 (1991).

NATURE OF CASE: Appeal from decision in an action requesting dissolution of a corporation.

FACT SUMMARY: Charland (P), a minority shareholder in a Rhode Island closely held corporation that operated an eighteen-hole golf course, Country View Golf Club, Inc. (Country View) (D), appealed from a decision awarding him $139,095.73 for his shares of Country View's (D) stock after Charland (P) brought a dissolution action against Country View (D) alleging that one of their corporate officers engaged in illegal activities.

CONCISE RULE OF LAW: When a corporation buys out a shareholder's stock in response to a dissolution petition, the shares may not be discounted solely because of their minority status or their lack of marketability.

FACTS: Charland (P), a minority shareholder in Country View (D), a Rhode Island closely held corporation that owned and operated an eighteen-hole golf course, filed a complaint asking that Country View (D) be dissolved because one of Country View's (D) officers was engaging in illegal activities. After filing its answer, Country View (D), acting pursuant to state law, elected to purchase Charland's (P) fifteen shares of Country View's (D) stock. Under a Rhode Island statute, when a petition for corporate dissolution is filed by a shareholder, the corporation may avoid dissolution by electing to purchase shares owned by the petitioner at a price equal to their fair value. Charland (P) and Country View (D) could not agree on the fair value of Charland's (P) shares. Therefore, the court appointed an appraiser, Joseph Smith, to determine the fair value of Charland's (P) shares. Smith concluded that a "minority discount" would be appropriate in determining the fair value of the shares. Based on his calculations, the trial court awarded Charland (P) the sum of $139,095.73. Charland (P) appealed, contending he did not receive fair value for his shares.

ISSUE: When a corporation buys out a shareholder's stock in response to a dissolution petition, may the shares be discounted because of their minority status or lack of marketability?

HOLDING AND DECISION: (Kelleher, J.) No. When a corporation buys out a shareholder's stock in response to a dissolution petition, the shares may not be discounted because of their minority status or lack of marketability. If shares are placed on the open market, their minority status would substantially decrease their value. However, when the shares are to be purchased by the corporation, the fact that they are noncontrolling shares is irrelevant. Moreover, had Charland (P) proved his case and dissolved Country View (D), each

shareholder would have been entitled to the same amount per share regardless of status. A lack of marketability discount, on the other hand, is separate from and bears no relation to a minority discount. However, Rhode Island law states that valuation should be made at the close of business on the day on which the petition is filed. Therefore, a lack of marketability discount is also inapposite when a corporation elects to buy out a shareholder who has filed for dissolution of a corporation. Since the trial court did apply a discount, thereby awarding Charland (P) less than the fair market value of his shares, the case is remanded.

EDITOR'S ANALYSIS: As noted by the court in Charland, many jurisdictions, including Rhode Island, have decided the question of determining the fair values of shares when a dissenting shareholder elects to require the fair value of his or her shares in the case of a merger or consolidation. In these cases, appraisers are generally given wide discretion to consider all relevant factors in determining the fair value of a dissenting shareholder's stock. This is a separate issue from whether a minority discount should be applied when a corporation elects to buy out a shareholder who has petitioned for dissolution proceedings, a question that few jurisdictions have addressed.

[For more information on dissolution of the close corporation, see Casenote Law Outline on Corporations, Chapter 3, § III, Viewing the Close Corporation from Within.]

QUICKNOTES

G.I. 1956 § 7-1.1-90 - Courts have power to liquidate corporation in a shareholder action dissolution would benefit shareholders due to acts of directors.

INVOLUNTARY DISSOLUTION - The termination of a corporation's existence through administrative or judicial action or insolvency.

NOTES:

CHAPTER 7
ALTERNATIVE FORMS OF BUSINESS

QUICK REFERENCE RULES OF LAW

1. **Liability of Limited Partner.** A limited partner may become liable for the obligations of the limited partnership under certain circumstances in which the limited partner has taken part in the control of the business. (Gateway Potato Sales v. G.B. Investment Co.)

   [For more information on limited partnerships, see Casenote Law Outline on Corporations, Chapter 1, § III, The Limited Partnership.]

2. **Corporate General Partner.** The duty of loyalty in a limited liability corporation extends to directors of the corporation's general partners sufficient to support a breach of duty claim by controlling shareholders. (In re USA Cafes, L.P. Litigation)

3. **Limited Liability Companies.** The participant in a limited liability company is not protected against a judgment creditor even if the basis for the judgment is an obligation unrelated to the activities of the company. (PB Real Estate, Inc. v. DEM II Properties)

4. **Limited Liability Companies.** The "veil of protection" afforded by a limited liability company towards its members can be pierced if the company was operating as an alter ego of the members or if the members were committing fraud or deceit on third parties. (Hollowell v. Orleans Regional Hospital)

5. **Limited Liability Companies.** A member of a limited liability company does not breach a fiduciary duty to the company by directly competing against it where the operating agreement expressly permits competition. (McConnell v. Hunt Sports Enterprises)

GATEWAY POTATO SALES v. G.B. INVESTMENT CO.
Creditor (P) v. Limited partnership (D)
Ariz. Ct. App., 822 P.2d 490 (1991).

NATURE OF CASE: Appeal from a court order granting summary judgment to a defendant and a denial of plaintiff's motion for reconsideration in a suit to recover payment for goods supplied.

FACT SUMMARY: Gateway (P), a creditor of Sunworth Packing Limited Partnership (D), brought suit against limited partner G.B. Investment (D) to recover payment for goods it had supplied to Sunworth (D).

CONCISE RULES OF LAW: A limited partner may become liable for the obligations of the limited partnership under certain circumstances in which the limited partner has taken part in the control of the business.

FACTS: Gateway Potato Sales (P), a creditor of Sunworth Packing Limited Partnership (D), brought suit to recover payment for goods it had supplied to Sunworth Packing (D). Gateway (P) also sought recovery from Sunworth Corporation (D) as a general partner and from G.B. Investment Company (D), a limited partner, pursuant to Arizona Revised Statutes Annotated § 29-319, which imposes liability on limited partners who control the business. At trial, G.B. Investment's (D) vice-president, Anderson, testified in his affidavit that G.B. Investment (D) had exerted no control over the daily management and operation of the limited partnership, Sunworth Packing (D). However, this testimony was contradicted by the affidavit testimony of Ellsworth, president of Sunworth Corporation (D). According to Ellsworth, G.B. Investment's (D) employees Anderson and McHolm, controlled the day-to-day affairs of the limited partnership (D) and made Ellsworth account to them for nearly everything he did. G.B. Investment (D) moved for summary judgment, urging that there was no evidence that the circumstances described in A.R.S. § 29-319 had occurred in this case. It argued that, as a limited partner, it was not liable to the creditors of Sunworth Packing (D) except to the extent of its investment. The trial court agreed, granting G.B. Investment's (D) motion for summary judgment. Gateway (P) appealed from the judgment and the denial of its motion for reconsideration, arguing the existence of conflicting evidence of material facts.

ISSUES: May a limited partner become liable for the obligations of the limited partnership under certain circumstances in which the limited partner has taken part in the control of the business?

HOLDING AND DECISION: (Taylor, J.) Yes. A limited partner may become liable for the obligations of the limited partnership under certain circumstances in which the limited partner has taken part in the control of the business. In enacting A.R.S. § 29-319(a), the legislature stopped short of expressly stating that if the limited partner's participation in the control of the business is substantially the same as the exercise of the powers of a general partner, he is liable to persons who transact business with a limited partnership even though they have no knowledge of his participation and control. It has made this statement by implication, though, by stating to the opposite effect that if the limited partner's participation in the control of the business is not substantially the same as the exercise of the powers of a general partner, he is liable only to persons who transact business with the limited partnership with actual knowledge of his participation in control. Moreover, in the absence of actual knowledge of the limited partner's participation in the control of the partnership business, there must be evidence from which a trier-of-fact might find not only control, but control that is substantially the same as the exercise of powers of a general partner. The evidence Gateway (P) presented in this case should have allowed it to withstand summary judgment. The affidavit testimony of Ellsworth raises the issue whether he was merely a puppet for the limited partner, G.B. Investment (D). Ellsworth's detailed statement raises substantial issues of material facts. It cannot be said, as a matter of law, that G.B. Investment (D) was entitled to summary judgment. Reversed and remanded.

EDITOR'S ANALYSIS: The decision in Gateway represents the general rule under the amended version of the Uniform Limited Partnership Act regarding the liability of limited partners who participate in the control of the business. Under this rule, limited partners may be found liable only to individuals engaging in business with the limited partnership reasonably believing, based upon the limited partner's conduct, that the limited partner is actually a general partner. This provision is widely considered to be the Act's most significant method of liability defense.

[For more information on limited partnerships, see Casenote Law Outline on Corporations, Chapter 1, § III, The Limited Partnership.]

NOTES

IN RE USACAFES, L.P. LITIGATION
Limited partnership (D) v. Holders (P)
600 A. 2d 43 (1992).

NATURE OF THE CASE: Consolidated class action seeking imposition of constructive trust.

FACT SUMMARY: The shareholders of a reorganized corporation filed breach of duty claims against the directors of the new corporation based on transactions that took place counter to the interests of the shareholders as reflected in the original prospectus.

CONCISE RULE OF LAW: The duty of loyalty in a limited liability corporation extends to directors of the corporation's general partners sufficient to support a breach of duty claim by controlling shareholders.

FACTS: USACafes L.P. (D) was formed after the reorganization of a Nevada corporation, which included the creation of a general partner that was also named as a defendant in the present case. Metsa Acquisition Corp. moved to purchase substantially all of the assets of USACafes (D), which triggered a breach of the duty of loyalty action against USACafes (D) by the holders (P) of the limited partnership. The holders (P) alleged that the sale of assets took place at a price favorable to Metsa Corporation, and that the directors of USACafes' (D) general partner received substantial side payments. In addition, the holders (P) asserted that the directors of USACafes' (D) general partner were not sufficiently informed to make a valid business judgment on the sale. Finally, the holders (P) asserted a breach of duty claim on behalf of the shareholders of the original Nevada corporation, based on the original shareholders' belief that a sale of substantially all the assets of the reorganized corporation required an affirmative majority vote by all the shareholders. In amending its complaint to include this assertion, the holders (P) requested judicial recognition of the right to vote on the Metsa transaction, or a rescission of the transaction.

ISSUE: Does the duty of loyalty in a limited liability corporation extend to directors of the corporation's general partners sufficient to support a breach of duty claim by controlling shareholders?

HOLDING: (Allen, J.) Yes. The duty of loyalty in a limited liability corporation extends to directors of the corporation's general partners sufficient to support a breach of duty claim by controlling shareholders. The directors of USACafes' general partner (D) concede that a fiduciary duty exists between the general partner and the limited partners of the corporation, but that no such duties are owed by the directors of the general partner towards the limited partners. In the view of the court, the directors' (D) assertion of the independence of the corporate general partner from its directors is incorrect. No precedents exist to directly address the question that the directors of a corporate general partner owe fiduciary duties to a corporation and its general partners. However, one who controls the property of another may not intentionally use that property to the detriment of the true owner without consent. Corporate directors are thus regarded as fiduciaries for corporate stockholders. Relevant authority extends the fiduciary duty of the general partner to a controlling shareholder. In addition, we recognize this duty in the directors of a general partner who are in control of the partnership's property, more so than a controlling shareholder. The directors (D) have breached a fiduciary duty imposed upon them as directors of the general partner, and the motion by the directors (D) to dismiss the claim is therefore denied.

EDITOR'S ANALYSIS: The court likened the role of a director owing fiduciary duties based on the control of property to that of a trustee. The law of trusts requires that a fiduciary may not waste property, even when there is no self-interest involved. In addition, a fiduciary is required to exercise due care when controlling property for the benefit of another. Eventually, courts of equity would extend these duties by analogy to corporate directors controlling the corporate enterprise. Thus, the appropriate remedy imposed by the court in the present case was a constructive trust, requiring the return of the value of the property as held in trust by the directors on the shareholders' behalf.

QUICKNOTES

CONSTRUCTIVE TRUST - A trust that arises by operation of law whereby the court imposes a trust upon property lawfully held by one party for the benefit of another, as a result of some wrongdoing by the party in possession so as to avoid unjust enrichment.

GENERAL PARTNERSHIP - A voluntary agreement entered into by two or more parties to engage in business whereby each of the parties is to share in any profits and losses therefrom equally and each is to participate equally in the management of the enterprise.

LIMITED LIABILITY - An advantage of doing business in the corporate form by safeguarding shareholders from liability for the debts or obligations of the corporation.

PB REAL ESTATE, INC. v. DEM II PROPERTIES
Real property broker (P) v. Mortgage holders (D)
50 Conn. App. 741 (1998)

NATURE OF THE CASE: Charging order to satisfy judgment against payments due towards defendants from limited liability company.

FACT SUMMARY: After plaintiffs obtained a deficiency judgment and court order to take payments made by a limited liability company owned by defendants, defendants moved to block the turnover based on protective statutes defining the limitations of the company's liability.

CONCISE RULE OF LAW: The participant in a limited liability company is not protected against a judgment creditor even if the basis for the judgment is an obligation unrelated to the activities of the company.

FACTS: PB Real Estate, Inc. (P) obtained a deficiency judgment against DEM II Properties (D) and moved to obtain payments from Botwick and Kurzawa, LLC, a limited liability company owned by the defendants. The trial court granted PB Real Estate, Inc.'s (P) application and directed the LLC to pay PB Real Estate (P) present and future shares of all distributions owing to DEM II Properties (D). The LLC and DEM II Properties (D) appealed the order, alleging that the payments owed by the LLC to DEM II Properties (D) were not proper subjects for deficiency payments, and asserting that the court order exceeded the scope of the statute authorizing payment to PB Real Estate (P).

ISSUE: Is the participant in a limited liability company protected against a judgment creditor when the basis for the judgment is an obligation unrelated to the activities of the company?

HOLDING: (Shea, J.) No. The participant in a limited liability company is not protected against a judgment creditor even if the basis for the judgment is an obligation unrelated to the activities of the company. The trial court characterized the payments made to the defendants as distributions, despite the defendants' contrary assertions that these payments were salaries made in compensation for their services rendered to the LLC. The ledgers show that the payments in question were not in the "salaries" column, but listed as significant earnings next to the initials of the defendants. This court concludes that the evidence properly supports the trial court's conclusion that the payments were distributions, making them proper subjects for turnover. The defendants further contend that the payments made to them do not constitute distributions because they never voted to order such distributions. However, the applicable statue explicitly defines a member's limited liability company interest, properly available for the satisfaction of a judgment, to include a member's share of the profits and losses of the LLC. The judgment issuing the turnover order is affirmed.

EDITOR'S ANALYSIS: The defendants in the present case relied on statutes requiring a formal vote from members in a limited liability company before distribution may be made, to protect the payments they received from the credit judgment. However, the court found the applicable statutes merely suggested an affirmative vote or approval process as alternatives, and implied consent on the behalf of the defendants based on their acceptance of the payments made to them in the past from a company which they owned and controlled. Thus, their characterizations to the contrary were found unrealistic and their appeal to overturn the payment order was denied.

QUICKNOTES

DEFICIENCY JUDGMENT - A judgment against a mortgagor for the difference between the amount obtained at a foreclosure sale and the amount of the mortgage debt that is due.

FORECLOSURE - An action to recover the amount due on a mortgage of real property where the owner has failed to pay their debt, terminating the owner's interest in the property which must then be sold to satisfy the debt.

LIMITED LIABILITY COMPANY - A business entity combining the features of both a corporation and a general partnership; the LLC provides its shareholders and officers with limited liability, but it is treated as a partnership for taxation purposes.

HOLLOWELL v. ORLEANS REGIONAL HOSPITAL
Hospital employees (P) v. Hospital (D)
WL 2832298 E.D.LA. (1998).

NATURE OF THE CASE: Motion for summary judgment and cross-motion for partial summary judgment pursuant to class action suit filed on behalf of employees of hospital for wrongful termination.

FACT SUMMARY: Employees of a New Orleans hospital filed a claim against their employer for being laid off without proper notice contrary to federal statute.

CONCISE RULE OF LAW: The "veil of protection" afforded by a limited liability company towards its members can be pierced if the company was operating as an alter ego of the members or if the members were committing fraud or deceit on third parties.

FACTS: Orleans Regional Hospital (ORH) (D) is a hospital providing psychiatric care for children and adolescents. As a limited liability company incorporated under Louisiana law, ORH (D) made changes to its operating procedures affecting the admission and length of stay of psychiatric patients. When the need for patient care decreased, ORH (D) began discharging employees (P). Hollowell (P) and other employees filed suit alleging that they had been laid off by ORH (D) without proper notice in violation of federal statute. The action was certified as a class action before being transferred to the present division. ORH (D) filed a motion to dismiss, and Hollowell and the class of plaintiffs filled a cross-motion for partial dismissal of the prior motion.

ISSUE: Can the "veil of protection" afforded by a limited liability company towards its members be pierced if the company was operating as an alter ego of the members or if the members were committing fraud or deceit on third parties?

HOLDING: (Lemmon, J.) Yes. The "veil of protection" afforded by a limited liability company towards its members can be pierced if the company was operating as an alter ego of the members or if the members were committing fraud or deceit on third parties. Policy considerations suggest that participants in a limited liability company may be found liable through the same evaluative process that the corporate veil is penetrated in traditional corporations. However, limited liability companies do not observe the same formalities as traditional corporations, such as annual elections for directors, the holding of meetings, or the keeping of meeting minutes. However, where the company was operating as an alter ego of the members or the members were committing fraud or deceit on third parties, the veil may be pierced in the same manner as that of a traditional corporation. Furthermore, under the applicable federal statute brought forth by Hollowell (P), ORH (D) may be treated as a "single business enterprise" based on the degree to which its members act independently from the parent. The common ownership of the parent, the de facto exercise of control, and the dependency of operations, are all relevant factors in both the determination of statutory eligibility and the misrepresentative activity of the members of ORH (D). Summary judgment is therefore inappropriate, as these aforementioned issues remain for trial. The defendant's motion is thus denied.

EDITOR'S ANALYSIS: Note that the protective "corporate veil" doctrine applies traditionally to corporations and not limited liability companies as suggested by the court in the present case. ORH (D), as a limited liability company, could have otherwise been found immune to the doctrine if not for the relevant degree of overlap between limited liability companies and traditional corporations. The court, as a matter of policy, thus extended the doctrine based on this overlap, to encompass limited liability companies such as the defendant, but ensured a degree of control by denying the motion for summary judgment and promulgating appropriate and explicit standards for the trial court to observe.

QUICKNOTES

CORPORATE VEIL - Refers to the shielding from personal liability of a corporation's officers, directors or shareholders for unlawful conduct engaged in by the corporation.

LIMITED LIABILITY COMPANY - A business entity combining the features of both a corporation and a general partnership; the LLC provides its shareholders and officers with limited liability, but it is treated as a partnership for taxation purposes.

SUMMARY JUDGMENT - Judgment rendered by a court in response to a motion by one of the parties, claiming that the lack of a question of material fact in respect to an issue warrants disposition of the issue without consideration by the jury.

McCONNELL v. HUNT SPORTS ENTERPRISES
Community leader (P) v. Soccer team investor (D)
WL 681757, 1999

NATURE OF THE CASE: Complaint for declaratory judgment against limited liability company requesting participation as franchise owner.

FACT SUMMARY: Members of a limited liability company formed to explore the possibility of applying for a new NHL franchise sought a declaration for breach of contract against each other based on the exclusion of certain members' ownership interests in the franchise.

CONCISE RULE OF LAW: A member of a limited liability company does not breach a fiduciary duty to the company by directly competing against it where the operating agreement expressly permits competition.

FACTS: Several community leaders in Columbus, Ohio, including McConnell (P), were contacted by the city mayor based on their involvement in professional sports to examine the possibility of applying for an NHL hockey franchise for Columbus. McConnell's (P) colleagues approached Hunt Sports Enterprises (HSE) (D) as a potential investor. Together, McConnell (P), HSE (D) and others formed Columbus Hockey Limited (CHL), a limited liability company whose general character was to invest in and operate a franchise in the NHL. Following an application for the franchise filed by CHL on behalf of the city of Columbus, difficulty arose when a planned tax to finance the construction of a required, appropriate arena failed to pass approval. When HSE (D) refused to accept an alternative lease proposal that would permit the required construction, McConnell (P) offered to lease the arena in HSE's (D) place. The offer was accepted and the NHL required that an ownership group be identified pursuant to its granting of a franchise. McConnell (P) signed the required documents in an individual capacity, in the place intended for CHL's participation as franchise owner, thus identifying him (P) as the majority owner. HSE (D), which continued to find the existing terms unacceptable, filed a complaint, and McConnell (P) requested a declaration permitting himself as a member of CHL to compete with CHL itself for the position of majority owner.

ISSUE: Does a member of a limited liability company breach a fiduciary duty to the company by directly competing against it where the operating agreement expressly permits competition?

HOLDING: (Per curiam.) No. A member of a limited liability company does not breach a fiduciary duty to the company by directly competing against it where the operating agreement expressly permits competition. Section 3.3 of the operating agreement states that "members may compete." However, HSE (D) contends that members of CHL may only compete in any business venture that is different from the business of the company, which includes investing in and operating an NHL franchise. We believe this interpretation goes beyond the plain language of section 3.3, which permits "any other venture of any nature." Appellees may therefore engage in activities that are competitive with CHL. The injury complained of is the direct competition of McConnell (P) as a member of CHL, against CHL and HSE (D) as a co-member of the same limited liability company. The evidence does not show McConnell (P) interfered with HSE's (D) own dealings with the NHL. Thus, there was not sufficient evidence presented to suggest any breach of fiduciary duty on the part of appellees to interfere tortiously with the business relationships of their limited liability parent. A directed verdict in favor of appellees was therefore appropriate.

EDITOR'S ANALYSIS: Similar to a partnership, a limited liability company involves a fiduciary relationship that precludes direct competition between the members of the company. However, the court conceded that the operating agreement explicitly permitted competition, making that issue moot. The real dispute here rested in the ability of the operating agreement to define the scope of any individual member's fiduciary duties towards the company. In the present case, the court found that the operating agreement did in fact have the power to define these duties, and gave the applicable clause appropriate weight when ruling in favor of McConnell (P) and other appellees.

QUICKNOTES

FRANCHISE - An agreement whereby one party (the franchisor) grants another (the franchisee) the right to market its product or service.

PARTNERSHIP - A voluntary agreement entered into by two or more parties to engage in business and to share any attendant profits and losses.

CHAPTER 8
THE DUTY OF CARE AND THE DUTY TO ACT LAWFULLY

QUICK REFERENCE RULES OF LAW

1. **The Duty of Care.** Where insiders have misappropriated corporate funds that were held in an implied trust for third parties, it is said that the director owes a fiduciary duty to the third parties and consequently, if the director fails to make an effort to fulfill his responsibilities as a director, he will be deemed to have breached his duty of care and thus will be held personally liable to the third parties for the misappropriated funds. (Francis v. United Jersey Bank)

   [For more information on director's fiduciary duties, see Casenote Law Outline on Corporations, Chapter4, IV, Special Problems Involving the Fiduciary Duties of Directors.]

2. **The Business Judgement Rule.** The question of whether or not a dividend is to be declared or a distribution made is exclusively a matter of business judgment for the board of directors and the courts will not interfere as long as the decision is made in good faith. (Kamin v. American Express Co.)

3. **The Business Judgement Rule.** Directors are bound to exercise good faith informed judgment in making decisions on behalf of the corporation. (Smith v. Van Gorkom)

   [For more information on a director's duty of care, see Casenote Law Outline on Corporations, Chapter 4, § II, The Duty of Care.]

4. **The Business Judgement Rule.** A board of directors has an affirmative duty to attempt in good faith to assure that a corporate information and reporting system exists and is adequate. (In re Caremark International Inc. Derivative Litigation)

   [For more information on duty of care, see Casenote Law Outline on Corporations, Chapter 4, § II, The Duty of Care.]

5. **The Duty to act Lawfully.** The sound business judgment rule eschews a court's intervention in corporate decision-making if the judgment of directors and officers is uninfluenced by personal considerations and is exercised in good faith. (Miller v. American Telephone & Telegraph Co.)

   [For more information on Business Judgment Rule, see Casenote Law Outline on Corporations, Chapter 4, § I, State Corporation Codes and the Business Judgment Rule.]

FRANCIS v. UNITED JERSEY BANK
Bankruptcy trustee (P) v. Estate administrator, executrix (D)
N.J. Sup. Ct., 87 N.J. 15, 432 A.d.. 814 (1981).

NATURE OF CASE: Action in negligence to recover misappropriated corporate funds.

FACT SUMMARY: Francis (P), the trustee in bankruptcy, sought damages from Lillian Overcash (D), Lillian Pritchard's executrix, for Lillian Pritchard's negligent performance of her duties as a director of Pritchard & Baird, which went bankrupt after Pritchard's four sons, Pritchard & Baird's directors, misappropriated corporate funds.

CONCISE RULE OF LAW: Where insiders have misappropriated corporate funds that were held in an implied trust for third parties, it is said that the director owes a fiduciary duty to the third parties and consequently, if the director fails to make an effort to fulfill his responsibilities as a director, he will be deemed to have breached his duty of care and thus will be held personally liable to the third parties for the misappropriated funds.

FACTS: Pritchard and Baird Intermediary Corp. (P&B) was a reinsurance broker. A reinsurance broker is the intermediary between the insurance company and the reinsurer, which is the entity that insures the insurance company. P&B, as a reinsurance broker, collected premiums from insurance companies, deducted a brokerage commission, and transmitted the balance to the reinsurer. When a loss occurred, P&B collected money from the reinsurer and transmitted it to the insurance company. Consequently P&B annually received millions of dollars of clients' money which, according to industry custom, should have been segregated. However, P&B ignored industry custom and commingled their clients' money with its own funds. Charles Pritchard, Sr., former chief executive of P&B, used to withdraw funds from the commingled account, but would only withdraw an amount that correlated to the corporation's profits and would repay the withdrawn amount at the end of the year. In 1968, Charles Sr. became seriously ill. Consequently he relinquished all management control to his two sons, William and Charles Jr., who continued the practice of withdrawing corporate funds from the commingled account. However, contrary to the practice of their father, the sons also withdrew their clients' money from the account and never repaid the withdrawn amounts. They continued to siphon ever-increasing amounts until they eventually forced P&B into bankruptcy in 1975. At all times during which the two sons managed P&B, their mother, Charles Sr.'s wife, Lillian Pritchard, was a director of P&B. Moreover, in 1973, when Charles Sr. died, she became the largest shareholder with 48% of the stock. However, not once did she read or obtain the annual financial statements. Nor did she make an effort to see that her sons' managerial practices complied with the industry standards. In short she was no more than a figurehead. Consequently,

Francis (P), the trustee in bankruptcy, sought damages from Lillian Overcash (D), Lillian Pritchard's executrix, for Lillian Pritchard's negligent performance of her duties as a director. In addition, United Jersey Bank (D), the administrator of Charles Sr.'s estate, was joined as a defendant. The trial court held for Francis (P) and entered a judgment for $10,355,736.91. The appellate division affirmed. Overcash (D) and United Jersey Bank (D) appealed.

ISSUE: Where insiders have misappropriated corporate funds that were held in as implied trust for third parties, does one director owe a fiduciary duty to the third parties?

HOLDING AND DECISION: (Pollock, J.) Yes. Where insiders have misappropriated corporate funds that were held in an implied trust for third parties, the director owes a fiduciary duty to the third parties. Consequently, if the director fails to make an effort to fulfill his responsibilities as a director, he will be deemed to have breached his duty of care and thus will be held personally liable to the third parties for the misappropriated funds. In this case, Mrs. Pritchard did not read the corporate financial statements, she did not supervise the business, nor even did she acquire a basic knowledge of the business. In short, she did not make the slightest effort to detect and prevent the illegal conduct of her two sons. In addition, it was no defense that she was ignorant of her sons' actions. Nor was it a defense that she did not actively participate in the misappropriation. Finally it should be noted that Mrs. Pritchard was not a director of an ordinary business but was a director of a reinsurance brokerage firm. Her duty was akin to that of a bank director to its depositors. As such she was held to a stricter accountability than if she had been a director of an ordinary business. Thus, based on all the circumstances discussed, the judgment of the appellate division is affirmed and Mrs. Pritchard's estate is personally liable in negligence for $10,355,736.91. Affirmed.

EDITOR'S ANALYSIS: This case held that the director was liable in negligence because of nonfeasance. Nonfeasance is the failure to act when there is a duty to do so, whereas malfeasance is an affirmative act made in a negligent manner. The courts are more likely to find a director liable for nonfeasance where the business itself is deemed fiduciary in nature, such as the banking business or as in the present case the reinsurance business.

[For more information on director's fiduciary duties, see Casenote Law Outline on Corporations, Chapter 4, § IV, Special Problems Involving the Fiduciary Duties of Directors.]

KAMIN v. AMERICAN EXPRESS CO.
Shareholder (P) v. Corporation (D)
N.Y. Sup. Ct., 86 Misc. 2d 809, 383 N.Y.S.2d 807 (1976).

NATURE OF CASE: Derivative action for damages for waste of corporate assets.

FACT SUMMARY: Kamin (P) brought a stockholders' derivative suit claiming American Express (D) had engaged in waste of corporate assets by declaring a certain dividend in kind.

CONCISE RULE OF LAW: The question of whether or not a dividend is to be declared or a distribution made is exclusively a matter of business judgment for the board of directors and the courts will not interfere as long as the decision is made in good faith.

FACTS: American Express (D) had acquired for investment almost two million shares of common stock in Donaldson, Lufken and Jenrette (DLJ) at a cost of $29.9 million. Kamin (P), a minority stockholder in American Express (D), charged that the subsequent decision to declare a special dividend to all stockholders resulting in a distribution of the shares of DLJ in kind was a negligent violation of the directors' fiduciary duty. He argued that the market value of the DLJ shares was only $4 million and that American Express (D) should have sold the DLJ shares on the market so as to be able to offset the $25 million capital loss against taxable capital gains on other investments and thus obtain an $8 million tax saving that would be otherwise unavailable. In a stockholders' derivative action, Kamin (P) sought a declaration that the dividend in kind constituted a waste of corporate assets and sought damages therefor. American Express (D) moved to dismiss the complaint.

ISSUE: Will the courts interfere with a board of directors' good faith business judgment as to whether or not to declare a dividend or make a distribution?

HOLDING AND DECISION: (Greenfield, J.) No. Whether or not to declare a dividend or make a distribution is exclusively a matter of business judgment for the board of directors, and thus the courts will not interfere with their decision as long as it is made in good faith. It is not enough to charge, as Kamin (P) has in this case, that the directors made an imprudent decision or that some other course of action would have been more advantageous. Such a charge cannot give rise to a cause of action. Thus, the motion for dismissal of the complaint is granted.

EDITOR'S ANALYSIS: The "business judgment rule" illustrated in this expresses the traditional and still valid view of a director's duty of care. This common-law standard is designed to allow the directors a wide berth in conducting the affairs of the corporation so that they can act effectively and efficiently in pursuing the corporation's best interests rather than being constantly influenced by the need to practice "defensive management" to prevent being held liable in this type of action.

QUICKNOTES
SELF-DEALING - Transaction in which a fiduciary uses property of another, held by virtue of the confidential relationship, for personal gain.

DIVIDEND - The payment of earnings to a corporation's shareholders in proportion to the amount of shares held.

NOTES:

SMITH v. VAN GORKOM
Shareholders (P) v. Board of directors (D)
Del. Sup. Ct., 488 A.2d. 858 (1985).

NATURE OF CASE: Appeal from denial of damages for breach of director's duties.

FACT SUMMARY: The trial court held that because Van Gorkom (D) and the other Trans Union directors (D) had three opportunities to reject the merger proposal, they acted with due deliberation and their conduct fell within the business judgment rule.

CONCISE RULE OF LAW: Directors are bound to exercise good faith informed judgment in making decisions on behalf of the corporation.

FACTS: In order to fully realize a favorable tax situation, Trans Union's chief executive, Van Gorkom (D), solicited a merger offer from an outside investor. Van Gorkom (D) acted on his own and arbitrarily arrived at a $55 per share price. Without any form of investigation, the full Trans Union board accepted the offer. The offer was proposed two subsequent times before its formal acceptance by the Board. Smith (P) and other shareholders brought this derivative suit on the basis that the Board (D) had not given due consideration to the offer. The trial court held that because it considered the offer three times before formally accepting it, the Board's (D) action fell within the business judgment rule. The appellate court affirmed, and this appeal was taken.

ISSUE: Are directors bound to exercise good faith informed judgment in making corporate decisions?

HOLDING AND DECISION: (Horsey, J.) Yes. Directors are bound to exercise good faith informed judgment in making corporate decisions. In this case, the Directors (D) tentatively approved the merger the first time it was presented to them. They had no, and requested no, substantiating data regarding the feasibility of the $55 per share price. No consideration was given to allowing time to study the proposal or to gain more information. As a result, their decision to accept the offer can be classified as nothing short of gross negligence. As a result, their actions cannot be foisted on the shareholders under protection of the business judgment rule. Remanded for a determination of the value of the shares and an appropriate damage award.

DISSENT: (McNeilly , J.) The Board (D) consisted of extremely well-educated, experienced, and successful business people. They were well aware of their duties and of the merits of the offer. Although their actions seem subjectively imprudent, this does not preclude application of the business judgment rule.

EDITOR'S ANALYSIS: The decisions of a corporation are left up to the Board of Directors. Some major decisions, such as mergers and acquisitions, require shareholder approval or ratification. Within certain parameters, decisions of the Board are upheld on review based on the business judgment rule. This rule grants immunity from liability for decisions a Board makes based on its business experience. In the absence of gross negligence, such decisions are generally upheld as falling within the Board's discretion.

[For more information on a director's duty of care, see Casenote Law Outline on Corporations, Chapter 4, § II, The Duty of Care.]

QUICKNOTES

BUSINESS JUDGMENT RULE - Doctrine relieving corporate directors and/or officers from liability for decisions honestly and rationally made in the corporation's best interests.

LEVERAGED BUY OUT - A transaction whereby corporate outsiders purchase the outstanding shares of a publicly held corporation mostly with borrowed funds.

NOTES:

IN RE CAREMARK INTERNATIONAL INC. DERIVATIVE LITIGATION

Shareholders (P) v. Board of directors (D)

Del. Ch. __A.2d__, 1996 WL 549894 (1996).

NATURE OF CASE: Motion to approve a settlement of a consolidated derivative action.

FACT SUMMARY: Caremark, a managed health-care provider, entered into contractual arrangements with physicians and hospitals, often for "consultation" or "research," without first clarifying the unsettled law surrounding prohibitions against referral fee payments.

CONCISE RULE OF LAW: A board of directors has an affirmative duty to attempt in good faith to assure that a corporate information and reporting system exists and is adequate.

FACTS: Caremark was involved in providing patient health care and managed health-care services. Much of Caremark's revenue came from third-party payments, insurers, and Medicare and Medicaid reimbursement programs. The Anti-Referral Payments Law (ARPL) applied to Caremark, prohibiting payments to induce the referral of Medicare or Medicaid patients. Caremark had a practice of entering into service contracts, including consultation and research, with physicians who at times prescribed Caremark products or services to Medicare recipients. Such contracts were not prohibited by the ARPL, but they raised the issue of unlawful kickbacks. Caremark's Board of Directors (D) attempted to monitor these contracts internally, seeking legal advice and devising guidelines for employees. However, the government began investigating Caremark. Caremark began making structural changes in response to the investigation, centralizing management. In spite of this, Caremark and two officers were indicted. Several shareholder derivative actions were subsequently filed, charging the Board of Directors (D) with failure to adequately monitor as part of its duty of care. Settlement negotiations began. Caremark agreed in the settlement to cease all payments to third parties that referred patients to Caremark and to establish an ethics committee, which it had, in effect, already done. Caremark also agreed to make reimbursement payments to private and public parties totalling $250 million. All other claims were waived in the proposed settlement. The proposed settlement was submitted to the court for approval.

ISSUE: Does a board of directors have an affirmative duty to attempt in good faith to assure that a corporate information and reporting system exists and is adequate?

HOLDING AND DECISION: (Allen, Chancellor) Yes. A board of directors has an affirmative duty to attempt in good faith to assure that a corporate information and reporting system exists and is adequate. Directors generally do not monitor day-to-day operations in a company. The Supreme Court has said that where there is no basis for suspicion, directors cannot be liable. However, it would be extending this holding too far to say that directors have no obligation whatsoever to determine whether they are receiving accurate information. The duty of care implies that a board will make a good faith effort to ensure that a corporate information and reporting system is adequate. In this case, acts that resulted in indictments do not, by themselves, prove that the Caremark Board (D) was not adequately monitoring corporate behavior. On the contrary, the Board (D) appears to have been making structural changes all along to gain greater centralized control of the company. And an ethics monitoring group was in place well before the settlement was reached. Given that the evidence on the record suggests that success in the derivative suit was unlikely, but that Caremark is giving up little in the way of concessions not already in place, the settlement is fair.

EDITOR'S ANALYSIS: A duty to monitor does not require a board to be aware of all the details of corporate activity. In fact, such oversight would be physically impossible in a large company. The duty does, however, require the board to be aware of major activities and related issues that could pose a threat to the company. The choice of what structure to use in informational gathering is still subject to the safe harbor of the business judgment rule; therefore, a claim that the duty to monitor has been breached is tremendously difficult to prove successfully.

[For more information on duty of care, see Casenote Law Outline on Corporations, Chapter 4, § II, The Duty of Care.]

NOTES:

MILLER v. AMERICAN TELEPHONE & TELEGRAPH CO.

Shareholder (P) v. Corporation (D)

507 F.2d 759 (3d Cir. 1974).

NATURE OF CASE: Appeal from dismissal of shareholder's derivative action.

FACT SUMMARY: In Miller's (P) stockholder's derivative action against AT&T (D) for failure to collect an outstanding debt of $1.5 million owed to the company by the Democratic National Committee (DNC) Miller (P) alleged that AT&T (D) breached its duty to exercise diligence in handling the affairs of the corporation.

CONCISE RULE OF LAW: The sound business judgment rule eschews a court's intervention in corporate decision-making if the judgment of directors and officers is uninfluenced by personal considerations and is exercised in good faith.

FACTS: AT&T (D) provided communications services to the Democratic National Committee (DNC) during the 1960 Democratic national convention. When AT&T (D) failed to collect the $1.5 million owed by the DNC to AT&T (D), Miller (P), an AT&T (D) stockholder, brought a shareholder's derivative action against AT&T (D), alleging that the company breached its duty to exercise diligence in handling the affairs of the corporation, resulting in affording a preference to the DNC in violation of the Communications Act of 1934. Miller (P) sought an injunction against AT&T (D) from providing further services to the DNC until the debt was paid. The district court denied Miller's (P) request for an injunction and dismissed the suit against AT&T (D) for failure to state a claim upon which relief could be granted. The court stated that collection procedures were properly within the discretion of the directors whose decisions would not be overturned absent an allegation that the conduct of the directors was plainly illegal or in breach of fiduciary duties. Miller (P) appealed.

ISSUE: Does the sound business judgment rule eschew a court's intervention in corporate decision-making if the judgment of directors and officers is uninfluenced by personal considerations and is exercised in good faith?

HOLDING AND DECISION: (Seitz, C.J.) Yes. The sound business judgment rule eschews a court's intervention in corporate decision-making if the judgment of directors and officers is uninfluenced by personal considerations and is exercised in good faith. Underlying the rule is the assumption that reasonable diligence was used in reaching the decision which the rule is invoked to justify. Here, had Miller's (P) complaint alleged only failure to pursue a corporate claim, application of the sound business judgment rule would support the district court's ruling that a shareholder could not attack the directors' decision. Where, however, as here, the decision not to collect a debt owed the corporation is itself alleged to have been an illegal act, the business judgment rule cannot insulate AT&T (D) directors from liability if they did breach the Communications Act. Because Miller (P) has alleged actual damage to the corporation from the transaction between AT&T (D) and the DNC in the form of a loss of a $1.5 million increment to AT&T's (D) treasury, this court concludes that the complaint does state a claim upon which relief can be granted sufficient to withstand a motion to dismiss. At the appropriate time, Miller (P) will be required to produce evidence sufficient to establish a violation of the Communications Act. Reversed and remanded.

EDITOR'S ANALYSIS: Bad faith may preclude the application of the business judgment defense where directors knowingly violate a statute or comparable expression of public policy, even if such a violation is undertaken in the corporation's best interests. However, a plaintiff bears the burden of proving causation and the amount of any losses incurred by the corporation or the shareholders as a result of a defendant's wrongdoing. A defendant is entitled to offset against such liability any gains to the corporation that the defendant can establish arose out of the same transaction.

[For more information on Business Judgment Rule, see Casenote Law Outline on Corporations, Chapter 4, § I, State Corporation Codes and the Business Judgment Rule.]

QUICKNOTES

BUSINESS JUDGMENT RULE - Doctrine relieving corporate directors and/or officers from liability for decisions honestly and rationally made in the corporation's best interests.

FIDUCIARY DUTY - A legal obligation to act for the benefit of another, including subordinating one's personal interests to that of the other person.

SHAREHOLDER'S DERIVATIVE ACTION - Action asserted by a shareholder in order to enforce a cause of action on behalf of the corporation.

18 U.S.C. § 610 - Prohibits certain corporate campaign spending.

9

CHAPTER 9
THE DUTY OF LOYALTY

QUICK REFERENCE RULES OF LAW

1. **Self Interested Transactions.** When a shareholder attacks a transaction in which the directors have an interest other than as directors of the corporation, the directors may not escape review of the merits of the transaction. (Lewis v. S.L. & E., Inc.)

    [For more information on Self-Dealing Corporations, see Casenote Law Outline on Corporations, Chapter 4, § III, The Duty of Loyalty.]

2. **Self Interested Transactions.** When a director, in selling corporate property to himself, represents or joins in the representation of the corporation, the transaction is voidable at the option of the corporation. (Talbot v. James)

    [For more information on Corporate Directors, Self-Dealing, see Casenote Law Outline on Corporations, Chapter 4, § IV, Special Problems Involving the Fiduciary Duties of Directors.]

3. **Statutory Approaches.** Directors who engage in self-dealing must establish that they acted in good faith, honesty, and fairness. (Cookies Food Products v. Lakes Warehouse)

    [For more information on duty of loyalty, see Casenote Law Outline on Corporations, Chapter 4, § III, The Duty of Loyalty.]

4. **Compensation.** Directors may breach a fiduciary duty by proposing a stock options plan that does not offer reasonable assurance to the corporation of adequate value exchanged by failing to disclose the present value of future options using a reasonable options-pricing formula. (Lewis v. Vogelstein)

5. **Use of Corporation Assets.** Directors of a corporation are not entitled to recover any compensation or salary for performing their ordinary duties unless a provision for such compensation is authorized by a resolution of the board of directors prior to the rendering of the services. (Hawaiian International Finances, Inc. v. Pablo)

    [For more information on directors' duty of loyalty, see Casenote Law Outline on Corporations, Chapter 4, § III, The Duty of Loyalty.]

6. **Use of Corporation Assets.** Corporate officers and directors must disclose all relevant information prior to taking personal advantage of any potentially corporate opportunity. (Northeast Harbor Golf Club, Inc. v. Harris)

7. **Duties of Controlling Shareholders.** Majority shareholders owe a duty to minority shareholders that is similar to the duty owed by a director, and when a majority stockholder is voting, he violates his duty if he votes for his own personal benefit at the expense of the stockholders. (Zahn v. Transamerica Corporation)

    [For more information on Fiduciary Duty, Controlling Shareholders, see Casenote Law Outline on Corporations, Chapter 4, § VI, Controlling Shareholders.]

8. **Duties of Controlling Shareholders.** Where a parent company controls all transactions of a subsidiary, receiving a benefit at the expense of the subsidiary's minority stockholders, the intrinsic fairness test will be applied, placing the burden on the parent company to prove the transactions were based on reasonable business objectives. (Sinclair Oil Corporation v. Levien)

[For more information on Fiduciary Duty, Controlling Shareholders, see Casenote Law Outline on Corporations, Chapter 4, § VI, Controlling Shareholders.]

9. **Duties of Controlling Shareholders.** In a challenged transaction involving self-dealing by a controlling shareholder, the substantive legal standard is that of entire fairness, with the burden of persuasion resting upon the defendants. (Kahn v. Tremont)

10. **Sale of Control.** Minority shareholders are not entitled to share in any premium price paid for the controlling shares of a corporation. (Zetlin v. Hanson Holdings, Inc.)

[For more information on controlling shareholders and a premium price, see Casenote Law Outline on Corporations, Chapter 4, § VI, Controlling Shareholders.]

11. **Duties of Controlling Shareholders.** (1) Even though a stockholder's derivative action exists in favor of a corporation, an individual stockholder is not precluded from bringing an individual action based on the same injury. (2) Majority shareholders have a fiduciary responsibility to minority shareholders and the corporation to use their power to control the corporation in a fair, just, and equitable manner and not to profit from that control at shareholder expense. (Jones v. H.F. Ahmanson & Co.)

[For more information on Derivative Suits, Individual Recovery, see Casenote Law Outline on Corporations, Chapter 9, § I, Derivative Suits.]

12. **Sale of Control.** Majority shareholders owe no fiduciary duties to other shareholders in sale of their stock; but, since officers and directors always stand in a fiduciary relationship to the corporation, its shareholders, and creditors, they cannot terminate their agency or accept the resignation of others if the immediate consequence would be to leave the interests of the corporation without proper care and protection. (Gerdes v. Reynolds)

[For more information on Sale of Control, see Casenote Law Outline on Corporations, Chapter 4, § VI, Controlling Shareholders.]

13. **Sale of Control.** A corporate director who is also a dominant shareholder stands in a fiduciary relationship to both the corporation and the minority stockholders, and, where such a director-shareholder sells controlling interest in the corporation, he is accountable to the extent that the sales price represents payment for the right to control. (Perlman v. Feldmann)

[For more information on Sale of Control, see Casenote Law Outline on Corporations, Chapter 4, § VI, Controlling Shareholders.]

14. **Sale of Control.** A director's agreement to transfer only a small percentage of shares, in exchange for a premium and a promise of resignation, constitutes a breach of fiduciary duty as an illegal sale of control. (Brecher v. Gregg)

15. **Sale of Control.** A seller of corporate control may not, as a general rule, profit by facilitating actions of the purchasers which operate to the detriment of the corporation or remaining shareholders; but where the facts do not indicate the existence of any such detriment, there is no question of the right of a controlling shareholder to derive a premium from the sale of a controlling block of stock. (Essex Universal Corp. v. Yates)

[For more information on Sale of Control, Premium Thereon, see Casenote Law Outline on Corporations, Chapter 4, § VI, Controlling Shareholders.]

LEWIS v. S. L. & E., INC.
Shareholder (P) v. Corporation (D)
629 F.2d 764 (2d Cir. 1980).

NATURE OF CASE: Appeal from judgment of derivative claim.

FACT SUMMARY: In Lewis' (P) derivative action against S.L.&E. (D) for waste of corporate assets, Lewis (P) argued, on appeal, that the trial court improperly allocated to him the burden of proving his claims of waste, and that since S.L.&E. (D) failed to prove that the transactions in question were fair and reasonable, Lewis (P) was entitled to judgment.

CONCISE RULE OF LAW: When a shareholder attacks a transaction in which the directors have an interest other than as directors of the corporation, the directors may not escape review of the merits of the transaction.

FACTS: Lewis (P), a shareholder of S.L.&E., Inc. (D), brought a derivative suit against directors of S.L.&E. (D), claiming that they had wasted the assets of S.L.&E. (D) by causing S.L.&E. (D) to lease business premises to L.G.T., Inc., another corporation operating a tire dealership. Lewis (P) claimed that the directors grossly undercharged L.G.T. for its occupancy and use of property owned by S.L.&E. (D). At trial, S.L.&E. (D) directors contended that the rental paid by L.G.T. was reasonable by offering evidence concerning the financial straits of L.G.T., the cost to L.G.T. of operating the property, and the rentals paid by two other properties in that neighborhood. The trial court held that Lewis (P) had failed to establish the rental value of the property during the period it was leased to L.G.T, and that S.L.&E. (D) was therefore entitled to judgment on the derivative claims. Implicit in the court's finding, granting judgment for S.L.&E. (D) upon Lewis' (P) failure to prove waste, was a determination that Lewis (P) bore the burden of proof on that issue. Lewis (P) appealed, arguing that the trial court improperly allocated to him the burden of proving his claims of waste, and that since S.L.&E. (D) failed to prove that the transactions in question were fair and reasonable, Lewis (P) was entitled to judgment.

ISSUE: When a shareholder attacks a transaction in which the directors have an interest other than as directors of the corporation, may the directors escape review of the merits of the transaction?

HOLDING AND DECISION: (Kearse, J.) No. When a shareholder attacks a transaction in which the directors have an interest other than as directors of the corporation, the directors may not escape review of the merits of the transaction. Under normal circumstances the directors of a corporation may determine, in the exercise of their business judgment, what contracts the corporation will enter into and what consideration is adequate, without review of the merits of their decisions by the courts. The business judgment rule presupposes that the directors have no conflict of interest. Here, the directors of S.L.&E. (D) were also directors of L.G.T. Thus, the directors of S.L.&E. (D) had the burden of proving that the rent paid by L.G.T for the property rented was fair and reasonable. The record shows that the directors failed to carry their burden. At trial, there was no direct testimony as to what would have been a fair rental during the relevant period, and the evidence that was introduced fell far short of establishing that rent paid was a fair annual rental value for the period. Thus, judgment should be entered against the directors in such an amount as the trial court shall determine to be equal to the amounts by which the annual fair rental value of the property exceeded the price paid by L.G.T. while it rented the property from S.L.&E. (D). Reversed and remanded.

EDITOR'S ANALYSIS: Under the rule that a disinterested majority of the directors of a corporation must approve a transaction with one of their number, the question has arisen whether this means a disinterested quorum or merely a disinterested majority of a quorum, so that the interested director could be counted to make up the quorum. Virtually all of the cases have held that the interested director could not be counted for quorum purposes. As the Calif & Dutch Co., 10 Cal. 349, the interested director for this purpose was "as much a stranger to the board as if he had never been elected a director."

[For more information on Self-Dealing Corporations, see Casenote Law Outline on Corporations, Chapter 4, § III, The Duty of Loyalty.]

QUICKNOTES

CLOSE CORPORATION - A corporation whose shares (or at least voting shares) are held by a closely knit group of shareholders or a single person.

BUSINESS JUDGMENT RULE - Doctrine relieving corporate directors and/or officers from liability for decisions honestly and rationally made in the corporation's best interests.

SELF-DEALING - Transaction in which a fiduciary uses property of another, held by virtue of the confidential relationship, for personal gain.

BUSINESS CORPORATION LAW § 713 - Provides that a contract between a corporation and an entity in which its directors are interested may be set aside unless the contract was fair and reasonable at the time of board approval.

TALBOT v. JAMES
Director (P) v. Director (D)
S.C. Sup. Ct., 259 S.C. 73 (1972).

NATURE OF CASE: Appeal from judgment in an action for an accounting.

FACT SUMMARY: In Talbot's (P) action against James (D) for an accounting as an officer and director of a corporation, Talbot (P) contended that James (D) violated his fiduciary relationship to the corporation and to Talbot (P), as a stockholder thereof, by diverting specific funds to himself.

CONCISE RULE OF LAW: When a director, in selling corporate property to himself, represents or joins in the representation of the corporation, the transaction is voidable at the option of the corporation.

FACTS: Talbot (P) and James (D) entered into a written agreement to form a corporation to construct and operate an apartment complex. The day following the election of officers and the issuance of capital stock, the board of directors of the corporation passed a resolution authorizing the corporation to borrow $850,700 from a mortgaging company. The record showed that James (D) personally received the sum of $25,025.31 from the proceeds of the mortgage loan. Talbot (P), after being advised that the corporation was in financial trouble, demanded an examination of the corporate records kept by James (D). James (D) refused. Talbot (P) then began an action against James (D) for an accounting as an officer and director of the corporation and contended that James (D) violated his fiduciary relationship to the corporation and to Talbot (P), as a stockholder thereof, by diverting the funds to himself. The Master found that James (D) had entered into a contract with himself, as president of the corporation, to receive funds from the proceeds of the mortgage loan without disclosing the identity of his interest to the other shareholders, and that James (D) would have to repay the sum received. James (D) appealed, and the court reversed the master's findings. Talbot (P) appealed.

ISSUE: When a director, in selling corporate property to himself, represents or joins in the representation of the corporation, is the transaction voidable at the option of the corporation?

HOLDING AND DECISION: (Moss, C.J.) Yes. When a director, in selling corporate property to himself, represents or joins in the representation of the corporation, the transaction is voidable at the option of the corporation. Here, James (D) entered into a contract with himself to receive benefits in the sum of $25,025.31 from the proceeds of the mortgage loan to the corporation without making full disclosure of his identity of interest to the other stockholders of the corporation. Thus, the corporation is entitled to judgment against James (D) in the amount of $25,025.31. Reversed and remanded.

DISSENT: (Bussey, J.) The judgment of the lower court should have been affirmed, but at the very least, if the corporation is to recover at all from James (D), its recovery should be limited to any profit actually received.

EDITOR'S ANALYSIS: In the simplest type of self-interested transaction, a corporation deals with a director or a senior executive. Sometimes, though, a corporation will deal with an enterprise or individual with whom a director or senior executive has a significant relationship. Such an enterprise or individual may be referred to as an "associate" of the director or senior executive and may be a spouse, child, parent, or sibling of a director or anyone for whom a director has financial responsibility.

[For more information on Corporate Directors, Self-Dealing, see Casenote Law Outline on Corporations, Chapter 4, § IV, Special Problems Involving the Fiduciary Duties of Directors.]

QUICKNOTES
SELF-DEALING - Transaction in which a fiduciary uses property of another, held by virtue of the confidential relationship, for personal gain.

NOTES:

COOKIES FOOD PRODUCTS, INC. v. LAKES WAREHOUSE DISTRIBUTING, INC.

Shareholders (P) v. Majority shareholder (D)

Iowa Sup. Ct., 430 N.W. 2d 447 (1988).

NATURE OF CASE: Appeal from a dismissal of a shareholders' derivative suit alleging breach of fiduciary duty.

FACT SUMMARY: After Herrig (D), a majority shareholder in Cookies Food Products (P), turned the company around by promoting and selling its products through his own distributing company, other Cookies (P) shareholders alleged that he had skimmed off profits through self-dealing transactions.

CONCISE RULE OF LAW: Directors who engage in self-dealing must establish that they acted in good faith, honesty, and fairness.

FACTS: Because Cookies Food Products (P) was in dire straits, its board of directors approached Herrig (D), a shareholder and owner of Lakes Warehouse Distributing (D), about distributing Cookies' (P) product. Under their agreement, Lakes (D) assumed all costs of warehousing, marketing, sales, delivery, promotion, and advertising. Cookies' (P) sales soared. Herrig (D) subsequently gained control of Cookies (P) by buying a majority of its stock. He then replaced four of the five board members. The exclusive distributorship contract was extended, as it had been before Herrig (D) became majority shareholder, and the newly configured board later authorized increased compensation for Herrig (D) and Lakes (D). No dividends were paid to Cookies (P) shareholders, however, due to the terms of Cookies' (P) SBA loan. The minority shareholders (P) filed suit, alleging that Herrig (D) had violated his duty of loyalty to Cookies (P). The district court ruled in Herrig's (D) favor. Cookies (P) appealed.

ISSUE: Must directors who engage in self-dealing establish that they acted in good faith, honesty, and fairness?

HOLDING AND DECISION: (Neuman, J.) Yes. Directors who engage in self-dealing must establish that they acted in good faith, honesty, and fairness. This is in addition to the requirement that any such transactions must be fully disclosed and consented to by the board of directors or the shareholders, or at least be fair and reasonable to the corporation. Self-dealing transactions must have the earmarks of arms-length transactions before a court can find them to be fair or reasonable. But financial success is not the only measure of fairness or reasonableness. Although Cookies (P) profited under Herrig's (D) authority, the court must also look to the fairness of the bargain that he struck with Cookies (P). In this case, given his hard work on Cookies (P) behalf, Herrig's (D) services were neither unfairly priced nor inconsistent with Cookies' (P) corporate interest. Furthermore, Herrig (D) furnished sufficient pertinent information to Cookies' (P) board to enable it to make prudent decisions concerning the contracts. To tinker with such a successful venture and to punish Herrig (D) for this success would be inequitable. Affirmed.

DISSENT: (Schultz, J.) It was Herrig's (D) burden to demonstrate that all of his self-dealing transactions were fair to Cookies (P). While much credit is due to Herrig (D) for the success of the company, this does not mean that these transactions were fair to the company. Cookies (P) has put forth convincing testimony that Herrig (D) has been grossly overcompensated for his services based on their fair market value. Cookies' (P) food broker expert witness testified that his company would have charged $110,865 for all of the services that Herrig (D) performed. Cookies (P) actually paid $730,637 for those services, a difference of $620,000 in one year.

EDITOR'S ANALYSIS: Corporate directors and officers may, under proper circumstances, transact business with the corporation, but it must be done in the strictest good faith and with full disclosure of the facts to, and with the consent of, all concerned. The burden is upon the corporate directors and officers to establish their good faith, honesty, and fairness. Such transactions are scanned by the courts with skepticism and the closest scrutiny, and may be nullified on slight grounds. These principles were embodied by the legislature in Iowa Code § 496A.34, applied by the court._____

[For more information on duty of loyalty, see Casenote Law Outline on Corporations, Chapter 4, § III, The Duty of Loyalty.]

QUICKNOTES

SHAREHOLDER'S DERIVATIVE ACTION - Action asserted by a shareholder in order to enforce a cause of action on behalf of the corporation.

FIDUCIARY DUTY - A legal obligation to act for the benefit of another, including subordinating one's personal interests to that of the other person.

SELF-DEALING - Transaction in which a fiduciary uses property of another, held by virtue of the confidential relationship, for personal gain.

MINORITY SHAREHOLDER - A stockholder in a corporation controlling such a small portion of those shares that are outstanding that its votes have no influence in the management of the corporation.

LEWIS v. VOGELSTEIN
Shareholders (P) v. Directors (D)
699 A.2D 327 (1997)

NATURE OF THE CASE: Shareholders' derivative challenge to a stock option compensation plan.

FACT SUMMARY: The directors of a corporation became the subject of a suit for breach of fiduciary duty by proposing a stock option plan for shareholder ratification which granted them future options without offering a reasonable means of pricing their estimated future value in the voting materials.

CONCISE RULE OF LAW: Directors may breach a fiduciary duty by proposing a stock options plan that does not offer reasonable assurance to the corporation of adequate value exchanged by failing to disclose the present value of future options using a reasonable options-pricing formula.

FACTS: A stock option plan was adopted and ratified by the shareholders (P) of Mattel at their annual meeting. The plan qualified each director (D) for a one-time grant of stock options exercisable over a period of ten years after the grant, in addition to a second type of options grant based on whether a director was re-elected to the board every year. However, the options granted under this second agreement also expired after ten years from the date of the initial grant. At the time of the shareholder ratification, the options had no estimated present value stated in the proxy materials. Lewis (P) and the other shareholders filed a complaint, asserting that the proxy materials were materially incomplete and misleading because they lacked the estimated present value of the stock to which the directors might become entitled under the option plan. In doing so, the shareholders (P) claimed that the company's directors (D) breached their fiduciary duty by failing to disclose the present value of future options based on an available option-pricing formula. In addition, the shareholders (P) claimed that the grants made under the options agreements were excessively large in relation to the value accrued to the corporation, which did not have reasonable assurance that the company would receive adequate value in exchange.

ISSUE: May directors breach a fiduciary duty by proposing a stock options plan that does not offer reasonable assurance to the corporation of adequate value exchanged by failing to disclose the present value of future options using a reasonable options-pricing formula?

HOLDING: (Allen, J.) Yes. Directors may breach a fiduciary duty by proposing a stock options plan that does not offer reasonable assurance to the corporation of adequate value exchanged by failing to disclose the present value of future options using a reasonable options-pricing formula. Although shareholder approval is not required for directors to make a proposal, the applicable law proscribes "fair process." It is thus reasonable to interpret the director's (D) failure to include an estimation of value as a breach of their duty of candor and loyalty, and the absence of this information constituted a material deficiency in the proxy materials. The options need not have a specific dollar valuation, but several reasonable option-pricing techniques are available, such as the Black-Scholes formula. To properly fulfill the applicable standard of care, the directors (D) should have at a minimum considered whether expert estimates of the present value of options, using available methods of calculation, would be reliable and helpful to the shareholders (P) and disclose their availability. The directors' (D) duty of disclosure does not require that the actual value of options be estimated, but only that a summary of the relevant facts and conditions be made, along with a disclosure of the directors' (D) current knowledge bearing on that estimation. However, given the facts of the present case, it is possible that the grant of options made constitutes an exchange of value made in good faith and within the limits of fiduciary duty as calculated by the prevailing methods of estimation. Currently, no facts have been presented to make that conclusion. Instead, the grants appear to be sufficiently unusual in size to require the court to refer to additional evidence when making an adjudication of validity. The motion to dismiss is therefore denied.

EDITOR'S ANALYSIS: Note that the court here only suggested that the one-time grant of options was potentially valid. In the absence of an adequate pricing formula, the second grant of options based on board tenure was ruled unreasonably risky, because such a transfer could be interpreted as having taken place in the absence of consideration, making it a gift. In addition, the duty of loyalty was addressed by examining whether the grant of options was actually fair to the corporation. The court did not believe so. By assuming that shareholder ratification was informed, it ruled that transactions where officers or directors were paid protected that transaction from judicial scrutiny except on the basis of waste, and that the exchange was best evaluated in light of a proportionality review at a later time.

QUICKNOTES:
STOCK OPTIONS - The right to purchase or sell a particular stock at a specified price within a certain time period.

HAWAIIAN INTERNATIONAL FINANCES, INC. v. PABLO
Corporation (P) v. President (D)
Haw. Sup. Ct., 53 Haw. 149, 488 P.2d 1172 (1971).

NATURE OF CASE: Appeal from judgment for defendants in an action to collect commissions on investment properties.

FACT SUMMARY: Hawaiian International Finances, Inc. (P) appealed a trial court decision that provided that Pablo (D), the president of Hawaiian (D), was not liable to Hawaiian (P) for certain commissions he received in the procurement of investment properties for Hawaiian (P).

CONCISE RULE OF LAW: Directors of a corporation are not entitled to recover any compensation or salary for performing their ordinary duties unless a provision for such compensation is authorized by a resolution of the board of directors prior to the rendering of the services.

FACTS: Pablo (D), president of Hawaiian (P), and his wife, Rufina (D), were also directors of Pablo Realty (D). Pablo (D) and three other nonlitigants traveled to California on behalf of Hawaiian (P), where agreements were entered into by Pablo (D) on behalf of Hawaiian (P) for two parcels of land. The sellers were represented by separate California real estate brokers who split their commissions from the sellers with Pablo (D). No formal agreements had been made between either of the brokers for any commission-splitting prior to the execution of the sales. Hawaiian (P) did not learn of the receipt of the commissions until the matter was brought up at a corporate meeting later. Hawaiian (P) then sued Pablo (D) to collect the commissions. The trial court ruled that Pablo (D) committed no wrong in accepting the partial commissions. Hawaiian (P) appealed.

ISSUE: Are directors of a corporation entitled to recover any compensation or salary for performing their ordinary duties if a provision for such compensation is authorized by a resolution of the board of directors prior to the rendering of the services?

HOLDING AND DECISION: (Kobayashi, J.) Yes. Directors of a corporation are not entitled to recover any compensation or salary for performing their ordinary duties unless a provision for such compensation is authorized by a resolution of the board of directors prior to the rendering of the services. Where a director also serves as an officer of the corporation, as Pablo (D) served as the president of Hawaiian (P) in this case, the director-officer cannot recover compensation unless it is expressly provided by statute, bylaw, regulation or contract. In this case, there is no evidence that any of the other directors who went with Pablo (D) to California received any compensation. Nor is there any evidence that the corporation expected to provide any compensation for the services rendered in the transactions in question. Pablo (D) was acting as a director for Hawaiian (P) when he went to California with the rest of the appointed subcommittee. He had no agreement, implied or otherwise, that he was to represent Hawaiian (P) as a compensated real estate broker. Had Hawaiian (P) known that Pablo (D) would be receiving a commission from Hawaiian's (P) purchase, it is reasonable to assume that Hawaiian (P) would have been more anxious to acquire the property at a price less than commission. Therefore, Pablo (D) is liable to Hawaiian (P) for the commissions he received. Reversed and remanded.

EDITOR'S ANALYSIS: Under the Restatement of Restitution, sec. 197, comment c, at 809-810, which speaks directly to the facts of the Pablo case and explains the rationale of the law in this area, where an agent purchasing property for his principal acts properly in making the purchase but subsequently receives a bonus from the seller, he holds the money received upon a constructive trust for his principal. The rule is not based on harm done to the beneficiary in the particular case but rests upon a broad principle of preventing a conflict of opposing interests in the minds of fiduciaries, whose duty it is to act solely for the benefit of the beneficiaries.

[For more information on directors' duty of loyalty, see Casenote Law Outline on Corporations, Chapter 4, § III, The Duty of Loyalty.]

QUICKNOTES
RESTATEMENT OF RESTITUTION, § 197 - Directors engaged in a transaction for the corporation cannot retain an undisclosed profit.

NOTES:

NORTHEAST HARBOR GOLF CLUB, INC. v. HARRIS

Corporation (P) v. President (D)

Me. Sup. Ct., 661 A.2d 1146 (1995).

NATURE OF CASE: Appeal from defense judgment in an action for breach of fiduciary duty.

FACT SUMMARY: Harris (D), president of the Northeast Harbor Golf Club (P), personally bought and developed adjoining property without advising the remaining board members.

CONCISE RULE OF LAW: Corporate officers and directors must disclose all relevant information prior to taking personal advantage of any potentially corporate opportunity.

FACTS: Harris (D) was the president of Northeast Harbor Golf Club (P) from 1971 to 1990. In 1979, a real estate broker informed Harris (D) that property adjoining the golf course was for sale. Harris (D) bought the property in her own name, disclosing this information to the Club's (P) board after the transaction was completed. Subsequently, Harris (D) obtained other adjoining property and eventually sought to develop homes on these properties. The Club's (P) board of directors opposed this development and asked Harris (D) to resign. The Club (P) then filed suit against Harris (D) for breaching her fiduciary duty by taking a corporate opportunity without disclosing it to the board. The trial court ruled for Harris (D), holding that acquiring property was not in the Club's (P) line of business. The Club (P) appealed.

ISSUE: Must corporate officers and directors disclose all relevant information prior to taking personal advantage of any potentially corporate opportunity?

HOLDING AND DECISION: (Roberts, J.) Yes. Corporate officers and directors must disclose all relevant information prior to taking personal advantage of any potentially corporate opportunity. Corporate officers bear a duty of loyalty to their corporation. This duty must be discharged in good faith with a view toward furthering the interests of the corporation. The American Law Institute has offered the most recently developed version of the corporate opportunity doctrine for this loyalty duty. ALI § 5.05 essentially states that a director may take advantage of a corporate opportunity only after meeting a strict requirement of full disclosure. This ALI standard should be adopted by the courts. In the present case, the case must be remanded to develop the factual record with regard to the principles of the ALI standard. Vacated and remanded.

EDITOR'S ANALYSIS: The trial court ruled for Harris (D) based largely on her good faith. The court found that she had made great financial and time contributions to the Club (P). The court also noted the Club's (P) inability to purchase the real estate.

QUICKNOTES

DUTY OF LOYALTY - A director's duty to refrain from self-dealing or to take a position that is adverse to the corporation's best interests.

CONSTRUCTIVE TRUST - A trust that arises by operation of law whereby the court imposes a trust upon property lawfully held by one party for the benefit of another, as a result of some wrongdoing by the party in possession so as to avoid unjust enrichment.

CORPORATE OPPORTUNITY - An opportunity that a fiduciary to a corporation has to take advantage of information acquired by virtue of his or her position for the individual's benefit.

ALI § 505 - Rules regarding directors or senior executives taking advantage of corporate opportunities.

NOTES:

ZAHN v. TRANSAMERICA CORP.
Zahn not identified (P) v. Majority shareholder (D)
162 F.2d 36 (1947).

NATURE OF CASE: Action to recover payments to be made upon liquidation of corporation.

FACT SUMMARY: Transamerica (D), owning a majority of voting stock, and thereby controlling the board of directors, had some of Axton-Fisher's stock redeemed so that Transamerica (D) would benefit from the liquidation.

CONCISE RULE OF LAW: Majority shareholders owe a duty to minority shareholders that is similar to the duty owed by a director, and when a majority stockholder is voting, he violates his duty if he votes for his own personal benefit at the expense of the stockholders.

FACTS: Axton-Fisher's stock was divided into three groups: preferred, class A, and class B. The charter provided that, upon liquidation of the corporation, a set amount was to be paid to the preferred shareholders, with the remainder of the assets to be divided between the class A and class B shareholders. The class A shareholders were to receive twice the amount per share as were the class B shareholders. The charter also provided that the board of directors could redeem the class A stock at its option by paying $60 per share and all unpaid dividends to the shareholders. Over a period of time, Transamerica (D) acquired 80% of the class B stock, and two-thirds of the overall voting stock of Axton-Fisher, and thereby controlled the board of directors. When the value of Axton-Fisher's assets increased greatly, the Transamerica (D) -controlled board redeemed the class A stock, and then sold the assets of the corporation, thereby liquidating it and benefitting Transamerica (D), which owned most of the remaining non-preferred stock.

ISSUE: Can a suit be maintained by minority shareholders against a majority shareholder where the majority shareholder uses his votes for personal benefit at the expense of the minority?

HOLDING AND DECISION: (Biggs, C.J.) Yes. There are two bases for the maintenance of such a suit. First, a dominant shareholder is held to the same duty as is a director, and when he benefits from dealings with the corporation, he has the burden of proving good faith of the transaction, and also fairness to minority interests. Second, when a director votes for the benefit of an outside interest, rather than for the benefit of the shareholders as a whole, there has been a breach of duty. Here, the vote of the board of directors was to benefit Transamerica (D), the majority shareholder, rather than the total shareholders of Axton-Fisher and, by exercising such power, Transamerica (D) breached its duty as a majority shareholder, and is thereby liable to the minority interests.

EDITOR'S ANALYSIS: This case points up the general rule that a majority shareholder owes some fiduciary duty to the minority, even though he is only acting as a shareholder. (At common law no such duty was recognized.)

[For more information on Fiduciary Duty, Controlling Shareholders, see Casenote Law Outline on Corporations, Chapter 4, § VI, Controlling Shareholders.]

QUICKNOTES

CONTROLLING SHAREHOLDER - A person who has power to vote a majority of the outstanding shares of a corporation, or who is able to direct the management of the corporation with a smaller block of stock because the remaining shares are scattered among small, disorganized holdings.

FIDUCIARY DUTY - A legal obligation to act for the benefit of another, including subordinating one's personal interests to that of the other person.

REDEMPTION - The repurchase of a security by the issuing corporation according to the terms specified in the security agreement specifying the procedure for the repurchase.

NOTES:

SINCLAIR OIL CORPORATION v. LEVIEN
Corporation (D) v. Shareholder (P)
Del. Sup. Ct., 280 A.2d 717 (1971).

NATURE OF CASE: Derivative suit for an accounting by parent company.

FACT SUMMARY: A minority stockholder in Sinven, Levien (P), accused Sinclair (D), the parent company, of using Sinven assets to finance its operations.

CONCISE RULE OF LAW: Where a parent company controls all transactions of a subsidiary, receiving a benefit at the expense of the subsidiary's minority stockholders, the intrinsic fairness test will be applied, placing the burden on the parent company to prove the transactions were based on reasonable business objectives.

FACTS: Sinclair (D) was a holding company that marketed, produced, and explored for oil. Sinclair (D) owned 97% of the stock of Sinclair Venezuelan Oil Company (Sinven), a company engaged in petroleum operations in South America. Levien (P) owned about 3,000 of Sinven's 120,000 publicly held shares. Sinclair (D) controlled the directors of Sinven. From 1960 to 1966, Sinclair (D) caused Sinven to pay out excessive dividends of $108,000,000, $38,000,000 above its earnings. In 1961, Sinclair (D) created Sinclair International to coordinate Sinclair's (D) foreign operations, then caused Sinven to contract to sell crude oil to International at specified rates and minimum quantities. When International failed to live up to the contract, Levien (P) and other minority shareholders of Sinven brought this derivative action requiring Sinclair to account for damages sustained by Sinven as a result of the excessive dividends and causing Sinven not to enforce the contract with International. The Court of Chancery found for Levien (P) and Sinclair (D) appealed.

ISSUE: Does the business judgment rule protecting fiduciaries from judicial scrutiny also protect a parent company where it exerts such complete control over its subsidiary that the parent receives a benefit at the subsidiary's expense?

HOLDING AND DECISION: (Wolcott, C.J.) No. Under the business judgment rule a court will not interfere with a board of directors' judgment unless there is a showing of gross and palpable overreaching. But this rule does not apply to a situation where a parent company appears to have benefitted from its control over a subsidiary to the detriment of the subsidiary's minority stockholders. In such a situation, any transactions will be tested by their intrinsic fairness if there is evidence of breach of the parent company's fiduciary duty coupled with self-dealing. For instance, in the present case, the allegation that Sinclair (D) caused excessive dividends to be paid out of Sinven is not enough to create a cause of action against the parent company for intrinsic unfairness. Levien (P) must meet the burden of proving the dividend was not based on a reasonable business objective.

However, the court found that the dividends were not self-dealing since Sinclair (D) had received nothing to the exclusion of Sinven and its minority shareholders. Thus, as to the dividends, the business judgment rule applied. As to the allegations that the dividends had prevented Sinven from expanding, the court held that Levien (P) had proved no loss of business opportunities due to the drain of cash from Sinven, so again the business judgment rule protected Sinclair (P). However, the court held that there was self-dealing by Sinclair (D) in contracting with its dominated subsidiary, International. Sinclair (D) caused International to breach its contract with Sinven to the detriment of Sinven's minority shareholders. But Sinclair (D) received products from Sinven through International and thus benefitted from the transaction. However, Sinclair (D) failed to cause Sinven to enforce the contract. Therefore, Sinclair's (D) inherent duty to its subsidiary, Sinven, coupled with its self-dealing, shifted the burden to it to show its breach of the International-Sinven contract was intrinsically fair. The court found that Sinclair (D) failed to meet the burden.

EDITOR'S ANALYSIS: The business judgment rule is an expression of the court's reluctance to interfere with corporate decision-making. It is a rule of evidence rather than a rule of law, and the standard of intrinsic fairness is an extension of the business judgment rule in this respect. For instance, in the present case, the court applied the business judgment rule and refused to interfere with Sinclair's (D) decisions on the dividends. In short, the burden to prove overreaching in order to knock down the business judgment rule was on Levien (P), and it was not met. But as to the breach of the International-Sinven contract, the burden shifted to Sinclair (D) to prove it was intrinsically fair, a burden it failed to meet. In such cases, the shift of burden of proof from the controlling stockholder-management to the accusing minority pivots on evidence of overreaching and self-dealing by the majority.

[For more information on Fiduciary Duty, Controlling Shareholders, see Casenote Law Outline on Corporations, Chapter 4, § VI, Controlling Shareholders.]

QUICKNOTES

INTRINSIC FAIRNESS TEST - A defense to a claim that a director engaged in an interested director transaction by showing the transaction's fairness to the corporation.

SUBSIDIARY - A company a majority of whose shares are owned by another corporation and which is subject to that corporation's control.

8 DEL. C. § 170 - Authorities dividend payments out of surplus or net profits.

KAHN v. TREMONT CORP.
Shareholder (P) v. Board of Directors (D)
Del. Sup. Ct., 694 A.2d 422 (1997).

NATURE OF CASE: Appeal by a shareholder in a derivative suit from lower court's approval of a parent-subsidiary stock purchase.

FACT SUMMARY: Kahn (P), a stockholder, alleged that Tremont's (D) board of directors participated in a series of improper transactions for the benefit of one controlling member.

CONCISE RULE OF LAW: In a challenged transaction involving self-dealing by a controlling shareholder, the substantive legal standard is that of entire fairness, with the burden of persuasion resting upon the defendants.

FACTS: Kahn (P), a shareholder of Tremont (D), alleged that one member of Tremont's (D) board of directors controlled a subsidiary and another related company, and had structured a stock purchase in a manner that benefitted himself at the expense of the corporation. The court of chancery found that the transaction had to be evaluated under the entire fairness standard of review and not the more deferential business judgment rule. The court found, however, that Tremont's (D) use of a Special Committee of disinterested directors was sufficient to shift the burden on the fairness issue to Kahn (P) and then concluded that the price and the process were both fair to Tremont (D). Kahn (P) appealed, claiming that the lower court erred in its burden of proof allocation regarding the entire fairness of the transaction and that the process and price were tainted and unfair.

ISSUE: In a challenged transaction involving self-dealing by a controlling shareholder, is the substantive legal standard is that of entire fairness, with the burden of persuasion resting upon the defendants?

HOLDING AND DECISION: (Walsh, J.) Yes. In a challenged transaction involving self-dealing by a controlling shareholder, the substantive legal standard is that of entire fairness, with the burden of persuasion resting upon the defendants. While approval of a transaction by an informed vote of a majority of the minority shareholders shifts the burden of proving the unfairness of the transaction entirely to the plaintiffs, the controlling shareholders must do more than establish a perfunctory special committee of outside directors. The court of chancery's determination that the Special Committee of Tremont's (D) outside directors was fully informed, active, and appropriately simulated an arm's length transaction is not supported by the record. The Special Committee did not function independently and in a manner entitling Tremont's (D) board to shift from themselves the burden that encumbers a controlled transaction.

The concept of entire fairness requires the court to examine all aspects of the transaction. On remand, the court of chancery will determine whether Tremont's (D) board demonstrated the entire fairness of the disputed transaction and will grant appropriate relief if necessary. Reversed.

CONCURRENCE: (Quillen, J.) The burden of proof in this case clearly should not shift from Tremont (D) to Kahn (P) on the issue of fairness. The Chancellor's opinion found that a parent-subsidiary transaction existed, the context in which the greatest risk of undetectable bias may be present.

DISSENT: (Berger, J.) The majority's decision to reverse is based on the court of chancery's erroneous evaluation of the facts, not its legal analysis. The trial court was satisfied, after six days of trial, that the Special Committee members were informed, active, and loyal to Tremont (D). That finding is supported by the record and should be accorded deference.

EDITOR'S ANALYSIS: The concept of fairness has two components: fair dealing and fair price. Fair dealing refers to how the transaction was initiated, structured, negotiated, and timed. Fair price relates to the economic and financial considerations of the proposed merger. The test for fairness is not to be bifurcated, however, and all aspects of the issue must be examined as a whole since the question is one of entire fairness.

NOTES:

ZETLIN v. HANSON HOLDINGS, INC.
Minority shareholder (P) v. Corporation (D)
N.Y. Ct. App., 48 N.Y.2d 684, 421 N.Y.S.2d 877, 397 N.E.2d 387 (1979).

NATURE OF CASE: Appeal from denial of recovery by minority shareholders.

FACT SUMMARY: Zetlin (P) contended minority shareholders should share in the premium price paid to Hanson (D) for its controlling shares in the corporation.

CONCISE RULE OF LAW: Minority shareholders are not entitled to share in any premium price paid for the controlling shares of a corporation.

FACTS: Zetlin (P) owned 2% of Gable Industries. Hanson (D) and Sylvestri (D) owned a controlling 44.4% of the corporation, which they sold for $8 over the open market price. Zetlin (P) sued, contending minority shareholders should share in the premium price paid for control. The trial and intermediate appellate courts held for Hanson (D) and Sylvestri (D), and Zetlin (P) appealed.

ISSUE: Are minority shareholders entitled to share in the premium price paid for controlling shares?

HOLDING AND DECISION: No. Minority shareholders are not entitled to share in the premium price paid for controlling shares of stock. The opposite rule would require that a controlling interest be transferred only through a tender offer to all shareholders. Such a radical departure from accepted corporate principles would more properly be brought about legislatively. Affirmed.

EDITOR'S ANALYSIS: It is undisputed that controlling shares of a corporation are more valuable than minority interests. Control affords the holder the power to direct corporate activities and to govern the allocation of corporate assets. The greater the ownership interest, the greater that the input in corporate affairs should be recognized.

[For more information on controlling shareholders and a premium price, see Casenote Law Outline on Corporations, Chapter 4, § VI, Controlling Shareholders.]

QUICKNOTES
TENDER OFFER - An offer made by one corporation to the shareholders of a target corporation to purchase their shares subject to number, time, and price specifications.

CORPORATE OPPORTUNITY - An opportunity that a fiduciary to a corporation has to take advantage of information acquired by virtue of his or her position for the individual's benefit.

CONTROLLING SHAREHOLDER - A person who has power to vote a majority of the outstanding shares of a corporation, or who is able to direct the

management of the corporation with a smaller block of stock because the remaining shares are scattered among small, disorganized holdings.

NOTES:

JONES v. H. F. AHMANSON & CO.
Minority Shareholder (P) v. Majority Shareholder (D)
Cal. Sup. Ct., 1 Cal. 3d 93, 460 P.2d 464 (1969).

NATURE OF CASE: Individual shareholder suit against a majority shareholder for breach of fiduciary duty.

FACT SUMMARY: When Ahmanson & Co. (D), majority shareholders, excluded minority shareholders from participating in United, one minority shareholder, Jones (P), brought suit.

CONCISE RULE OF LAW: (1) Even though a stockholder's derivative action exists in favor of a corporation, an individual stockholder is not precluded from bringing an individual action based on the same injury. (2) Majority shareholders have a fiduciary responsibility to minority shareholders and the corporation to use their power to control the corporation in a fair, just, and equitable manner and not to profit from that control at shareholder expense.

FACTS: H. F. Ahmanson & Co. (D) owned a majority of stock in the United Savings and Loan Association (Association). Jones (P) owned only 25 shares of the Association. Ahmanson & Co. (D) and other majority shareholders formed a holding company called United Financial Corporation (United) and exchanged their Association shares for a "derived block" of 250 United shares for each Association share. As a result, United held 85% of the Association's 6,568 outstanding shares of stock. Jones (P) and other minority stockholders of the Association were given no opportunity to exchange their shares for United stock. In 1960 and 1961, United created a substantial public trading market for its stock through offerings of stock and debentures. The first offering consisted of 60,000 units, each unit comprising two United shares and one $100 5% interest-bearing bond. The Ahmanson (D) faction stood to gain a $927.50 return of capital on each "derived block" of United shares. To secure United's debt on the bonds, Ahmanson (D) and other majority shareholders pledged the assets and earnings of the Association. When the market for Association stock declined, United offered at first to buy Association shares worth $1,400 plus $300 earnings each for $1,100 per share. When this proved somewhat successful, Association management, controlled by United's majority shareholder, Ahmanson (D) and friends, lowered dividends on Association shares, then proposed an exchange of 51 United shares, book value of $210 and annual earnings of $134, for each share of Association stock with book value of more than $1,700 and annual earnings of $651. Ahmanson (D) and friends filed for a permit allowing the exchange, but this was withdrawn when Jones (P) and other minority shareholders objected that the exchange failed to meet the statutory standard of fairness. Jones (P) sued individually and on behalf of other minority stockholders of the Association, seeking damages and other relief. The lower courts entered judgment for Ahmanson (D), but the California Supreme Court reversed.

ISSUE: (1) Where an injury suffered by a group of minority shareholders is also suffered by their corporation, making any suit by them derivative in nature, does this preclude an individual shareholder of that group from bringing a suit for the same injury in an individual capacity? (2) Do majority shareholders have the right to dispose of their stock without regard to the wishes and desires or knowledge of the minority shareholders?

HOLDING AND DECISION: (Traynor, C.J.) (1) No. The Shaw test, holding that where injury to a minority shareholder is no different from that suffered by other minority shareholders and any action must be brought derivatively, is in error. In a stockholder's derivative suit, the corporation is the real plaintiff and the stockholders enjoy no direct benefits from any recovery. However, the stockholder's individual suit enforces a right against the corporation which the stockholder holds individually. Here, Jones (P) does not seek recovery for the corporation for the diminished value of her stock due to Ahmanson & Co. (D) action. The gravamen of her cause of action consists of injury to her, and other minority stockholders of the Association. If the injury is not incidental to any injury suffered by the corporation, there exists an individual cause of action. (2) No. Majority shareholders' control over a corporation must benefit all shareholders proportionately. Any transactions challenged by minority shareholders as unfair to their interests will be subjected by the courts to close scrutiny. Directors and controlling shareholders will suffer the burden of proving that their use of controlling power was in good faith and inherently fair, carrying the earmark of an arm's length bargain. Here, Ahmanson & Co (D) claim they, as controlling shareholders of United and the Association, breached no fiduciary duty to minority shareholders. They assert the majority rule that majority shareholders, unlike directors and officers, owe no duty to the minority shareholders unless the majority had information relative to the value of corporate stock that was not available to the minority. Ahmanson & Co. (D) claim they possessed no such information and thus they are free to dispose of their stock as they see fit, without concern to the wishes of the minority. But California recognizes the minority rule that directors, officers, and controlling shareholders owe a duty to all shareholders individually not to benefit at their expense from their official or controlling position in the corporation. Here, Ahmanson & Co. (D) used their control to exclude the minority shareholders of the Association from participating in the purchase of United stock and also pledged the Association's assets and earnings to meet the debt of United bonds. Such exercise of controls over a corporation is to the detriment of its minority stockholders and the

Continued on next page.

conduct of the controlling stockholders is inconsistent with their duty of good faith and inherent fairness to the minority. The court demanded in equity that Jones (P) and other affected minority shareholders be placed in as favorable a position as the majority placed itself. Jones (P) was also given an election of damages between recovery for the appraised value of her shares on the date Association shares were exchanged for United shares, or the equivalent of the fair market value of a "derived block" of United stock on the date this action was commenced, plus interest.

EDITOR'S ANALYSIS: This case presents a conflict between the traditional right of a shareholder to sell his stock as he pleases and the modern trend toward protection of minority shareholders from the self-serving interests of the majority. The traditional rule allows majority shareholders the "perfect right to dispose of their stock" without consulting minority stockholders. Certainly, there is an argument for such a position in the doctrine of laissez faire. Courts are loath to interfere in corporate affairs unless absolutely necessary. However, the courts eventually recognized the need for government control in corporate transactions to the extent that if "special facts" could be proved by minority shareholders that evidenced an injury to a corporation or shareholders through sale of controlling shares, then the courts would impose a fiduciary duty on controlling shareholders to the minority stockholders. This was a rule of evidence, placing the burden to prove "special facts" on the minority. What the California rule in the present case adds to minority shareholder protection is to shift the burden of proof to the controlling shareholder not only to prove the good faith of a sale transaction, but to also show its inherent fairness.

[For more information on Derivative Suits, Individual Recovery, see Casenote Law Outline on Corporations, Chapter 9, § I, Derivative Suits.]

NOTES:

GERDES v. REYNOLDS

Bankruptcy trustee (P) v. Former director (D)

N.Y. Sup. Ct., Special Term, 28 N.Y.S. 2d 622 (1941).

NATURE OF CASE: Action for breach of fiduciary duty to stockholders.

FACT SUMMARY: Reynolds (D) and others (officers, directors, and majority stockholders of Reynolds Investment Co.) sold out their majority interests and resigned from their corporation without checking the purchasers, who proceeded to waste the corporate assets.

CONCISE RULE OF LAW: Majority shareholders owe no fiduciary duties to other shareholders in sale of their stock; but, since officers and directors always stand in a fiduciary relationship to the corporation, its shareholders, and creditors, they cannot terminate their agency or accept the resignation of others if the immediate consequence would be to leave the interests of the corporation without proper care and protection.

FACTS: Reynolds (D) and Woodward (D) were officers, directors, and majority shareholders of the Reynolds Investment Co. (though they owned voting control their interests were junior to the non-voting debentures and preferred stock). They sold their stock and controlling interest thereby to the firm of Prentice and Bailey without either investigating the buyers or notifying other shareholders. As part of the sale, they also resigned as officers and directors, appointing people designated by Prentice in their stead. No inquiry was made as to any designated individual or of Prentice other than a superficial bank inquiry which noted that the company tended to spread its assets out quite thinly. After the purchase, Prentice proceeded to waste the assets of the corporation which ultimately went bankrupt. Gerdes (P), trustee in bankruptcy, sued Reynolds (D) and Woodward (D) to account for the losses on the grounds that their conduct in the sale here constituted a breach of fiduciary duty.

ISSUE: May directors and officers of a corporation, who hold controlling interest in that corporation, be held to any fiduciary duty to the corporation in sales of that controlling interest?

HOLDING AND DECISION: (Walter, J.) Yes. Majority shareholders owe no fiduciary duties to other shareholders in sale of their stock, but, since corporate officers and directors always stand in a fiduciary relationship to the corporation, its shareholders, and creditors, they cannot terminate their agency or accept the resignation of others if the immediate consequence would be to leave the interests of the corporation without proper care and protection. All stockholders, majority or otherwise, act for themselves in matters of selling stock. No fiduciary duties are owed. Here, however, it is clear that resignation from corporate office was a condition of sale. While such officers undoubtedly

have a right to resign, they are limited in their actions by their fiduciary duties (as officers and directors) to the corporation. It is illegal for officers and directors to resign and elect in their stead persons who intend to loot the corporate treasury. Such is the case here, however. The officers knew that, by resigning, they were placing in the hands of their successors securities which had not been fully paid for. Yet, they made no serious attempt to investigate them. Judgment must be for Gerdes (P). The measure of damage is to be that increment in the sales price of the stock which represents the purchase of control of the corporation. (Sales price actual value, or $2 - 0.75 = $1.25/share.)

EDITOR'S ANALYSIS: This case points up the general rule re majority and/or controlling stockholders' duties toward minority stockholders. Though the general maxim that when majority stockholders act as stockholders they act for themselves holds true, as soon as they act as "controlling" stockholders, courts begin to place equitable limitations on them. Thus, when, as above, their sale of stock involves sale of control, they are liable to the corporation and other (minority) stockholders for the control increment in the sales price. Similar controls are applied when majority stockholders contract with the corporation. Any increment in consideration extracted unfairly from the corporation merely because of the stockholders' controlling interest belongs to the corporation and must be accounted for.

[For more information on Sale of Control, see Casenote Law Outline on Corporations, Chapter 4, § VI, Controlling Shareholders.]

QUICKNOTES

DEBENTURES - Long-term unsecured debt securities issued by a corporation.

COMMON STOCK - A class of stock representing the corporation's ownership, the holders of which are entitled to dividends only after the holders of preferred stock are paid.

FIDUCIARY DUTY - A legal obligation to act for the benefit of another, including subordinating one's personal interests to that of the other person.

NOTES:

PERLMAN v. FELDMAN
Minority stockholder (P) v. Controlling shareholder (D)
218 F.2d 173 (2d Cir. 1955).

NATURE OF CASE: Stockholder derivative action for an accounting.

FACT SUMMARY: Feldman (D), a director and dominant stockholder of Newport Steel, sold the controlling interest, along with the right to control distribution.

CONCISE RULE OF LAW: A corporate director who is also a dominant shareholder stands in a fiduciary relationship to both the corporation and the minority stockholders, and, where such a director-shareholder sells controlling interest in the corporation, he is accountable to the extent that the sales price represents payment for the right to control.

FACTS: Feldman (D) was director and dominant stockholder (he and his family owned controlling interest) of Newport Steel Corp., a small steel-producing company. Though actually too small to compete with other steel suppliers, Newport was able to survive and thrive because of a severe steel shortage which existed at the time of this case and because of the so-called Feldman plan. Under this plan, Newport was able to exact from buyers (who were desperate for steel) interest-free advances which permitted it to expand and finance operations without incurring normal financing costs (allowing it to compete with other steel suppliers). To avoid this and to assure themselves of a higher percentage of Newport's steel, several independent steel users formed the Wilport Company. Though Newport stock had never been worth more than $12 per share, Wilport paid Feldman (D) and his family $20 per share for controlling interest in Newport, which included control over distribution of steel (since Feldman [D], directors, and officers quickly resigned and were replaced by Wilport nominees). Perlman (P), a minority stockholder in Newport, sued Feldman for an accounting for all profits gained from his sale of the controlling interest, charging a breach of fiduciary duty in depriving Newport of future Feldman plan benefits by selling to someone whose purpose in buying was to circumvent the Feldman plan pressures. From judgment for Feldman (D), Perlman (P) appealed.

ISSUE: May a controlling shareholder or corporate director be held accountable for profits from sale of controlling interest?

HOLDING AND DECISION: (Clark, C.J.) Yes. A corporate director, who is also a dominant shareholder, stands, in a fiduciary relationship to both the corporation and the minority stockholders, and, where such a director-shareholder sells controlling interest in the corporation, he is accountable to the extent that the sales price represents payment for the right to control. Directors of a corporation act in a strictly fiduciary capacity. Their office is a trust. They must not in any degree allow their official conduct to be determined by their private interests. This same rule should apply to controlling stockholders as well. In both cases, their actions are subject to strict scrutiny by the courts. The burden is upon them to justify their actions and establish their undivided loyalty to the corporation. Here, Feldman (D) quite obviously acted in self-interest and to the detriment of the corporation and the minority shareholders. His actions in siphoning off, for personal gain, the value of market advantages sold to Wilport, to the detriment of Newport (they lose Feldman plan advantages), violate his trust relationship with Newport. The decision below is reversed and remanded to the trial court for determination of damages, i.e., the exact increment in the sales price attributable to control.

DISSENT: (Swann, C.J.) Justice Swann points out that the majority does not clearly delineate what fiduciary duties are owed as directors and what duties are owed as controlling stockholders. Further, ignoring the loss of Feldman plan benefits, he sees no detriment to the minority here in permitting the sale to Wilport.

EDITOR'S ANALYSIS: This case points up the clear trend of authority which attributes liability to controlling stockholders for sale of corporate control. Note the manner of proof here. The fact that "control" was the object of Wilport is to be inferred from the fact that they obviously bought so as to avoid the Feldman plan. Minority shareholders, of course, feared worse. Even though it had not yet occurred, it is obvious that minority stockholders feared a Gerdes v. Reynolds situation in which control is purchased in order to permit waste of corporate assets. To be sure, Wilport companies have little reason to care about Newport progress, and every reason, in the steel shortage, to take Newport for all it was worth, forcing it to operate at little or no profit. As such, this case may be viewed as a further step in protecting minority stockholder interests from abuse.

[For more information on Sale of Control, see Casenote Law Outline on Corporations, Chapter 4, § VI, Controlling Shareholders.]

QUICKNOTES

MINORITY SHAREHOLDER - A stockholder in a corporation controlling such a small portion of those shares that are outstanding that its votes have no influence in the management of the corporation.

DERIVATIVE SUIT - Action asserted by a shareholder in order to enforce a cause of action on behalf of the corporation.

FIDUCIARY DUTY - A legal obligation to act for the benefit of another, including subordinating one's personal interests to that of the other person.

RESTITUTION - The return or restoration of what the defendant has gained in a transaction to prevent the unjust enrichment of the defendant.

BRECHER v. GREGG

Holder of common stock (P) v. Corporate director (D)

89 Misc.2d 457, 392 N.Y.S.2d 776 (1975)

NATURE OF THE CASE: Shareholders' derivative action based on the sale of shares by a corporate director.

FACT SUMMARY: The president of a broadcasting corporation accepted payment from another media company to resign his position in favor of the media company's own nominee, becoming the target of a derivative suit alleging breach of fiduciary duty based on an illegal sale of office.

CONCISE RULE OF LAW: A director's agreement to transfer only a small percentage of shares, in exchange for a premium and a promise of resignation, constitutes a breach of fiduciary duty as an illegal sale of control.

FACTS: Brecher (P) was a holder of common stock in Lin Broadcasting Corporation (LIN). Gregg (D) was LIN's founder and served as its president and a member of its board of directors. Gregg (D) conducted a transaction with the Saturday Evening Post where the Post bought all of Gregg's (D) shares of LIN's common stock, paying a premium for Gregg's (D) promise to resign as LIN's president and facilitating the election of the Post's own nominee for the vacant board position. Brecher (P) brought a shareholder's derivative suit on behalf of LIN, alleging that Gregg's (D) acceptance of the premium amounted to a sale of corporate office and was thus illegal as a breach of fiduciary duty.

ISSUE: Does a director's agreement to transfer only a small percentage of shares, in exchange for a premium and a promise of resignation, constitute a breach of fiduciary duty as an illegal sale of control?

HOLDING: (Harvey, J.) Yes. A director's agreement to transfer only a small percentage of shares, in exchange for a premium and a promise of resignation, constitutes a breach of fiduciary duty as an illegal sale of control. Brecher (P) contends that the corporation was entitled to receive a portion of the sale price paid by the Post to Gregg (D) as a premium. In addition, Brecher (P) contends that since the remaining directors acquiesced in Gregg's (D) favor and actually voted to elect the Post's nominee, they are jointly and severally liable with Gregg (D) for the premiums resulting from the sale. However, no evidence was introduced to show that these additional director defendants were involved in the negotiations resulting in the premium, nor was any evidence introduced to show they benefited from the sale in question. Regarding Gregg's (D) individual liability, we find that sufficient evidence does exist to show payment of a price exceeding $1.2 million above the price quoted for Gregg's (D) shares, and the inducement for this excess was Gregg's (D) promise to resign his position and deliver effective control to the Post. Gregg (D) is therefore liable and must forfeit the illegal profit from this sale to the corporation.

EDITOR'S ANALYSIS: It is well-accepted that a sale of corporate office or management control accompanied by insufficient stock to carry voting control is still illegal. This is based on the fact that the corporate director still illegally profited from his actions. Thus, the court in this case was quick to find in favor of the plaintiff despite the fact that no sale of corporate control actually took place.

QUICKNOTES

COMMON STOCK - A class of stock representing the corporation's ownership, the holders of which are entitled to dividends only after the holders of preferred stock are paid.

CONTROLLING SHAREHOLDER - A person who has power to vote a majority of the outstanding shares of a corporation, or who is able to direct the management of the corporation with a smaller block of stock because the remaining shares are scattered among small, disorganized holdings.

SHAREHOLDER'S DERIVATIVE ACTION - Action asserted by a shareholder in order to enforce a cause of action on behalf of the corporation.

ESSEX UNIVERSAL CORP. v. YATES
Buyer (P) v. Seller (D)
305 F.2d 572 (2d Cir. 1962).

NATURE OF CASE: Action for breach of contract.

FACT SUMMARY: Yates (D) contracted to sell shares in and control of Republic Pictures Corp. to Essex Universal (P), but then reneged.

CONCISE RULE OF LAW: A seller of corporate control may not, as a general rule, profit by facilitating actions of the purchasers which operate to the detriment of the corporation or remaining shareholders; but where the facts do not indicate the existence of any such detriment, there is no question of the right of a controlling shareholder to derive a premium from the sale of a controlling block of stock.

FACTS: Essex Universal (P) contracted with Yates (D) to purchase his controlling interest in Essex Universal. One provision of the contract provided that Yates (D) was to arrange for a special meeting of the Republic Board of Directors to be called at which Yates' (D) directors were to resign one at a time (seriatum) and Essex (P) directors were to be elected in their place. The purpose of this special meeting clearly was to effect immediate transfer of control. Had Essex (P) been forced to wait until the next annual meeting to elect any directors and until the meeting after that to gain control (directors were elected for three-year terms, one-third elected at each annual meeting), it would have taken 18 months. When Yates (D) refused to close the deal, however, Essex (P) sued for breach of contract, claiming damages of $ 2.7 million. As a defense, Yates (D) set up illegality of the contract, claiming that a contract for the sale of control of a corporation should be deemed invalid as against public policy. From summary judgment for Yates (D), Essex (P) appealed.

ISSUE: Is a contract for sale of corporate stock invalid as against public policy solely because it includes a provision guaranteeing a takeover of control (by replacement of the board of directors)?

HOLDING AND DECISION: (Lumbard, J.) No. A seller of corporate control may not, as a general rule, profit by facilitating actions of the purchasers which operate to the detriment of the corporation or remaining shareholders; but, where the facts do not indicate the existence of any such detriment, there is no question of the right of a controlling shareholder (under New York law) to contract to sell or derive a profit from the sale of controlling stock. It is, of course, illegal to sell corporate office or management control by itself (i.e., separate from sale of stock). Such control of a corporation is held by fiduciaries on behalf of all stockholders. Directors, as such fiduciaries, hold control for all the stockholders, as their representatives. So, while sale of a controlling block of stock is not illegal, sale of the board of directors would be. Here, the summary judgment below does not indicate whether or not a determination of fact was made as to whether the contract involved merely a sale of stock or, in fact, a sale of the board. As such, the

judgment is reversed and remanded for determination of whether the clause accelerating takeover constituted an illegal sale of corporate control. In dicta, Chief Judge Lombard answers the remand question in the negative. It would be unreasonable to prohibit a group who has bought a controlling block of stock from taking control of the corporation. With no evidence of detriment here to the other stockholders, the contract should be upheld.

CONCURRENCE: (Clark, J.) Circuit Judge Clark concurs with the opinion of the court. Summary judgment was clearly improper. On remand, however, he would avoid any restraining instruction to the trial court. In light of the complexity of corporate transfers and the court's limited knowledge of such matters, he would leave the general determination of illegality to the trier of fact, as a question of fact.

CONCURRENCE: (Friendly, J.) Circuit Judge Friendly concurs with remand but would hold the contract here violative of public policy. A seriatum resignation procedure such as this would be valid if the stock involved were over 50% of voting stock, since in that case all stockholders would, as a matter of "practical certainty," know that such transfer would mean transfer of control. But where, as here, only 28% of the stock was to be sold, circumventing the normal stockholder elections does constitute a detriment to the stockholders and corporation which must be violative of public policy. The contract should be held invalid.

EDITOR'S ANALYSIS: This case points up both the general standards for measuring the legality of transfer of control clauses in stock sale contracts and three differing applications of those standards. The proper application (in New York) was determined two years later in Re Caplan, in which the New York court stated, "Where there has been a transfer of a majority of the stock, or even such a percentage as gives working control, a change of directors by resignation and filling of vacancies is proper." As such, the view of Chief Judge Lombard that forcing controlling shareholders to wait for board control is unreasonable was adopted. Note that under SEC Act § 14(f), when a corporation comes within SEC Act jurisdiction, information about the nominees for election (in transfer of control such as here) must be sent to all stockholders at least 10 days prior to the election unless (1) less than a majority of the board, or (2) less than 10% of outstanding stock, was involved.

[For more information on Sale of Control, Premium Thereon, see Casenote Law Outline on Corporations, Chapter 4, § VI, Controlling Shareholders.]

QUICKNOTES

MINORITY SHAREHOLDER - A stockholder in a corporation controlling such a small portion of those shares that are outstanding that its votes have no influence in the management of the corporation.

PROXY - A person authorized to act for another.

10

CHAPTER 10
INSIDER TRADING

QUICK REFERENCE RULES OF LAW

1. **The Common Law Background.** A director of a corporation may not personally seek out a stockholder for the purpose of buying his shares without disclosing material facts within his peculiar knowledge as a director and not within reach of the stockholder; but, the fiduciary obligations of directors are not so onerous as to preclude all dealing in the corporation's stock where there is no evidence of any such fraud. (Goodwin v. Agassiz)

   [For more information on Director Self-Dealing, see Casenote Law Outline on Corporations, Chapter 4, § III, The Duty of Loyalty.]

2. **Securities Exchange Act.** The violation of a legislative enactment makes the actor liable for an invasion of an interest of another if: (a) the intent of the enactment is to protect an interest of the other as an individual; and (b) the interest invaded is one which the enactment is intended to protect. (Kardon v. National Gypsum)

   [For more information on insider trading and Rule 10b-5, see Casenote Law Outline on Corporations, Chapter 7, § I, Rule 10b-5.]

3. **Securities Exchange Act..** (1) Where corporate employees come into possession of material information, they are under no duty to disclose that information if there is a valid business reason for nondisclosure, but they may not benefit from transactions in the corporation's securities by reason of that nondisclosure. (2) A corporation that issues public statements concerning a matter which could affect the corporation's securities in the marketplace must fully and fairly state facts upon which investors can reasonably rely. (Securities and Exchange Commission v. Texas Gulf Sulphur Co.)

   [For more information on insider trading in breach of fiduciary duty, see Casenote Law Outline on Corporations, Chapter 7, § I, Rule 10b-5.]

4. **Securities Exchange Act..** A public statement issued by a corporation is violative of § 10(b) of the Securities and Exchange Act if it is materially misleading. (Basic Inc. v. Levinson)

   [For more information on Misleading Statements, see Casenote Law Outline on Corporations, Chapter 7, § II, Rule 10b5 Prohibits Issuance of Misleading Statements in Securities Trading.]

5. **Securities Exchange Act..** A purchaser of stock who has no duty to a prospective seller because he is neither an insider nor a fiduciary has no obligation to disclose material information he has acquired, and his failure to disclose such information does not, therefore, constitute a violation of § 10(b) of the Securities Exchange Act of 1934. (Chiarella v. U.S.)

   [For more information on the regulation of insider trading, see Casenote Law Outline on Corporations, Chapter 7, Introduction.]

6. **Securities Exchange Act..** Before a tippee will be held liable for openly disclosing nonpublic information received from an insider, the tippee must derivatively assume and breach the insider's fiduciary duty to the shareholders. (Dirks v. Securities and Exchange Commission)

   [For more information on Insider Information, see Casenote Law Outline on Corporations, Chapter 7, § I, Rule 10b-5.]

7. **Securities Exchange Act..** (1) A person who trades in securities for personal profit, using confidential information misappropriated in breach of a fiduciary duty to the source of the information, is guilty of violating Securities Exchange Act § 10(b) and Rule 10b-5. (2) The Securities and Exchange Commission did not exceed its rulemaking authority by adopting Rule 14e-3(a), which proscribes trading on undisclosed information in the tender offer setting, even in the absence of a duty to disclose. (United States v. O'Hagan)

   [For more information on Rules 10b-5 and 14e-3(a), see Casenote Law Outline on Corporations, Chapter7, I, Rule 10b-5.]

8. **Securities Exchange Act..** Before a claim of fraud or breach of fiduciary duty may be maintained under 10(b) or Rule 10b-5, there must first be a showing of manipulation or deception. (Santa Fe Industries, Inc. v. Green)

   [For more information on Elements, 10b-5 Actions, see Casenote Law Outline on Corporations, Chapter 7, § III, Private Civil Actions Under Rule 10b-5.]

9. **Liability for Short-Swing Trading Under 16(b).** The prohibition against short-swing profits by insiders is constitutional. (Gratz v. Claughton)

   [For more information on Short-Swing Trading, see Casenote Law Outline on Corporations, Chapter 7, § IV, Section 16 of the 1934 Act.]

10. **Liability for Short-Swing Trading Under 16(b).** Section 16(b) is not applied in circumstances where the possibility of the abuse sought to be prevented does not exist. (Kern County Land Co. v. Occidental Petroleum Corp.)

   [For more information on Scope, § 16(b) of the 1934 Act, see Casenote Law Outline on Corporations, Chapter 7, § IV, Section 16 of the 1934 Act.]

11. **Liability for Short-Swing Trading Under 16(b).** Any person who acquires special knowledge by virtue of a confidential or fiduciary relationship must account to his principal for any profits derived therefrom, regardless of whether the principal suffered any damage. (Diamond v. Oreamuno)

   [For more information on Fiduciary Duties of Directors, see Casenote Law Outline on Corporations, Chapter 4, § IV, Special Problems Involving the Fiduciary Duties of Directors.]

12. **The Common Law Revisited.** When the directors disseminate information to stockholders when no stockholder action is sought, the fiduciary duties of care, loyalty and good faith apply. (Malone v. Brincat)

GOODWIN v. AGASSIZ

Stock seller (P) v. Director (D)

Mass. Sup. Jud. Ct., 283 Mass. 358, 186 N.E. 659 (1933).

NATURE OF CASE: Action for rescission of sale of stock.

FACT SUMMARY: Agassiz (D) and another, director and president of the corporation, purchased stock of Goodwin (P) in the corporation without disclosing inside information which turned out to be important.

CONCISE RULE OF LAW: A director of a corporation may not personally seek out a stockholder for the purpose of buying his shares without disclosing material facts within his peculiar knowledge as a director and not within reach of the stockholder; but, the fiduciary obligations of directors are not so onerous as to preclude all dealing in the corporation's stock where there is no evidence of any such fraud.

FACTS: Agassiz (D) and another, director and president of the Cliff Mining Co., purchased Goodwin's (P) stock in that corporation through a broker on the Boston Stock Exchange. Prior to the sale, certain corporate property had been explored for mineral deposits, unsuccessfully. The director and president, however, had knowledge of a geological theory by which they expected to discover minerals on that land. They decided not to disclose it publicly, however, so that another mining company, in which they were also stockholders, could acquire options on adjacent land. Goodwin (P) sued to force a rescission of the stock sale on the grounds that the director and president had breached their fiduciary duties by failing to disclose the geological theory, their belief in it, and its subsequent successful testing. From a dismissal of the complaint, Goodwin (P) appealed.

ISSUE: May a director of a corporation deal in the corporation's shares where his action is based upon inside knowledge?

HOLDING AND DECISION: (Rugg, C.J.) Yes. A director of a corporation may not personally seek out a stockholder for the purpose of buying his shares without disclosing material facts within his peculiar knowledge as a director and not within reach of the stockholder, but the fiduciary obligations of directors are not so onerous as to preclude all dealing in the corporation's stock where there is no evidence of any such fraud. Business must be governed by practical rules. An honest director would be in a difficult situation if he could neither buy nor sell stock in his own corporation without seeking out the other actual ultimate party to such transaction. Absent fraud, he must be permitted to deal. Here, there is no evidence of any fraud: (1) Agassiz (D) did not personally solicit Goodwin (P) to sell his stock; (2) Agassiz (D) was an experienced stock dealer who made a voluntary decision to sell; (3) at the time of sale, the undisclosed theory had not yet been proven; and, (4) had the director and president disclosed it

prematurely, they would have exposed themselves to litigation if it proved to be false. The judgment below must be affirmed.

EDITOR'S ANALYSIS: Prior to the SEC Act of 1934, this case pointed up the general standard for "insider" liability: fraud. The use of inside information by corporate officers to gain personal profit could be proscribed only if some showing of fraud could be made. Note that this is consistent with the general common-law caveat emptor approach to the relationship between shareholders and management. At common law, it was held that no fiduciary relationship existed between management and shareholders, so, by caveat emptor, any trading done by either was legal unless provably fraudulent. Note, finally, that even where a common-law duty was found to exist, it was always limited to direct dealings between directors and shareholders. Shareholders selling to or buying from third parties were never protected.

[For more information on Director Self-Dealing, see Casenote Law Outline on Corporations, Chapter 4, § III, The Duty of Loyalty.]

QUICKNOTES

SELF-DEALING - Transaction in which a fiduciary uses property of another, held by virtue of the confidential relationship, for personal gain.

NOTES:

KARDON v. NATIONAL GYPSUM

Parties not Identified.

69 F. Supp. 512 (E.D. Pa. 1946)

NATURE OF CASE: Motion to dismiss in action charging conspiracy, fraudulent misrepresentations and suppression of truth in pursuance of conspiracy and inducement to sell stock shares for less than their true value.

FACT SUMMARY: National Gypsum (D) and the Slavins, accused by Kardon (P) of conduct in violation of § 10(b) of the Securities Exchange Act of 1934, contended that the Act did not provide for private suits by persons injured as a result of a § 10(b) violation, and that Congress did not intend to permit civil liability.

CONCISE RULE OF LAW: The violation of a legislative enactment makes the actor liable for an invasion of an interest of another if: (a) the intent of the enactment is to protect an interest of the other as an individual; and (b) the interest invaded is one which the enactment is intended to protect.

FACTS: Kardon (P) sued National (D) and the Slavins (D), alleging conspiracy, fraudulent misrepresentations, suppression of truth in pursuance of conspiracy and inducement to sell shares of stock for less than their true value in violation of § 10(b) and Rule 10b-5 of the Securities Exchange Act. The Slavins and National (D) moved to dismiss on the grounds that service was invalid, and the complaint failed to state a valid cause of action against them. They argued that § 10(b) of the Act did not provide for civil liability, and thus, Congress had specifically withheld from private parties the right to recover damages arising from a § 10(b) violation.

ISSUE: Does the violation of a legislative enactment make the actor liable for an invasion of an interest of another if: (a) the intent of the enactment is to protect an interest of the other as an individual; and (b) the interest invaded is one which the enactment is intended to protect?

HOLDING AND DECISION: (Kirkpatrick, J.) Yes. The violation of a legislative enactment by doing a prohibited act or by failing to perform a required act makes the actor liable for an invasion of an interest of another if: (a) the intent of the enactment is exclusively or in part to protect an interest of the other as an individual; and (b) the interest invaded is one which the enactment is intended to protect. Although there is no provision in § 10 or elsewhere expressly allowing civil suits by persons injured as a result of violations of § 10 or the Rule, disregard of the command of the statute is a wrongful act and a tort. Here, the question is whether an intention by Congress can be implied to deny a remedy and wipe out a liability which, normally by virtue of basic principles of tort law, accompanies the doing of a prohibited act. Where, as here, the whole statute discloses a broad purpose to regulate securities transactions of all kinds to eliminate all manipulative or deceptive methods in such transactions, the mere omission of an express provision for civil liability is not sufficient to negate what the general law implies. National (D) and the Slavins (D) also argue that under the general rule of law, civil liability for violation of a statute accrues only to a member of a class of "investors" for whose special benefit the statute was enacted. However, the term "investors" is not just limited to persons about to invest in a security or own less than the total issue of stock. Moreover, the complaint can be sustained both under the Act and the common law because it alleges that: (1) a conspiracy between the Slavins (D) to defraud Kardon (P) by making untrue statements of material facts existed; (2) acts by the Slavins (D) in pursuance of conspiracy consisted of falsely representing to Kardon (P) that no negotiations were pending for the sale of corporate assets; (3) an agreement with National (D) during the pendency of the conspiracy and prior to its consummation to sell the assets of the company to National existed (D); and (4) that, during the pendency of the conspiracy and prior to its consummation, the Slavins (D) and National (D) induced Kardon (P) by fraud and deceit to sell his stock. Thus, the Slavins' (D) and National's (D) motions to dismiss are denied.

EDITOR'S ANALYSIS: Section 27 of the Securities Exchange Act allows suits to enforce any liability created by the Act to be brought in any jurisdiction "wherein the defendant is found or is an inhabitant or transacts business" or "wherein any act or transactions constituting the violation occurred." As soon as venue is based on Section 27, process may be served on defendants in districts in which they are inhabitants, or "wherever the defendant may be found" whether inside or out of the state in which the action is brought. Section 27 also allows a plaintiff into federal court even when there is not complete diversity among the parties because, under the Section, the federal courts have exclusive jurisdiction of violations of the Securities Exchange Act and of all suits in equity and actions at law brought to enforce any duty or liability created by the Act.

[For more information on insider trading and Rule 10b-5, see Casenote Law Outline on Corporations, Chapter 7, § I, Rule 10b-5.]

QUICKNOTES

SECURITIES EXCHANGE ACT, § 10(b) - Makes it unlawful for any person to use manipulation or deception in the buying or selling of securities.

SEC v. TEXAS GULF SULPHUR

Government agency (P) v. Corporation (D)

401 F.2d 833 (2d Cir. 1968).

NATURE OF CASE: Suit by SEC against individuals and a corporation for Rule 10b-5 violations.

FACT SUMMARY: Texas Gulf Sulphur (D) made a significantly large discovery of mineral deposits. While concealing the magnitude of the find, certain corporate employees purchased large amounts of TGS (D) stock. A misleading press release was issued to suppress the effect of rumors of the large discovery. Some nonemployees bought TGS (D) stock just prior to public release of the discovery based on their advance knowledge of the release.

CONCISE RULE OF LAW: (1) Where corporate employees come into possession of material information, they are under no duty to disclose that information if there is a valid business reason for nondisclosure, but they may not benefit from transactions in the corporation's securities by reason of that nondisclosure. (2) A corporation that issues public statements concerning a matter which could affect the corporation's securities in the marketplace must fully and fairly state facts upon which investors can reasonably rely.

FACTS: Texas Gulf Sulphur (TGS) (D) was a corporation engaged in, among other things, exploration for and mining of certain minerals. Pursuant to this activity, TGS (D) conducted aerial and ground surface surveys of an area near Timmins, Ontario, Canada. A particular tract, known as Kidd 55, looked very promising as a source of desired minerals. The procedure to determine if commercially feasible quantities and qualities were present involved drilling a hole to a specified depth and examining and analyzing the contents of the core of the hole. TGS (D) did not have ownership or mineral rights to Kidd 55. In order to determine if acquisition was warranted, a test hole was drilled on November 8, 1963, and was designated Kidd 55-1. Present at the drilling site were various employees and consultants of TGS (D). Included in that group were the TGS (D) employees Clayton (D) and Holyk (D). An on-the-spot analysis of the core sample of Kidd 55-1 revealed a rich deposit of copper, zinc, and silver. In order to conceal the find, a second hole was drilled in an adjacent area that showed no signs of minerals. Kidd 55-1, was covered over. On the basis of the content of the Kidd 55-1 TGS (D) commenced acquisition of the entire Kidd tract and surrounding tracts. The president of TGS (D), Stephens (D), instructed all on-site personnel to keep absolute secrecy of the find to facilitate the acquisitions. A laboratory analysis revealed the on-site estimate of quality to be slightly conservative and that the find was of amazing quality. Commencing March 31, 1964, TGS (D) drilled three additional holes, Kidd 55-3, Kidd 55-4, and Kidd 55-5, to determine the depth and lateral extent of the deposits. The results of these three core samples indicated the real possibility of a substantial commercially feasible deposit of copper and zinc. The results of the latter three core samplings were communicated daily to TGS (D) by Stephens (D). The last drilling in this series, Kidd 55-5, was completed April 10, 1964. The amount of activity surrounding the drilling of these core sample holes had resulted in a number of rumors as to the size and quality of the find. On April 11, Stephens (D) read stories in two New York newspapers based, apparently, on these rumors. To counteract the rumors, Stephens (D) determined that a press release should be prepared stating the company's position. Two TGS (D) employees, Fogarty (D) and Carroll (D), prepared the release. The press release was issued on April 12, 1964. The release was attributed to Fogarty (D), describing him as executive vice president of TGS (D). The release denied the validity of the rumors and described them as excessively optimistic. It described various unsuccessful ventures in Canada in general and stated that as to the core drilling near Timmins, Ontario, insufficient data or information was available to evaluate the company's prospects there. The only indication that was available to date was that further drilling was necessary before any conclusions could be reached. The release ended by stating that when sufficient data was available to reach any conclusions a public statement would be issued. The release was stated to be the company's position based on information in its possession through April 12. Drilling of core samples continued through April 15, by which time five additional holes were drilled and the analysis complete by April 16. Based on this additional information, a reporter for a widely read Canadian mining journal was invited to this site to report on the discovery. The report was prepared April 13 and submitted to Mollison (D), Holyk (D), and Darke (D), the three TGS (D) employees interviewed. They made no changes in the report, which stated that a 10-million-ton strike had been made, and the article was published April 16, 1964. A report prepared by the three was also submitted to Ontario government officials for their release on April 15. It was, in fact, not released until April 16, for unknown reasons. At 10:00 A. M., a 10- to 15-minute statement was read to representatives of the American financial press detailing the discovery and announcing its size as 25 million tons. The first release was over a brokerage house wire service at 10:29 A.M. Dow Jones reported it at 10:54 A.M. A review of the market price of TGS (D) stock as quoted on the New York Stock Exchange was made for the period from November 8, 1963, when drilling of Kidd 55-1 was begun, to May 15, 1964. On November 8, the stock sold for about $17.50. When Kidd 55-1 had been completed, the stock was selling for $18. When the results of the chemical tests of the Kidd 55-1 core were completed in December, the shares were quoted at almost $21. On February 21, 1964, the shares were selling at $24. By March 31, 1964, the price had risen to $26. On April 10, it was traded at $30. As a result of the press release of

Continued on next page.

April 12, the stock rose temporarily to $32, but by April 15 had dropped back to just over $29. April 16, 1964, the date of the official announcement of the size of the strike, showed sales at around $37. By May 15, 1964, TGS (D) stock was selling at just over $58 per share. What gave rise to the action by the Securities and Exchange Commission (P) against the individual defendants and Texas Gulf Sulphur (D) was that during the period from November 8, 1963, through April 16, 1964, the named defendants had purchased either shares in TGS (D) or had been granted options by the company to buy shares at 95% of the current market value. In addition, certain earlier named individuals who were not connected with TGS (D) were also named as defendants due to their purchases of shares or calls to buy shares as a result of learning of the strike prior to complete dissemination of the news to the public. One of the directors of TGS (D), Coates (D), made purchases through his son-in-law, a broker, of 2,000 shares at 10:20 A.M., April 16, for certain family trusts for which he was trustee but not beneficiary. As a result of the call from Coates (D), the son-in-law also made substantial other purchases for his customers at the same time. Many of the people buying shares during this period, including several employees, had not previously been buyers of any stock of any corporation or had never engaged in the somewhat speculative practice of buying calls. Of the named defendants, prior to November 12, 1963, they collectively owned 1,135 shares of TGS (D) stock and no calls. By March 31, 1964, they owned 8,235 shares and calls on 12,300 more shares. The aggregate investment of four employees alone was in excess of $100,000. The stock options to five employee-defendants were granted by the TGS (D) board of directors on February 20, 1964. The facts of the discovery had been concealed from the members of the board. The recipients of the options did not notify the New York Stock Exchange as required. The SEC filed charges against all named defendants and the corporation alleging their actions violated § 10(b) and Rule 10b-5 of the Securities Exchange Act of 1934. Specifically, they charged that by simultaneously concealing the information about the size of the find while purchasing shares and calls and accepting options, the defendant-employees violated the provisions; that others acting on inside information purchased shares; and that TGS (D) violated the provisions by the press release of April 12, 1964. Trial was had in United States District Court for the Southern District of New York. The judge, in a lengthy opinion, declared all defendants, save two individuals, were not guilty of violations for any offenses charged. The two defendants found to have committed illegal acts had traded in TSG (D) stock between April 9, 1964, and April 16, 1964. The trial judge determined that prior to April 9, no material information had been concealed and, therefore, any trading prior to that date did not violate the act and that the press release was not misleading in that there were no material facts to misstate at that time.

ISSUE: (1) May individual employees and directors of a corporation be held to have violated § 10(b) and Rule 10b-5 by purchasing securities and accepting options to purchase securities in their corporation while in possession of information that could affect the price of those securities which is not available to the public? May persons they communicate this information to privately, who then purchase those securities, be similarly held liable? (2) Can a corporation be held liable to the investing public for issuing a report that misstates a material fact about an activity of the corporation?

HOLDING AND DECISION: (Waterman, J.) (1) Yes. The court laid a foundation for its decision by examining the purpose and intent of Congress and the Securities Exchange Commission in enacting the Securities Exchange Act of 1934 and the promulgation of Rule 10b-5 pursuant to the Act. The basic thrust of the Act was to promote fairness in securities transactions generally and to prevent specific unfair and inequitable practices in securities transactions. The regulations and controls so imposed were to apply to all transactions, whether face-to-face or in the impersonal markets of the organized exchanges and the over-the-counter market. Rule 10b-5 was designed to insure that all investors trading in the impersonal securities markets should have relatively equal access to material information relating to their transactions. The court found that the essence of Rule 10b-5 was to prevent a person who has direct or indirect access to internal corporate information which is not, nor intended to be, publicly known from making use of that information for his personal benefit by trading in corporate securities. As to the individual defendants, the court examined their individual conduct as it related to the circumstances as they developed over the period involved. Since the major thrust of the trial courts dismissal of most charges was a finding that no material information existed prior to April 9, 1964, this court first dealt with that issue. The court stated that the test for a determination of materiality is whether a reasonable man would consider the information important in forming a decision in relation to transacting in the security involved. Implicit in this definition is the existence of any fact which objectively and reasonably could be expected to influence the price or value of the security involved. Rule 10b-5 does not require a corporate insider to make public any information within his knowledge that would be expected to affect the shares of his corporation. There are many circumstances in which such information may rightfully be withheld. But, if a legitimate decision to withhold is made, the insider may not transact in the securities of the corporation unless and until it is effectively disclosed to the public. An insider is not to be expected to make public disclosure of his predictions or educated guesses derived from his expert analytical abilities or superior financial acumen. What must be disclosed is the factual basis for his analysis results. In determining whether facts are material, there must be a balancing of the indicated probability of the occurrence against the magnitude of the occurrence in relation to the size of the corporate enterprise. Applying this principal to the results of the analysis of the core sample obtained from Kidd 55-1 indicates that this was material information. The results of that core sample analysis were described by various

Continued on next page.

experts as "most impressive" and "beyond your wildest expectation." But perhaps the most significant objective indicator of the material nature of the initial core sample was that four employees who had direct knowledge invested over $100,000 in the stock of TGS (D). Some of these individuals had never invested before. It should be clearly evident that outside investors, had they been in possession of the core analysis information, would have taken that information to be a significant factor in determining their investment course. This is not to say that the information must have been made public, only that the insiders could not trade on that information for their benefit without disclosing it. TGS (D) and the individuals had a valid reason for withholding the information, since they had yet to acquire the Kidd tract or the surrounding tracts which they desired. Yet, they chose to purchase the stock and, in Darke's (D) case, pass along tips to associates who purchased while the information was suppressed. In addition, the corporate employee who directed the land acquisition program while also buying TGS (D) stock must be considered to have had sufficient knowledge that the find was valuable to subject him to liability as well. A different situation is presented by the purchases of Crawford (D) and Coates (D). Crawford's (D) purchases were ordered on April 15 and April 16. Coates' (D) purchases were made on April 16 immediately after the reading of the complete public statement issued by TGS (D). Both contend that their purchases occurred after the public disclosure of the material information. But public disclosure means effective public disclosure, not just technical disclosure. At the time of their purchases, there had not been any wide dissemination of the TGS (D) statement. Both purchases were made before even the Dow Jones wire service had published the contents of the statement. Both defendants assert, however, that they honestly believed the information had been effectively disclosed. A finding of liability under the federal securities laws and, in particular, Rule 10b-5 does not require proof of a specific intent to defraud. While the standard to be applied must contain some measure of scienter, this requirement will be satisfied by a showing of negligent conduct, lack of diligence, or unreasonable conduct. We find that it cannot be said that either Crawford (D) or Coates (D) could have reasonably believed that the material information had been fully and effectively disseminated to the public at the time of their purchases. The third type of conduct that must be examined was the acceptance of the stock options by the corporate officers and directors. There can be no reasonable distinction made between this type of transaction and a transaction involving an actual purchase or sale. When the board of directors granted the options in February 1964, the defendants had withheld from the granting directors the information about the Timmins discovery that has already been determined to have been material. Before accepting the proffered options, the defendants were under a duty to disclose the material information. The fact that they did not disclose subjects the options to a remedy of rescission under Rule 10b-5. Since the trial court determined that no liability attached to the acceptance of the options by two employees who

were not considered top management personnel and the SEC (P) did not see fit to appeal that judgment, we need not render an opinion as to their liability. (2) The court's decision then moved to a determination of the liability, if any, of TGS (D) itself for violation of Rule 10b-5. The determination of liability would be made on the basis of an examination of the statement issued, in the form of a press release, on April 12, 1964. TGS (D) contended that no liability could be found based on four defenses. First, there was no showing that the statement produced any significant market action, and therefore, secondly, there was no showing of an intent to affect the market price for the benefit of TGS (D) or to TGS (D) insiders. Third, that the lack of a showing of intent to benefit TGS (D) or insiders established that the release was not issued in connection with any purchases or sales by TGS (D) or the insiders. Finally, the company contended that even if the statement were found to be issued in connection with the security transactions, there was no showing that it was false, misleading, or deceptive. In determining the proper meaning and application of the term "in connection with the purchase or sale of any security" clause of § 10b and Rule 10b-5, the court made an extensive examination of the legislative history of the statute. Their conclusion was that the thrust of the legislation was to prevent false, misleading, or deceptive devices or information from affecting the securities market. By examining other legislation (e.g., the Securities Act of 1933), the court found that if Congress intended to limit 10b and 10b-5 to transactions made by the parties charged, different, more specific language to that effect would have been employed. The court determined the legislative intent to be the protection of the investing public and that the broad language of § 10b did not limit its application to situations in which the perpetrator had engaged in transactions. To find liability, therefore, the SEC need only establish that the statement was false or misleading and that the issuer knew, or should have known, that the statement was of such a nature. There need not be a finding that the statement was issued with a wrongful purpose, that is, to benefit the corporation or the insiders. To apply that standard could conceivably allow the wrongdoer to gamble a little in the issuance of the statement. If the statement is issued but does not have the desired effect, then no liability would be found. But, if the desired effect does result, then the wrongdoer can hope he is not found out and escape liability. The fact that the April 12 release did not produce any significant market activity is only indicative that its desired purpose may not have been achieved. This interpretation imposes a duty on corporate management to ascertain that any proposed public statement fairly and accurately represents the whole truth in regard to the subject matter of the release. Where statements are made that are calculated to influence the market in a corporate security, if those statements are false or misleading, then Rule 10b-5 has been violated if the officers of the corporation cannot establish that every reasonable effort was made to ascertain the accuracy and completeness of the statement. By application of these standards, the court considered the effect of the April 19 release. It found that the

Continued on next page.

statements in the release were less than candid and complete and certainly did not describe the actual state of the facts, which were apparently known to its authors. If the company felt compelled to make a statement on April 12, then that statement should have consisted of the details of what was actually known to that time, thus allowing the individual investor to form his own conclusions. Since the point was not fully developed by the trial court, this court remanded the case back to the trial court for a determination of whether the statement was, in fact, misleading and whether discretion should be exercised in the favor of the SEC's request for an injunction against future violations.

CONCURRENCE: (Friendly, J.) The junior officers, Holyk (D) and Mollison (D), were entitled to a dismissal, as it is unreasonable to expect a minor officer to reject an option such as was offered here. Stephens (D), Fogarty (D), and Kline (D), as senior officers, had a duty to inform that this was not the right time to grant the option.

EDITOR'S ANALYSIS: The Texas Gulf Sulphur case is one of the most important decisions to date on judicial interpretation of Rule 10b-5. It provided some indication of the all-inclusive nature of the rule. Corporate officers may not take advantage of undisclosed material information to trade in the securities of their corporation. Even if the insiders do not transact, they cannot reveal the information to outsiders who may then trade to their advantage. A person who learns of inside information, even though an outsider, may not trade if he knows or has reason to know the information has not been effectively disseminated to the public. In Texas Gulf alone, the remedies granted included money damages, rescission (of the options), and injunction. While the plaintiff in Texas Gulf was the SEC, previous decisions have found an implied right of private action under 10b-5. The scope of 10b-5 is, therefore, enormous. Both the government and private plaintiffs may hold liable corporate insiders, persons they tip, persons who independently learn of inside information, and the corporation itself. The concept of privity is abandoned and the requirement of scienter greatly limited. And, based on the opinion of a New York State court, violations of 10b-5 can be asserted in a state action. Many authorities have expressed alarm at the potential scope of Rule 10b-5. They fear that the evils of the marketplace sought to be corrected may be replaced by another equally damaging evil — that is, that conduct by individuals and corporations that would not have gotten by the complaint stage in a traditional lawsuit will subject the individuals and corporations to staggering penalties.

[For more information on insider trading in breach of fiduciary duty, see Casenote Law Outline on Corporations, Chapter 7, § I, Rule 10b-5.]

QUICKNOTES

RULE 10b-5 - Unlawful to defend or make untrue statements in connection with purchase or sale of securities.

MATERIALITY - Importance; the degree of relevance or necessity to the particular matter.

INSIDER - Any person within a corporation who has access to information not available to the public.

SECURITIES EXCHANGE ACT, § 10(b) - Makes it unlawful for any person to use manipulation or deception in the buying or selling of securities.

NOTES:

BASIC, INC. v. LEVINSON

Corporation (D) v. Shareholder class representative (P)

485 U.S. 224, 108 S.Ct. 978 (1988).

NATURE OF CASE: Action brought under § 10(b) of the Securities and Exchange Act.

FACT SUMMARY: Levinson (P), representing a class of shareholders, brought an action against Basic, Inc. (D) and its directors, asserting that Basic (D) issued three false or misleading public statements and thereby was in violation of § 10(b) of the Securities and Exchange Act.

CONCISE RULE OF LAW: A public statement issued by a corporation is violative of § 10(b) of the Securities and Exchange Act if it is materially misleading.

FACTS: Prior to December 20, 1978, Basic, Inc. (D) was a publicly traded company primarily engaged in the business of manufacturing chemical refractors for the steel industry. Beginning in 1976, Combustion Engineering, Inc., a company producing aluminum refractors, sought a merger with Basic (D). During 1977 and 1978, Basic (D) made three public statements denying it was engaged in merger negotiations. On December 18, 1978, Basic (D) asked the New York Stock Exchange to suspend trading in its shares and issued a release stating that it had been "approached" by another company concerning a merger. On December 20, 1978, Basic (D) publicly announced its approval of Combustion's tender offer for all outstanding shares of Basic (D). Levinson (P), a shareholder of Basic (D), then brought a class action against Basic (D) asserting that Basic (D) and its directors had issued three false or misleading public statements and thereby were in violation of § 10(b) of the Securities and Exchange Act. Levinson (P) contended that the class was injured because class members sold Basic (D) shares at artificially depressed prices in a market affected by Basic's (D) misleading statements and in reliance thereon. The district court granted summary judgment for Basic (D), holding that as a matter of law, any misstatements made by Basic (D) were immaterial. The court of appeals reversed, holding that Basic's (D) statements were misleading. Basic (D) appealed.

ISSUE: Is a public statement issued by a corporation violative of § 10(b) of the Securities and Exchange Act if it is materially misleading?

HOLDING AND DECISION: (Blackmun, J.) Yes. A public statement issued by a corporation is violative of § 10(b) of the Securities and Exchange Act if it is materially misleading. Whether merger discussions in any particular case are material will depend on the facts. To assess the magnitude of the transaction to the issuer of the securities allegedly manipulated, a fact-finder will need to consider such facts as the size of the two corporate entities and of the potential premiums over market value. No particular event or factor short of closing the transaction need be either necessary or sufficient by itself to render merger discussions material. Materiality depends on the significance the reasonable investor would place on the misrepresented information. Here, in the merger context, materiality depended upon the probability that the transaction would be consummated and its significance to the issuer of securities, Basic, Inc. (D). The court of appeals adopted the argument, with respect to materiality, that once Basic (D) made a statement denying the existence of merger discussions, even discussions that might not have been material in absence of the denial were material because they made the statement untrue. This Court rejects the proposition that information becomes material by virtue of a public statement denying it, and, thus, remands the matter to that court to decide the issue of materiality consistent with this opinion. Remanded.

DISSENT: (White, J.) A congressional policy that the majority's opinion ignores is the strong preference the securities laws display for widespread public disclosure and distribution to investors of material information concerning securities. This congressionally adopted policy is expressed in the numerous and varied disclosure requirements found in the federal securities law scheme. This Court should limit its role in interpreting § 10(b) and Rule 10b-5 to one of giving effect to such policy decisions by Congress.

EDITOR'S ANALYSIS: The determination of an appropriate remedy is a private action under § 10(b) and Rule 10b-5 is a difficult problem whose solution depends on a number of variables. These include whether the corporation is closely or publicly held, whether the plaintiff is a buyer or a seller, and whether the wrong is a misrepresentation or a wrongful disclosure. Oftentimes, as in many Rule 10b-5 problems, rules governing analogous torts provide a good framework of analysis, especially since Rule 10b-5 cases often rely upon tort concepts in the area of remedies.

[For more information on Misleading Statements, see Casenote Law Outline on Corporations, Chapter 7, § II, Rule 10b5 Prohibits Issuance of Misleading Statements in Securities Trading.]

QUICKNOTES

MATERIALITY - Importance; the degree of relevance or necessity to the particular matter.

RULE 10b-5 - Unlawful to defend or make untrue statements in connection with purchase or sale of securities.

SECURITIES EXCHANGE ACT, § 10(b) - Makes it unlawful for any person to use manipulation or deception in the buying or selling of securities.

CHIARELLA v. UNITED STATES
Printer (D) v. Government (P)
445 U.S. 222 (1980).

NATURE OF CASE: Appeal from conviction for violating federal securities law.

FACT SUMMARY: While employed as a printer, Chiarella (P) saw information that one corporation was planning to attempt to secure control of another, and he used this information by going out and trading stock.

CONCISE RULE OF LAW: A purchaser of stock who has no duty to a prospective seller because he is neither an insider nor a fiduciary has no obligation to disclose material information he has acquired, and his failure to disclose such information does not, therefore, constitute a violation of § 10(b) of the Securities Exchange Act of 1934.

FACTS: In the course of his job as a printer at Pandick Press, Chiarella (P) was exposed to documents of one corporation revealing its plan to attempt to secure control of a second corporation. Although the identities of the corporations were concealed by blank spaces or false names until the true names were sent over on the night of the final printing, Chiarella (P) had deduced the names of the target companies beforehand from other information contained in the documents. Without revealing any of this information to the prospective sellers, he went about purchasing shares in the target corporations. He sold them after the takeover attempts were made public, thus realizing a gain of more than $30,000 in the course of 14 months. The SEC began an investigation, which culminated in Chiarella's (P) entering into a consent decree agreeing to return his profits to the sellers of the shares. He was, that same day, fired by Pandick Press. Eight months later, he was indicted on 17 counts of violating § 10(b) of the Securities Exchange Act of 1934 and SEC Rule 19b-5. Chiarella (P) argued that his silence about the information he had obtained did not constitute a violation of § 10(b) because he was under no duty to disclose the information to the prospective sellers, inasmuch as he was neither an insider nor a fiduciary. The district court charged the jury that Chiarella (P) should be convicted if it found he had willfully failed to inform sellers of target companies securities that he knew of a forthcoming takeover bid that would make their shares more valuable. In affirming the resulting conviction, the court of appeals held that "(a)nyone — corporate insider or not — who regularly receives material non-public information may not use that information to trade in securities without incurring an affirmative duty to disclose." The Supreme Court granted certiorari.

ISSUE: If a stockholder owed no duty of disclosure to the party from whom he purchased securities, does his failure to disclose to the seller material information he has acquired constitute a violation of § 10(b) of the Securities Exchange Act of 1934?

HOLDING AND DECISION: (Powell, J.) No. If one who purchases stock is neither an insider nor a fiduciary, and thus owes no duty to the prospective seller, his failure to disclose inside material information he has acquired does not constitute a fraud in violation of § 10(b) of the Securities Exchange Act of 1934. Administrative and judicial interpretations have established that silence in connection with the purchase or sale of securities may operate as a fraud actionable under § 10(b) despite the absence of statutory language or legislative history specifically addressing the legality of nondisclosures. However, such liability is premised upon a duty to disclose arising from a relationship of trust and confidence between parties to a transaction. In this case, the charges of the lower courts did not reflect his duty requirement adequately. Furthermore, both courts failed to identify a relationship between Chiarella (P) and the sellers that could give rise to a duty and thus provide a basis for his conviction under § 10(b) for failure to disclose the information he had. It may well be that he breached a duty to the acquiring corporation when he acted upon information he obtained by virtue of his position as an employee of the printer employed by the corporation. Whether this breach of duty would support a conviction under § 10(b) for fraud need not be decided, for this theory was not presented to the jury. Reversed.

DISSENT: (Burger, C.J.) I would read § 10(b) and Rule 10b-5 to mean that a person who has misappropriated nonpublic information has an absolute duty to disclose that information or to refrain from trading. The broad language of the statute and Congress' intent to use it as an elastic "catchall" provision to protect the uninitiated investor from misbehavior evidences the propriety of such an interpretation.

EDITOR'S ANALYSIS: The SEC has not made a practice of challenging trading by noninsiders on the basis of undisclosed market information. In fact, it has generally pointed to some fiduciary duty or special relationship between the purchase or seller and the outsider trader as a basis for such challenges. For example, in SEC v. Campbell, the writer of a financial column engaged in "scalping," i.e., purchasing stocks shortly before recommending them in his column and then selling them when the price rose after the recommendation was published. The SEC went to great lengths to equate his relationship with his readers to that of an adviser's relationship with his clients.

[For more information on the regulation of insider trading, see Casenote Law Outline on Corporations, Chapter 7, Introduction.]

QUICKNOTES

SECURITIES EXCHANGE ACT, § 10(b) - Makes it unlawful for any person to use manipulation or deception in the buying or selling of securities.

RULE 10b-5 - Unlawful to defend or make untrue statements in connection with purchase or sale of securities.

DIRKS v. SECURITIES AND EXCHANGE COMMISSION

Tippee (D) v. Government agency (P)

Sup. Ct. Of the U.S.; 103 S. Ct. 3255 (1983).

NATURE OF CASE: SEC action for violation of § 10(b).

FACT SUMMARY: Dirks (D), who, based on some nonpublic information he received and a subsequent investigation, aided the SEC (P) in convicting EFA for corporate fraud, and was then sued by the SEC (P) for violating § 10(b) because he openly disclosed tho nonpublic information to investors.

CONCISE RULE OF LAW: Before a tippee will be held liable for openly disclosing nonpublic information received from an insider, the tippee must derivatively assume and breach the insider's fiduciary duty to the shareholders.

FACTS: Dirks (D), the tippee and officer of a brokerage firm, was told by Secrist, the insider, that Equity Funding of America (EFA) was engaging in corporate fraud. Dirks (D) then investigated EFA to verity Secrist's information. Neither Dirk (D) nor his firm owned or traded EFA stock. However, during Dirks' (D) investigation he openly revealed the information to investors and caused many of them to sell their EFA stock. Consequently the price of EFA stock dropped from $26 to $15. However, largely due to Dirks' (D) investigation, the SEC (P) was able to convict the officers of EFA for corporate fraud. Still, the SEC (P) sued and reprimanded Dirks (D) for his disclosure of the nonpublic information to the investors. The court of appeals affirmed. Dirks (D) then applied for and was granted certiorari by the U.S. Supreme Court.

ISSUE: Will a tippee automatically be liable for openly disclosing nonpublic information received from an insider?

HOLDING AND DECISION: (Powell, J.) No. Before a tippee will be held liable for openly disclosing nonpublic information received from an insider, the tippee must derivatively assume and breach the insider's fiduciary duty to the shareholders of not trading on nonpublic information. The tippee will be deemed to have derivatively assumed and breached such a duty only when he knows or should know that the insider will benefit in some fashion for disclosing the information to the tippee. Mere receipt for nonpublic information by a tippee from an insider does not automatically carry with it the fiduciary duty of an insider. In this case, Secrist, the insider, did not receive a benefit for his disclosure. He disclosed the information to Dirks (D), the tippee, solely to help expose the fraud being perpetrated by the officers of EFA. Therefore, since Secrist, the insider, did not receive a benefit for his disclosure of nonpublic information to Dirks (D), the tippee, Secrist did not breach his fiduciary duty to the shareholders. Consequently since Secrist, the insider, did not breach his duty to the shareholders, there was no derivative breach by Dirks (D) when he passed on the nonpublic information to investors. Reversed.

DISSENT: (Blackmun, J.) It is not necessary that an insider receive a benefit from his disclosure of nonpublic information before a court can hold that he breached his duty to the shareholders. All that is necessary is that the shareholders suffer an injury. Here Secrist's disclosure to Dirks (D) resulted in Dirks' (D) clients trading on the information which in turn resulted in a market loss of $11 per share for the shareholders. Consequently, Secrist the insider, breached his duty and therefore Dirks (D), as tippee, derivatively breached. Thus, Dirks (D) violated § 10(b).

EDITOR'S ANALYSIS: This case is consistent with the Court's decision in Chiarella v. U.S. where the Court found that there is no general duty to disclose before trading on material nonpublic information and held that a duty to disclose under § 10(b) does not arise from mere possession of nonpublic market information. Rather, such a duty, the Court found, arises from the existence of a fiduciary relationship.

[For more information on Insider Information, see Casenote Law Outline on Corporations, Chapter 7, § I, Rule 10b-5.]

QUICKNOTES

INSIDER - Any person within a corporation who has access to information not available to the public.

FIDUCIARY DUTY - A legal obligation to act for the benefit of another, including subordinating one's personal interests to that of the other person.

TIPPEE - A person who obtains material nonpublic information from another standing in a fiduciary relationship to the corporation that is the subject of such information.

RULE 10b-5 - Unlawful to defend or make untrue statements in connection with purchase or sale of securities.

NOTES:

UNITED STATES v. O'HAGAN

Corporation (D) v. Shareholder (P)

521 U.S. 642 138 L.Ed.2d 724 (1997).

NATURE OF CASE: Appeal of the reversal of convictions for violations of § 10(b) and § 14(e) of the Securities Exchange Act.

FACT SUMMARY: O'Hagan (D) began purchasing call options on Pillsbury stock when his law firm was retained to handle a potential tender offer by Grand Met for Pillsbury stock. When the tender offer was announced, O'Hagan (D) sold his options, profiting by more than $4.3 million.

CONCISE RULE OF LAW: (1) A person who trades in securities for personal profit, using confidential information misappropriated in breach of a fiduciary duty to the source of the information, is guilty of violating Securities Exchange Act § 10(b) and Rule 10b-5. (2) The Securities and Exchange Commission did not exceed its rulemaking authority by adopting Rule 14e-3(a), which proscribes trading on undisclosed information in the tender offer setting, even in the absence of a duty to disclose.

FACTS: O'Hagan (D) was a partner in the law firm of Dorsey & Witney. Grand Met retained the law firm to represent Grand Met regarding a potential tender offer for the common stock of Pillsbury Company. O'Hagan (D) did no work on the representation in the firm. He did, however, buy 2,500 Pillsbury options. When Grand Met announced its tender offer, O'Hagan (D) sold his call options, making a profit of more than $4.3 million. The SEC (P) investigated O'Hagan's (D) transactions, eventually issuing a fifty-seven-count indictment, including violations of § 10(b), § 14(e), Rule 10b-5, and Rule 14e-3(a). O'Hagan (D) was convicted on all fifty-seven counts and received a forty-one-month term of imprisonment. He appealed, and all the convictions were reversed when the court reasoned that a "misappropriation theory" was not a proper basis for securities fraud and that Rule 14e-3(a) exceeded SEC (P) rulemaking authority. The SEC (P) appealed.

ISSUE: (1) Is a person who trades in securities for personal profit, using confidential information misappropriated in breach of a fiduciary duty to the source of the information, guilty of violating Securities Exchange Act § 10(b) and Rule 10b-5? (2) Did the Securities and Exchange Commission exceed its rulemaking authority by adopting Rule 14e-3(a), which proscribes trading on undisclosed information in the tender offer setting, even in the absence of a duty to disclose?

HOLDING AND DECISION: (Ginsburg, J.) (1) Yes. A person who trades in securities for personal profit, using confidential information misappropriated in breach of a fiduciary duty to the source of the information, is guilty of violating Securities Exchange Act § 10(b) and Rule 10b-5. A fiduciary's undisclosed, self-serving use of a principal's information to purchase or sell securities, in breach of a duty of loyalty and confidentiality, defrauds the principal of the exclusive use of that information. In this case, O'Hagan (D) owed a duty of loyalty and confidentiality to his law firm and the firm's client. O'Hagan (D) took information that was the exclusive property of the client and used it to make securities trades. His actions fall squarely within behaviors that the Exchange Act sought to eliminate to "insure the maintenance of fair and honest markets." While prior cases have held that there is no general duty to disclose between members of the marketplace, when a special relationship exists, misappropriation is a sufficient basis upon which to rest a conviction for violations of § 10(b) and Rule 10b-5. Reversed. (2) No. The Securities and Exchange Commission did not exceed its rulemaking authority by adopting Rule 14e-3(a), which proscribes trading on undisclosed information in the tender offer setting, even in the absence of a duty to disclose. The Williams Act amended the Exchange Act to include a prohibition against "any fraudulent, deceptive, or manipulative acts or practices, in connection with any tender offer." Given the SEC's charge to take measures designed to prevent fraud, the SEC may prohibit acts, not themselves fraudulent under the common law, if the prohibition is "reasonably designed to prevent . . . acts and practices [that] are fraudulent." In that light, the "disclose or abstain from trading" requirement of Rule 14e-3(a) is reasonable in that it seeks to prevent frauds surrounding tender offers. Here, O'Hagan (D) made no disclosure, and his $4.3 million profit indicates the extent of his trading on tender offer information. Reversed.

CONCURRENCE AND DISSENT: (Scalia, J.) Criminal statutes must be interpreted in accord with the principle of lenity. The statutory language that says no "manipulative or deceptive device or contrivance" may be used in connection with the purchase or sale of any security must be construed as requiring the manipulation or deception of a party to a securities transaction. Such was not clearly the case here.

EDITOR'S ANALYSIS: Chiarella v. United States, 445 U.S. 222 (1980), which involved securities trades by a printer privy to corporate takeover plans, left open the questions posed in this case. In Chiarella, the Court held that there was no general duty between all participants in market transactions to forgo action based on material, nonpublic information. The Court suggested that a special relationship was necessary to give rise to a duty to disclose or abstain form trading. However, the Court did not specify whether the only relationship prompting liability was the relationship between a corporation's insiders and shareholders. Another issue left undecided until this case was whether misappropriation of information could be a basis for criminal liability.

[For more information on Rules 10b-5 and 14e-3(a), see Casenote Law Outline on Corporations, Chapter 7, § I, Rule 10b-5.]

SANTA FE INDUSTRIES v. S. WILLIAM GREEN
Corporation (D) v. Shareholder (P)
97 S. Ct. 1292 (1977).

NATURE OF CASE: Action for violation of § 10(b) of the Securities Act of 1934 and Rule 10b-5.

FACT SUMMARY: Santa Fe Industries merged with Kirby Lumber for the sole purpose of eliminating minority shareholders.

CONCISE RULE OF LAW: Before a claim of fraud or breach of fiduciary duty may be maintained under 10(b) or Rule 10b-5, there must first be a showing of manipulation or deception.

FACTS: Santa Fe Industries (D) owned 90% of Kirby Lumber's stock. Under Delaware law, a parent could merge with a subsidiary without prior notice to minority shareholders and could pay them the fair market value of the stock. Solely to eliminate these minority shareholders, Santa Fe (D) merged with Kirby. A complete audit was run of the business and shareholders were sent an offer of $150 a share plus the asset appraisal report and an opinion letter that the shares were worth $125. Green (P) and other shareholders did not appeal the price offered them as provided by state law. Instead, they initiated suit under § 10(b) of the Securities Act of 1934 and Rule 10b-5. Green (P) alleged that the merger had not been made for a business purpose and no prior notice was given shareholders. Green (P) further alleged that the value of the stock as disclosed in the appraisal should have been $722 per share based on the assets of Kirby divided by the number of shares. The court held that the merger was valid under state law which did not require a business purpose or prior notice for such mergers. The court held there was no misrepresentation, manipulation, or deception as to the value of the shares since all relevant information appeared in the appraisal report. The court of appeals reversed, finding a breach of fiduciary duty to the minority shareholders, no business purpose or notice.

ISSUE: Is breach of duty alone, without a showing of deception or manipulation, a ground for a § 10(b) or Rule 10b-5 action?

HOLDING AND DECISION: (White, J.) No. Before any action may be brought under § 10(b) or Rule 10b-5, there must be a showing of manipulation or deception. The Act and Rule speak plainly in these terms. Not every act by a corporation or its officers was intended to be actionable under § 10(b) or Rule 10b-5. Here, there was full disclosure. If the minority shareholders were dissatisfied they could seek a court appraisal under the state statute. Neither notice nor a business purpose is required under state law. If minority shareholders feel aggrieved they must pursue state remedies since no private right of action has ever been granted under § 10(b) or Rule 10b-5 in cases such as this

one. Ample state remedies exist for breach of fiduciary duty actions and for appraisals. Reversed.

CONCURRENCE: (Blackmun and Stevens, JJ.) The entire discussion of standing under § 10(b) and Rule 10b-5 was unnecessary and may be misread. I feel the controlling shareholders did not breach their duty since there was full disclosure and the minority was entitled to their fair share.

EDITOR'S ANALYSIS: In Blue Chip Stamps v. Manor Drug Stores the court also held that mere negligence is not grounds for an action under § 10(b) and Rule 10b-5. In Ernst & Ernst v. Hochfelder, 425 U.S. 185 (1976), the court held that the SEC could not enact rules which conflicted with plain expressions of congressional intent. Hence, Rule 10b-5 could not be more restrictive in nature than could actions under § 10(b) of the Securities Act of 1934.

[For more information on Elements, 10b-5 Actions, see Casenote Law Outline on Corporations, Chapter 7, § III, Private Civil Actions Under Rule 10b-5.]

QUICKNOTES

RULE 10b-5 - Unlawful to defend or make untrue statements in connection with purchase or sale of securities.

SECURITIES EXCHANGE ACT, § 10(b) - Makes it unlawful for any person to use manipulation or deception in the buying or selling of securities.

FIDUCIARY DUTY - A legal obligation to act for the benefit of another, including subordinating one's personal interests to that of the other person.

NOTES:

GRATZ v. CLAUGHTON
Parties not identified
187 F.2d 46 (2d Cir. 1951).

NATURE OF CASE: Action by shareholder under § 16(b) of the Securities Exchange Act.

FACT SUMMARY: Claughton (D) appealed from a judgment under § 16(b) of the Securities and Exchange Act.

CONCISE RULE OF LAW: The prohibition against short-swing profits by insiders is constitutional.

FACTS: Claughton (D) appealed from a judgment under § 16(b) of the Securities and Exchange Act. The two major issues in this case were the constitutionality of § 16(b), i.e., the prohibition of insider stock trading resulting in short-swing profits, and the computations of profits from the sale of the stock.

ISSUE: Is the prohibition of short-swing profits and their method of computation in connection with insiders constitutional?

HOLDING AND DECISION: (Learned Hand, C.J.) Yes. The prohibition of short-swing profits and their method of computation in connection with insiders is constitutional. Section 16(b) declares that "any profit realized ... from any purchase and sale, or any sale and purchase ... within any period of less than six months ... shall inure to and be recoverable by the issuer." Congress is not obliged to limit the means which it chooses so exactly to its ends that correspondence is exact. If only those persons were liable, who could be proved to have a bargaining advantage, the execution of the statute would be so encumbered as to defeat its whole purpose. The method of matching sales and purchases so as to increase them to the greatest possible amount is valid. Affirmed.

EDITOR'S ANALYSIS: Another case held that the "partners of an investment banking partnership are not caught as statutory insiders when one of their number becomes a director of the company whose shares are purchased and sold in a six-month period." Blau v. Lehman, 368 U. S. 403 (1961).

[For more information on Short-Swing Trading, see Casenote Law Outline on Corporations, Chapter 7, § IV, Section 16 of the 1934 Act.]

QUICKNOTES
SECURITIES EXCHANGE ACT, § 16(b) - Provides that corporations may recover profits realized by an owner of more than 10% of shares when that owner buys and sells stock within a 6 month period.

NOTES:

KERN COUNTY LAND COMPANY v. OCCIDENTAL PETROLEUM CORP.

Target corporation (P) v. Takeover corporation (D)

93 S. Ct. 1736 (1983).

NATURE OF CASE: Action to recover "insider profits" under § 16(b) of the Securities Exchange Act of 1934.

FACT SUMMARY: Occidental (D) attempted a tender offer takeover of Kern (P) and in the process acquired over 10% of Kern's (P) stock. In reaction, Kern (P) arranged a defensive merger with Tenneco which forced a conversion of Occidental's (D) Kern (P) stock to Tenneco stock within six months of Occidental (D) becoming a 10% holder of Kern (P) shares.

CONCISE RULE OF LAW: Section 16(b) is not applied in circumstances where the possibility of the abuse sought to be prevented does not exist.

FACTS: Occidental Petroleum Corporation (D) had tried unsuccessfully to arrange a merger with Kern County Land Company (P). Occidental (D) then determined to attempt a takeover of Kern (P) by way of a tender offer for Kern (P) shares at $83.50 per share. The initial offer was to accept 500,000 shares starting May 8, 1967, until June 8, 1967. By May 10, 500,000 shares had been tendered and Occidental (D) enlarged its offer to accept another 500,000 shares. By June 8, the closing date of the offer, Occidental (D) had acquired 887,549 shares of Kern (P). On May 10, Occidental (D) had acquired sufficient shares to become a 10% owner of all outstanding Kern (P) shares. It thereupon registered as an "insider" as required by the SEC Occidental (D) reported all share acquisitions thereafter as required. Meanwhile the Kern (P) board of directors had been resisting the tender offer by letters exhorting shareholders not to tender their shares. It also began merger negotiations with Tenneco to merge Kern (P) into Tenneco. An agreement of this merger was announced by the Kern (P) board on May 19. The terms of the merger were that Kern (P) shareholders would receive one share of Tenneco cumulative, convertible preference stock for each share of Kern (P) stock they owned. Occidental (D) appraised the Tenneco stock at $105 per share. Occidental (D) conceded that its attempted takeover would not succeed and that it might be subject to liability for insider trading under § 16(b). It granted an option for Tenneco to buy back whatever shares Occidental (D) received in the merger at $105 per share. The option was not to be exercised before December 9, 1967, and was granted in return for an option fee of $10 per share to be credited against the purchase price if the option were exercised. The option was granted on June 2, and the option price paid. December 9 was chosen as the earliest possible exercise date, because it was six months and one day after the expiration of the tender offer on June 8. The merger plan with Tenneco was approved by shareholders at a meeting on July 17, 1967.

Occidental (D) did not vote its shares, but expressed no opposition to the plan at that time. Various attempts were made to delay the completion of the merger so as not to subject Occidental (D) to 16(b) liability. None succeeded, and on August 30, 1967, after approval for the merger was obtained from the California Corporations Commissioner, the merger was completed. At that point the right to exchange the Kern County (P) shares for the Tenneco shares was vested and in fact was mandatory. Occidental (D) did not actually make the exchange until December 11, 1967, at which point Tenneco exercised its option and purchased all of Occidental (D) shares with a resulting profit to Occidental (D) of $19,506,419.22. Kern (P) then instituted a suit to recover these profits under § 16(b) of the Securities Exchange Act of 1934. That section provides that any officer, director, or holder of more than 10% of a corporation's securities would be liable for any profits involving a purchase and sale or sale and purchase of the corporation's shares within a six-month period. By its tender offer of May 8, Occidental (D) became a 10% shareholder of Kern (P).

ISSUE: Where a 10% holder of a corporation's stock is forced to make a sale of those shares within six months of their acquisition by reason of a merger over which the 10% holder had no control, is § 16(b) applicable to any resulting profits?

HOLDING AND DECISION: (White, J.) No. The congressional intent in enacting 16(b) was to prevent the use by insiders of information not generally available to the investing public for their own benefit by short-term transactions in their own company's shares. The rule was stated in absolute terms because the class of transactions referred to was so obviously subject to abuse of the use of insider information. There has developed a practice in the Federal Appellate Court to only apply the rule where the circumstances indicated the potential for the abuse, that is, to apply it only where it would accomplish its goals. The first consideration in this case is to determine if a sale occurred within six months of Occidental (D) becoming a 10% shareholder. The finalization of the merger on August 30 irrevocably committed Occidental (D) to make the share exchange and we must view that the exchange took place on that day no matter when the formal ritual took place. The granting of the option would not have been a sale, since it was possible that Tenneco would not exercise the offer. The real question to be determined is whether that sale, occurring within the six-month period since acquisition, would subject Occidental (D) to the provisions of 16(b). In view of the adversary atmosphere that existed between Occidental (D) and Kern (P), it is unrealistic to assume that Occidental (D) had access to any inside information. In fact, Occidental (D) had tried to gain access to Kern's (P) records and had to resort to the courts to do so. It would appear that no possibility existed for access to beneficial inside information. Occidental (D) took no part in the vote approving the merger which caused the sale. Its votes could not have defeated the proposal. It was, in effect, trapped. It is argued that at the time Occidental (D) made the tender offer, it

101

Continued on next page.

could anticipate the defensive merger and that Occidental (D) could only profit by such a merger. Even if this tenuous argument is accepted, the profit would not come from any inside information, since Occidental (D) could not know who the defensive merger partner would be or what price would result. But there are many other possible results of a tender offer, not the least of which is success. The option itself was not reasonably susceptible to speculative abuse, since at the time the $105 call price was agreed upon no market had been established for the shares involved. If the actual price had dropped below $95 at the time of exercise, Tenneco would simply drop the option. If, on the other hand, the price had risen above $105 at that time, Occidental (D) would be selling at a bargain price. The true motivation for the option was an attempt to avoid the liability of § 16(b) since Occidental (D) had no interest in being a non-influential minority shareholder in Tenneco and Tenneco wished to be rid of Occidental (D) as a shareholder. We hold that since there was no real possibility of abuse of insider information, § 16(b) should not be applied in this instance.

DISSENT: (Douglas, J.) Section 16(b) is written in absolute terms with specified exemptions. If Congress intended there be other exemptions for situations such as the present case, it would have written them in. This transaction falls squarely within the prohibitions of that section. The section was written in strict terms so there would have to be no examination of intent or actual use of inside information, since the proof of those elements was so difficult as to be almost impossible. There is ample SEC and Congressional intent enunciated to show that while there was a realization that strict interpretation of the rule would result in application to situations not subject to the abuse protected against, the evil was great enough to justify the occasional application to innocent situations. The majority now sanctions a case-by-case examination of circumstances to determine if the rule should be applied. This is exactly the opposite of the intention and language of the section. I would further disagree with the majority's conclusion that the granting of an option was not a sale within the meaning of § 16(b). The $10 per share option price was substantial enough, particularly in the aggregate of over $8 million to make it imperative that Tenneco exercise the option rather than forfeit that money.

EDITOR'S ANALYSIS: While the decision of the majority was justified in terms of fairness, the language of the statute is absolute. The dissent makes a telling point by arguing that no exceptions were allowed in the statute because of the difficulty in proving the wrongful intent or motive. The case seems particularly troublesome in view of the conceded attempt to evade the application of § 16(b) by Occidental (D). If the animosity between Tenneco and Occidental (D) was so great, why did

Tenneco agree to try to help Occidental (D) bail out of this situation? On the other hand, it seems clear that Occidental (D) initiated the merger attempt with every intention it would be successful. It would seem to be unfair to subject Occidental (D) to liability simply because it attempted a legitimate business transaction and was thereafter caught up in a revolving door over which it had no control. The "sale" of the shares was totally involuntary on Occidental (D)'s part. The statute contemplates a voluntary action in both the buying and selling of the shares. Courts are very reluctant to give absolute force to statutes even if they are written in absolute terms. No legislature can adequately cover all possible permutations of a given fact circumstance and the courts exist to try to apply the statutes to the circumstances intended. It is a harsh rule of law, indeed, that allows for no exceptions, no matter how compelling the circumstances.

[For more information on Scope, § 16(b) of the 1934 Act, see Casenote Law Outline on Corporations, Chapter 7, § IV, Section 16 of the 1934 Act.]

QUICKNOTES

SECURITIES EXCHANGE ACT, § 16(b) - Provides that corporations may recover profits realized by an owner of more than 10% of shares when that owner buys and sells stock within a 6 month period.

TENDER OFFER - An offer made by one corporation to the shareholders of a target corporation to purchase their shares subject to number, time, and price specifications.

NOTES:

DIAMOND v. OREAMUNO
Shareholder (P) v. Director (D)
N.Y. Ct. of App., 24 N.Y.2d 494, 301 N.Y.S.2d 78, 248 N.E.2d 910 (1969).

NATURE OF CASE: Derivative action for an accounting.

FACT SUMMARY: Oreamuno (D) and others, directors of a corporation, sold off shares in their corporation acting on inside information that was not available to ordinary shareholders like Diamond (P).

CONCISE RULE OF LAW: Any person who acquires special knowledge by virtue of a confidential or fiduciary relationship must account to his principal for any profits derived therefrom, regardless of whether the principal suffered any damage.

FACTS: Management Assistance Inc. (MAI) was in the business of financing computer installations through "sale and lease back" arrangements. MAI was supposed to provide maintenance services for the computers as well, but lacked the capacity to handle this service itself and, so, had to contract that work out to IBM. In 1966, IBM sharply increased its prices, causing a dramatic 75% decline in MAI net earnings (in one month), and a decline in the market price of stock from $28 to $11. After notification of the price increase by IBM to the Board of MAI, but prior to any public announcement, Oreamuno (D), chairman of the board, and Gonzalez, President of MAI, sold off their MAI stock at $28 per share. Diamond (P), an ordinary stockholder, not privy to the inside information, filed a derivative action against both for an accounting for the profits they realized from acting on their inside information (i.e., the difference between the amount realized from sale at $28, and the amount which would have been realized at $11). The trial court dismissed the complaint, but an intermediate Appellate Court reinstated it. This appeal followed.

ISSUE: May the officers and directors of a corporation be held accountable for gains realized by them from transactions in the company's stock as a result of their use of material inside information, even though the corporation itself suffers no damage?

HOLDING AND DECISION: (Fuld, C.J.) Yes. Any person (including corporate officers and directors) who acquires special knowledge by virtue of a confidential or fiduciary relationship with another is not free to exploit that knowledge for his own benefit, but must account to his principal for any profits derived therefrom, regardless of whether such principal suffered any damage. The function of an action for an accounting and return of profits such as this is not merely to compensate plaintiffs, but also to prevent and deter wrongful acts by insider defendants. As such, proof of actual damage is hardly necessary since that is what is to be deterred. Furthermore, a corporation's reputation for integrity, not reducible to dollars and cents is, nevertheless, valuable.

Federal law has recognized this position in § 16(b) of the Securities and Exchange Act of 1934, which establishes a conclusive presumption that whenever a director, officer, or 10% shareholder buys and sells securities of his corporation within a six-month period, he is trading on inside information. Here, even though Oreamuno (D) and Gonzalez held their stock longer than six months, there is no reason why relief cannot be had from the state courts. The complaint is proper and the appellate decision below must be affirmed.

EDITOR'S ANALYSIS: This case points up the modern trend of authority for the extent that insiders may be held accountable for profits realized as a result of their use of material inside information. Oreamuno establishes the proposition that any shareholder may institute a derivative action on the part of the corporation, in order to recover such profits, even if there is no evidence of any damage to the corporation from the insider dealing. (Question, however, whether the selling off of large blocks of stock by corporate insiders might not have a depressing effect on the stock's worth, in and of itself.) This is, of course, in sharp contrast with Goodwin, wherein the court held that no action could be maintained against such insiders without affirmative proof of fraud. Note, finally, that the form of action here is a derivative suit. A derivative suit is one in which a shareholder derives his standing to sue from the corporation, which must be a necessary party to the suit, sues to enforce corporate rights, and seeks relief in the form of a judgment against third parties and in favor of the corporation.

[For more information on Fiduciary Duties of Directors, see Casenote Law Outline on Corporations, Chapter 4, § IV, Special Problems Involving the Fiduciary Duties of Directors.]

QUICKNOTES
FIDUCIARY DUTY - A legal obligation to act for the benefit of another, including subordinating one's personal interests to that of the other person.

RULE 10b-5 - Unlawful to defend or make untrue statements in connection with purchase or sale of securities.

SECURITIES EXCHANGE ACT, § 16(b) - Provides that corporations may recover profits realized by an owner of more than 10% of shares when that owner buys and sells stock within a 6 month period.

MALONE v. BRINCAT
Shareholders (P) v. Corporation (D)
Del. Sup. Ct., 722 A.2d 5 (1998).

NATURE OF CASE: Appeal from dismissal with prejudice of a class action suit alleging breach of fiduciary duty.

FACT SUMMARY: Malone (P) and other stockholders alleged that Brincat (D) and the other directors of Mercury Finance Company, a Delaware corporation, had breached their fiduciary duty of disclosure by overstating the company's earnings.

CONCISE RULE OF LAW: When the directors disseminate information to stockholders when no stockholder action is sought, the fiduciary duties of care, loyalty and good faith apply.

FACTS: Malone (P) and other shareholders alleged that Brincat (D) and the other directors had intentionally inflated the company's earnings and has thereby breached their fiduciary duties. The Court of Chancery held that directors have no fiduciary duty of disclosure under Delaware law in the absence of a request for shareholder action, reasoning that the shareholders must seek a remedy under federal securities law. The Court of Chancery dismissed the complaint with prejudice pursuant to rule 12(b)(6) for failure to state a claim upon which relief may be granted. Malone (P) appealed.

ISSUE: When the directors disseminate information to stockholders when no stockholder action is sought, do the fiduciary duties of care, loyalty and good faith apply?

HOLDING AND DECISION: (Holland, J.) Yes. When the directors disseminate information to stockholders when no stockholder action is sought, the fiduciary duties of care, loyalty and good faith apply. Dissemination of false information could violate one or more of those duties. Directors who knowingly disseminate false information that results in corporate injury or damage to an individual stockholder violate their fiduciary duty, and may be held accountable in a manner appropriate to the circumstances. If Malone (P) intends to assert a derivative claim, he should be permitted to replead to assert such a claim. The Court of Chancery properly dismissed the complaint before it against the individual director defendants, in the absence of well-pleaded allegations stating a derivative, class or individual cause of action and remedy. We disagree, however, with the Court of Chancery's holding that such a claim cannot be articulated on these facts. The case should have been dismissed without prejudice. Reversed and remanded.

EDITOR'S ANALYSIS: The court in this case decided that the plaintiffs should be allowed to amend their complaint. Delaware law may provide a basis for equitable relief. This court found that

federal securities law may not be involved since the purchase or sale of securities was not at issue. The court stated that the 1998 Securities Litigation Uniform Standards Act would not apply retroactively to the case at bar.

QUICKNOTES
1998 SECURITIES LITIGATION UNIFORM STANDARDS ACT - requires securities class actions such as these to be brought exclusively in federal court.

CHAPTER 11
SHAREHOLDER SUITS

QUICK REFERENCE RULES OF LAW

1. **The Nature of the Derivative Action.** Where the main thrust of a complaint concerns an injury to the corporation or all of its stock, the action enforces a corporate right and is properly characterized as a derivative action. (Sax v. World Wide Press,Inc.)

    [For more information on requirements for derivative suits, see Casenote Law Outline on Corporations, Chapter 9, § I, Derivative Suits.]

2. **The Nature of the Derivative Action.** In the case of a closely held corporation, the trial court has discretion to decide whether a plaintiff must proceed by direct or derivative action. (Barth v. Barth)

    [For more information on derivative suits and close corporations, see Casenote Law Outline on Corporations, Chapter 9, § I, Derivative Suits.]

3. **Individual Recovery in Derivative Action.** Where a shareholder's derivative suit seeks to vindicate a wrong done to the corporation, any recovery belongs to the injured corporation. (Glenn v. Hoteltron)

    [For more information on recovery of damages in a derivative suit, see Casenote Law Outline on Corporations, Chapter 9, § I, Derivative Suits.]

4. **Individual Recovery in Derivative Action.** Equitable principles preclude use of the corporate fiction to evade the "contemporaneous ownership rule," which provides that the complaining shareholder in a derivative action must have been a shareholder at the time of the wrong of which he complains. (Bangor Punta Operations, Inc. v. Bangor & Aroostook R.R.)

    [For more information on Contemporaneous Ownership, see Casenote Law Outline on Corporations, Chapter 9, § I, Derivative Suits.]

5. **The Contemporaneous-Ownership Rule.** A corporation cannot maintain an action for wrongs that occurred before the new shareholders' acquisition of the shares. (Rifkin v. Steele Platt)

    [For more information on the contemporaneous ownership rule, see Casenote Law Outline on Corporations, Chapter 9, § I, Derivative Suits.]

6. **Demand on the Board and Termination of Derivative actions of the board or a committee.** Demands on boards of directors are futile if a complaint alleges with particularity that: (1) a majority of the directors are interested in the transaction; (2) the directors failed to inform themselves to a degree reasonably necessary about the transaction; or (3) the directors failed to exercise their business judgment in approving the transaction. (Marx v. Akers)

    [For more information on requirements for shareholder derivative suits, see Casenote Law Outline on Corporations, Chapter 9, § I, Derivative Suits.]

7. **Demand on the Board and Termination of Derivative actions of the board or a committee.** Although the substantive aspects of a decision to terminate a stockholders' derivative action against corporate directors made by a committee of disinterested directors appointed by the corporation's board of directors are beyond judicial inquiry under the business judgment doctrine, the court may inquire as to the disinterested independence of the

members of that committee and as to the appropriateness and sufficiency of its investigative procedures. (Auerbach v. Bennett)

[For more information on Special Litigation Committees, see Casenote Law Outline on Corporations, Chapter 9, § I, Derivative Suits.]

8. **Demand on the Board and Termination of Derivative actions of the board or a committee.**   Where the making of a prior demand upon the directors of a corporation to sue is excused and a stockholder initiates a derivative suit on behalf of the corporation, the board of directors or an independent committee appointed by the board can move to dismiss the derivative suit as detrimental to the corporation's best interests and the court should apply a two-step test to the motion: (1) has the corporation proved independence, good faith, and a reasonable investigation?; and (2) does the court feel, applying its own independent business judgment, that the motion should be granted? (Zapata Corp. v. Maldonado)

[For more information on Demand on Directors, see Casenote Law Outline on Corporations, Chapter 9, § I, Derivative Suits.]

9. **Plaintiff's Counsel fees.**   Attorneys for shareholder plaintiffs are entitled to a fair percentage of the benefit inuring to the corporation and its stockholders as a result of their efforts. (Sugarland Industries, Inc. v. Thomas)

[For more information on recovery of counsel fees, see Casenote Law Outline on Corporations, Chapter 9, § I, Derivative Suits.]

10. **Plaintiff's Counsel fees.**   Attorney's fees may not be awarded where the settlement of a derivative action provides no substantial benefit to a corporation or its shareholders (Kaplan v. Rand)

11. **Security for Expenses.**   California state law contains no provision for an award of attorney fees where security is not sought or posted. (Alcott v. M.E.V. Corp.)

[For more information on security for expenses statutes, see Casenote Law Outline on Corporations, Chapter 9, § I, Derivative Suits.]

12. **Indemnification and Insurance.**   Delaware's mandate that a corporation indemnify directors or officers for the successful defense of certain claims includes those cases where a third- party settlement induced dismissal of those claims. (Waltuch v. Conticommodity Services,Inc.)

For more information on mandatory indemnification, see Casenote Law Outline on Corporations, Chapter 9, § II, Mandatory or Permissive Indemnification.]

13. **Settlement of Derivative Actions.**   A derivative action by a stockholder plaintiff suing on behalf of the corporation belongs primarily to the corporation and any recovery, whether by judgment or by settlement, belongs to the corporation. (Clarke v. Greenberg)

SAX v. WORLD WIDE PRESS, INC.

Shareholder (P) v. Corporation (D)

809 F.2d 610 (9th Cir. 1987).

NATURE OF CASE: Appeal from a dismissal of an amended complaint in a private shareholder action seeking damages.

FACT SUMMARY: When World Wide Press, Inc. (D) breached an agreement to sell stock to its employee Sax (P), Sax (P) filed a direct shareholder action alleging a conspiracy, which World Wide (D) claimed must be brought derivatively.

CONCISE RULE OF LAW: Where the main thrust of a complaint concerns an injury to the corporation or all of its stock, the action enforces a corporate right and is properly characterized as a derivative action.

FACTS: World Wide (D) hired Sax (P) as its general manager to create and build a plant in Montana. Their oral employment agreement gave Sax (P) an option to purchase up to 75,000 shares of stock in World Wide (D). After Sax (P) successfully started the business and had acquired about 5% of World Wide's (D) outstanding stock, World Wide (D) refused to sell Sax (P) any more stock. Sax (P) terminated his employment and filed a complaint as an individual shareholder for actual and punitive damages caused by an alleged conspiracy to depreciate the value of his stock. The district court dismissed the counts for damages in Sax's (P) amended complaint, however, on the ground that the claims stated a derivative cause of action, not a private complaint as an individual shareholder. Sax (P) appealed.

ISSUE: Where the main thrust of a complaint concerns an injury to the corporation or all of its stock, does the action enforce a corporate right which is properly characterized as a derivative action?

HOLDING AND DECISION: (Nelson, J.) Yes. Where the main thrust of a complaint concerns an injury to the corporation or all of its stock, the action enforces a corporate right and is properly characterized as a derivative action. The damages sought by Sax (P) for the loss of interest income on his stock investment are incidental to injuries to World Wide (D). Even if World Wide's (D) assets were depleted with the sole purpose of decreasing the value of Sax's (P) stock and destroying his return on his investment, the action would nonetheless be derivative. Sax (P) does not request damages for World Wide's (D) refusal to sell him the promised stock but for the unmarketability of his stock as a result of World Wide's (D) actions. This is an injury suffered by all of World Wide's (D) shareholders, not just Sax (P) alone. Thus, the dismissal is affirmed.

EDITOR'S ANALYSIS: The characterization of an action as derivative or direct is a question of state law. The official comment in the annotations to Mont. Code Ann. § 35-1-514

states that the need for the derivative remedy is best illustrated when those in control of the corporation are the alleged wrongdoers. Once state law characterizes the action as either derivative or direct, the applicable procedural rules are determined by federal law, in this instance Fed. R. Civ. P. 23.1, with which Sax (P) failed to comply.

[For more information on requirements for derivative suits, see Casenote Law Outline on Corporations, Chapter 9, § I, Derivative Suits.]

QUICKNOTES

SHAREHOLDER'S DERIVATIVE ACTION - Action asserted by a shareholder in order to enforce a cause of action on behalf of the corporation.

GRAVAMEN - The material part of a cause of action, setting forth the injury that is sought to be redressed.

NOTES:

BARTH v. BARTH
Minority Shareholder (P) v. Majority Shareholder (D)
Sup. Ct. Of Ind., 659 N.E.2d 559 (1995).

NATURE OF CASE: Appeal in derivative action by minority shareholder of a close corporation after reversal of dismissal of suit.

FACT SUMMARY: Robert Barth (P), minority shareholder Barth Electric Co., brought suit individually against president and majority shareholder Michael Barth (D), alleging that Michael (D) had taken certain actions that substantially reduced the value of Robert's (P) shares of common stock in the corporation.

CONCISE RULE OF LAW: In the case of a closely held corporation, the trial court has discretion to decide whether a plaintiff must proceed by direct or derivative action.

FACTS: Michael Barth (D) was the president and majority shareholder of Barth Electric Co., a close corporation. Minority shareholder Robert Barth (P) brought suit against Michael Barth (D) alleging that Michael (D) had: (1) paid excessive salaries to himself and to members of his immediate family; (2) used corporate employees to perform services on his and his son's homes without compensating the corporation; (3) dramatically lowered dividend payments; and (4) apportioned corporate funds for personal investments. Michael Barth (D) moved to dismiss the complaint arguing that a derivative action was required, and the trial court granted the motion. The court of appeals reversed, holding that requiring a derivative action would put form over substance and that the rationales for requiring a derivative action do not apply to close corporations. Michael Barth (D) appealed, seeking transfer.

ISSUE: In the case of a closely held corporation, does the trial court have the discretion to decide whether a plaintiff must proceed by direct or derivative action?

HOLDING AND DECISION: (Sullivan, J.) Yes. In the case of a closely held corporation, the trial court has discretion to decide whether a plaintiff must proceed by direct or derivative action. Although generally the shareholders of a corporation may not maintain actions at law in their own names to redress injury to the corporation, there are two important reasons that this rule should not apply in the case of close corporations. First, shareholders in a close corporation stand in a fiduciary relationship to each other, and as such, must deal fairly, honestly, and openly with the corporation and their fellow shareholders. Second, shareholder litigation in the closely-held corporation context will often not implicate the policies that mandate requiring derivative litigation when more widely-held corporations are involved. In determining whether to allow a direct action, the court must make certain that to do so will not unfairly expose the corporation or defendants to a multiplicity of actions, materially prejudice the interests of creditors of the corporation, or interfere with a fair distribution of the recovery among all interested persons. The opinion of the court of appeals is vacated, and transfer is granted for reconsideration in light of the rule adopted in the opinion. Remanded.

EDITOR'S ANALYSIS: This decision will likely have a significant impact on the way litigation evolves in the area of close corporations. Many minority shareholders in close corporations will undoubtedly be more inclined to bring a suit directly against another shareholder than they would have been if they had to file a derivative action. While some may view this as a great victory, it can also be viewed as a step backwards in an increasingly litigious society.

[For more information on derivative suits and close corporations, see Casenote Law Outline on Corporations, Chapter 9, § I, Derivative Suits.]

QUICKNOTES

CLOSE CORPORATION: A corporation whose shares (or at least voting shares) are held by a closely knit group of shareholders or a single person.

COMMON STOCK: A class of stock representing the corporation's ownership, the holders of which are entitled to dividends only after the holders of preferred stock are paid

DERIVATIVE SUIT Action asserted by a shareholder in order to enforce a cause of action on behalf of the corporation.

NOTES:

GLENN v. HOTELTRON SYSTEMS, INC.
Derivative suit bringer (P) v. Company (D)
N.Y. Ct. of App., 547 N.Y.S.2d 816, 547 N.E.2d 71 (1989).

NATURE OF CASE: Appeal from a judgment awarding damages to a closely held corporation in a shareholder derivative action.

FACT SUMMARY: After filing a successful derivative suit against Schachter (D), his co-owner of Ketek Electric Corporation, Kulik (P) argued that the damages should be awarded to him and not to Ketek.

CONCISE RULE OF LAW: Where a shareholder's derivative suit seeks to vindicate a wrong done to the corporation, any recovery belongs to the injured corporation.

FACTS: Schachter (D) and Kulik (P) founded Ketek Electric Corporation with each owning half of the corporation's shares and serving as the corporation's only officers. Schachter (D) was also the sole owner of Hoteltron Systems, Inc. (D). Kulik (P) filed a derivative action against Schacter (D) alleging that Schacter (D) diverted Ketek assets and opportunities to Hoteltron (D). On a prior appeal, the appellate division found Schachter (D) liable for diverting Ketek assets and opportunities. Following a trial on damages, the supreme court found that Hoteltron (D) had earned profits of $362,242 as a result of Schachter's (D) actions. On Schachter's (D) appeal, the appellate division concluded that Hoteltron's (D) profits should be awarded to the injured corporation, Ketek, rather than the innocent shareholder, Kulik (P). Kulik (P) appealed.

ISSUE: Where a shareholder's derivative suit seeks to vindicate a wrong done to the corporation, does any recovery belongs to the injured corporation?

HOLDING AND DECISION: (Wachtler, C.J.) Yes. Where a shareholder's derivative suit seeks to vindicate a wrong done to the corporation, any recovery belongs to the injured corporation. Kulik (P) argues that this result is inequitable because Schachter (D), as a shareholder of Ketek, will ultimately share in the proceeds of the damage award. But that prospect exists in any successful derivative action in which the wrongdoer is a shareholder of the injured corporation. An exception based on that fact alone would effectively nullify the general rule. It is true that this anomaly is magnified in cases involving closely held corporations, but this consideration does not require a different damage rule for close corporations. Affirmed.

EDITOR'S ANALYSIS: This court emphasized that, while awarding damages directly to an innocent shareholder may seem equitable, other interests should not be overlooked. The fruits of a diverted corporate opportunity are properly a corporate asset. Awarding that asset directly to the innocent shareholder could impair the rights of creditors whose claims may be superior to that of the innocent shareholder. However, the court did not rule out the possibility that an award to innocent shareholders rather than to the corporation would be appropriate in some circumstances. One way to adjust the equities would be to allow a pro rata recovery, as illustrated in Perlman v. Feldmann, 219 F.2d 173 (2d Cir. 1955).

[For more information on recovery of damages in a derivative suit, see Casenote Law Outline on Corporations, Chapter 9, § I, Derivative Suits.]

QUICKNOTES
DERIVATIVE SUIT - Action asserted by a shareholder in order to enforce a cause of action on behalf of the corporation.

NOTES:

BANGOR PUNTA OPERATIONS, INC. v. BANGOR & AROOSTOOK R.R.

Stock owner (D) v. Corporation (P)

417 U.S. 703 (1974).

NATURE OF CASE: Action for damages for mismanagement, misappropriation, and waste.

FACT SUMMARY: Bangor Punta (D) had once held 98% of the stock in Bangor & Aroostook Railroad (P), which claimed that Bangor Punta (D) had engaged in acts of mismanagement, misappropriation, and waste in controlling the affairs of Bangor & Aroostook Railroad (P).

CONCISE RULE OF LAW: Equitable principles preclude use of the corporate fiction to evade the "contemporaneous ownership rule," which provides that the complaining shareholder in a derivative action must have been a shareholder at the time of the wrong of which he complains.

FACTS: Bangor & Aroostook Corporation (B & A) had held 98.3% of the stock in Bangor & Aroostook Railroad (BAR) (P) which it subsequently sold to Bangor Punta (D). Bangor Punta (D) later sold the stock to Amoskeag Co., which set about acquiring enough other stock to bring its ownership of BAR (P) up to more than 99%. BAR (P) filed an action alleging that both B & A and Bangor Punta (D) had engaged in securities law violations and acts of mismanagement, misappropriation, and waste of corporate assets with regard to the running of BAR (P). The district court dismissed the action. It held the real party in interest was Amoskeag, the present owner of more than 99% of the stock; that it had paid a fair price and received fair value in purchasing the stock; that it would be the principal beneficiary of any damages that would be recovered, and that it could not have satisfied the "contemporaneous ownership rule" had it not been evaded by having the corporation, BAR (P), bring suit in its name. The contemporaneous ownership rule provides that the complaining shareholder in a derivative action must have been a shareholder at the time of the wrong of which he complains to bring an action thereon. The district court reasoned that equitable principles would not allow Amoskeag to evade this rule by using the corporate fiction to have BAR (D) bring suit in its own name when Amoskeag was the one who would be recovering any benefit resulting therefrom. Finally, the district court noted that the contemporaneous ownership rule was found in both federal procedural rules and state substantive law. Thus, it made no difference which procedure applied, for the present action could not be maintained. The court of appeals reversed, holding that the benefit of any damage recovery in this action would accrue to the public through the improvement in BAR's (P) economic position and the quality of its services. This, it concluded, rendered any windfall to Amoskeag irrelevant and prevented looking at the suit as if it were one brought by Amoskeag in corporate disguise.

ISSUE: Can a shareholder use the corporate fiction to evade the contemporaneous ownership rule?

HOLDING AND DECISION: (Powell, J.) No. It is most certain that equitable principles do not permit a shareholder to use the corporate fiction to evade the contemporaneous ownership rule, as was attempted by Amoskeag in this case. The courts will look behind the corporate entity to the true substance of the claims and the actual beneficiaries and disregard the corporate form where it is being used to defeat an overriding public policy. Here, Amoskeag will be the principle beneficiary of any recovery, but it is estopped from bringing suit in its own name because it did not own stock at the time of the alleged wrongs. Furthermore, it is a settled principle of equity that a shareholder may not complain of acts of corporate mismanagement if he acquired his shares from those who participated or acquiesced in the allegedly wrongful transactions. This principle has been invoked with special force where a shareholder purchases all or substantially all the shares of a corporation from a vendor at a fair price, and then seeks to have the corporation recover against the vendor for prior corporate mismanagement. The object is to preclude precisely the type of windfall Amoskeag would recover in this case, for it is probable that the damages would not be put back into the business but would go primarily to the benefit of the 99% stockholder, Amoskeag. This action was instituted by BAR (P) for the benefit of Amoskeag, which could not have brought the suit itself. It was not brought to obtain relief for those of the 20 shareholders owning less than 1% of the stock who might have been owners of stock at the time of the alleged wrongs, and who thus would satisfy the contemporaneous ownership rule and be eligible to bring suit. What is being attempted in this action is a suit by Amoskeag camouflaged in corporate clothes, which equity will not permit. The action must be dismissed. Reversed.

DISSENT: (Marshall, J.) There were a few minority shareholders who owned stock at the time of the alleged wrongs, and BAR (P) owes them a duty to seek recovery for the wrongs they suffered. This is not like the Home Fire case, which held that a party who had purchased 100% of the shares in the "wronged" corporation from the "wrongdoers" could not be heard to complain of those acts because any recovery would be a "windfall" inasmuch as it paid fair value for the shares and got what it paid for.

EDITOR'S ANALYSIS: Most jurisdictions have some form of the contemporaneous ownership rule in effect. However, at common law, the cases were split as to whether contemporaneous ownership should be a requirement in shareholder derivative actions. Even where the rule exists, there are exceptions thereto. One important exception is where "continuing wrongs" are involved. A shareholder is free to bring a derivative action where the alleged wrong began prior to his acquisition of stock but continued thereafter.

[For more information on Contemporaneous Ownership, see Casenote Law Outline on Corporations, Chapter 9, § I, Derivative Suits.]

QUICKNOTES

DERIVATIVE SUIT - Action asserted by a shareholder in order to enforce a cause of action on behalf of the corporation.

RIFKIN v. STEELE PLATT
Company buyer (P) v. Seller (D)
Colo. Ct. App., 824 P.2d 32 (1991).

NATURE OF CASE: Appeal from a judgment in favor of a corporate plaintiff in a shareholder suit for breach of fiduciary duty and cross-appeal by plaintiffs of a damages award.

FACT SUMMARY: When Rifkin (P) and other buyers of The Boiler Room (P), a corporation, discovered inaccuracies in financial representations made in the purchase agreement, they filed suit, but the sellers (D) argued that The Boiler Room (P) could not recover for wrongful conduct that occurred before the buyers (P) acquired their shares.

CONCISE RULE OF LAW: A corporation cannot maintain an action for wrongs that occurred before the new shareholders' acquisition of the shares.

FACTS: Through a stock purchase agreement, Steele Platt (D) and Fas-Wok, Inc. (D) agreed to sell The Boiler Room, Inc. (P), a corporation, which owned a restaurant in a shopping center in Denver. After closing, the buyers, including Rifkin (P), discovered inaccuracies in financial representations made in the agreement. Consequently, they filed suit, alleging breach of contract, breach of good faith, breach of fiduciary duty, and unjust enrichment. Platt (D) counterclaimed, seeking rescission of the agreement. The trial court entered judgment for Rifkin (P) and the other buyers on the breach of contract claim and for the Corporation (P) on the breach of fiduciary duty claim. Platt (D) appealed the judgment on the breach of fiduciary duty claim arguing that The Boiler Room (P) would improperly receive a windfall because the purchase price reflected the prior wrongdoing.

ISSUE: Can a corporation maintain an action for wrongs that occurred before the new shareholders' acquisition of the shares?

HOLDING AND DECISION: (Plank, J.) No. A corporation can not maintain an action for wrongs that occurred before the new shareholders' acquisition of the shares. If the purchase price was reduced due to the prior wrongdoings of the sellers, the shareholders would improperly receive a windfall if allowed to recover damages. Here, it is undisputed that the acts which constituted Platt's (D) breach of fiduciary duty occurred prior to Rifkin (P) and the other buyers' acquisition of stock in The Boiler Room (P). However, the parties dispute whether the purchase price reflected the prior wrongdoings. The trial court did not make a finding on this issue. Therefore, the case is remanded for further findings. If the court finds that the price reflected Platt's (D) wrongdoings, it must dismiss the breach of fiduciary duty claim. However, if it finds that the purchase price did not reflect the wrongdoings, then the previous damage award may stand.

EDITOR'S ANALYSIS: The holding employed in this case is known as the contemporaneous ownership rule. It is the majority rule. However, it will not apply in the following three circumstances: (1) When the noncontemporaneous owner receives her shares "by operation of law; (2) when former shareholders are engaged in a continuing wrong; and (3) when the noncontemporaneous owner is challenging short-swing profits.

[For more information on the contemporaneous ownership rule, see Casenote Law Outline on Corporations, Chapter 9, § I, Derivative Suits.]

QUICKNOTES
FIDUCIARY DUTY - A legal obligation to act for the benefit of another, including subordinating one's personal interests to that of the other person.

RESCISSION - The canceling of an agreement and the return of the parties to their positions prior to the formation of the contract.

NOTES:

MARX v. AKERS

Shareholder (P) v. Corporation (D)

88 N.Y.2d 189, 644 N.Y.S.2d 121, 666 N.E.2d 1034 (1996).

NATURE OF CASE: Appeal from ruling by Appellate Division dismissing complaint for failure to make a demand on the board and failure to state a cause of action.

FACT SUMMARY: Marx (P), shareholder of IBM (D), brought a derivative action against the corporation alleging that the directors violated their fiduciary duty by voting for unreasonably high compensation for company executives.

CONCISE RULE OF LAW: Demands on boards of directors are futile if a complaint alleges with particularity that: (1) a majority of the directors are interested in the transaction; (2) the directors failed to inform themselves to a degree reasonably necessary about the transaction; or (3) the directors failed to exercise their business judgment in approving the transaction.

FACTS: Marx (P), a shareholder of IBM (D), commenced a derivative action against IBM (D) alleging that Akers (D), a former chief executive officer of IBM, and other directors violated their fiduciary duty and engaged in self-dealing by awarding excessive compensation to other directors on the board. IBM (D) moved to dismiss the complaint for failure to state a cause of action and failure to serve a demand on IBM's board to initiate a lawsuit based on these allegations. The supreme court dismissed the complaint stating that Marx (P) failed to show that demand would have been futile, and the Appellate Division affirmed. Marx (P) appealed.

ISSUE: Is a demand on the board of directors futile if a complaint alleges with particularity that: (1) a majority of the directors are interested in the transaction; (2) the directors failed to inform themselves to a degree reasonably necessary about the transaction; or (3) the directors failed to exercise their business judgment in approving the transaction?

HOLDING AND DECISION: (Smith, J.) Yes. Demands on boards of directors are futile if a complaint alleges with particularity that: (1) a majority of the directors are interested in the transaction; (2) the directors failed to inform themselves to a degree reasonably necessary about the transaction; or (3) the directors failed to exercise their business judgment in approving the transaction. Directors are self-interested in a transaction if they receive a direct financial benefit from the transaction that is different from the benefit to the shareholders generally. Voting oneself a raise excuses a demand. However, the inquiry must still be made as to whether this is a sufficient basis to support a cause of action. Courts have repeatedly held that a cause of action will not stand alone on the basis of excessive salary raises unless wrongdoing, oppression, or abuse of a fiduciary position is also demonstrated. The evidence presented is not ample to support Marx's (P) allegations of wrongdoing, so the Appellate Division's order should stand. Affirmed.

EDITOR'S ANALYSIS: In setting forth the instances in which demand will be excused, the court rejected both the Delaware rule and the universal demand rule proposed by the American Law Institute and adopted by eleven states. Although a Universal Demand requirement would decrease the number of cases such as this one, it would also be a waste of time in many circumstances. On the other hand, until the standards excusing demand are tested and clarified, there will still be an increase in the number of cases on this issue.

[For more information on requirements for shareholder derivative suits, see Casenote Law Outline on Corporations, Chapter 9, § I, Derivative Suits.]

NOTES:

AUERBACH v. BENNETT
Shareholder (P) v. Director (D)

N.Y. Ct. of App., 47 N.Y.2d 619, 419 N.Y.S.2d 920, 393 N.E.2d 994 (1979).

NATURE OF CASE: Shareholders' derivative action charging directors with breach of their duties.

FACT SUMMARY: Auerbach (P), a shareholder in General Telephone, brought a suit charging that Bennett (D) and other directors had breached their duty to the corporation by personal involvement in the payment of bribes and kickbacks, but a "disinterested" committee appointed by the board found the suit not to be in the corporation's best interests and sought its dismissal.

CONCISE RULE OF LAW: Although the substantive aspects of a decision to terminate a stockholders' derivative action against corporate directors made by a committee of disinterested directors appointed by the corporation's board of directors are beyond judicial inquiry under the business judgment doctrine, the court may inquire as to the disinterested independence of the members of that committee and as to the appropriateness and sufficiency of its investigative procedures.

FACTS: General Telephone found that certain of its employees and directors had been engaged in paying out approximately $11 million in bribes and kickbacks. Almost immediately, Auerbach (P) instituted a shareholders' derivative suit charging the directors with breach of their duty to the corporation and asking that they be made to account for the payments made. The board of directors proceeded to create a special litigation committee comprised of three disinterested directors who had joined the board after the challenged transactions had occurred. It empowered the committee to act for the board with respect to the litigation. The committee found that the litigation would not be in the best interest of the company because of the bad publicity, the waste of corporate management's time, the inordinate cost in view of the unlikelihood of success, etc. The corporation thus moved to dismiss the complaint, and the trial court granted the motion on the ground that the business judgment rule precluded the court from inquiring into the committee's actions. The appellate division reversed.

ISSUE: When the board of directors appoints a committee of disinterested directors to decide whether to terminate a stockholders' derivative suit against corporate directors, does the business judgment rule prevent judicial inquiry into the substantive aspects of the committee's decision but allow such inquiry as to the disinterested independence of the committee members and as to the appropriateness and sufficiency of the committee's investigative procedures?

HOLDING AND DECISION: (Jones, J.) Yes. In a case like this, where a committee of disinterested directors is appointed by the board of directors to determine whether to terminate a stockholders' derivative action against corporate directors, the business judgment rule precludes judicial inquiry into the substantive aspects of the committee's decision but permits such inquiry as to the disinterested independence of the committee members and as to the appropriateness and sufficiency of the committee's investigative procedures. The business judgment rule shields the deliberations and conclusions of the chosen representatives of the board only if they possess a disinterested independence and do not stand in a dual relation which prevents an unprejudicial exercise of judgment. This flows from the fact that the business judgment rule only covers board action taken in good faith. In applying these principles to this case, there is a lack of evidence that the committee members were anything other than disinterested and independent or that their investigative procedures were inappropriate or insufficient. To allow a fishing expedition by withholding summary judgment until there is an opportunity for disclosure proceedings, in the hope such evidence might turn up, would not be proper. Speculation that something might thus turn up is no basis for postponing decisions on a summary judgment motion under the authority of the applicable statute. Anyway, the disclosure proposed would go only to particulars as to the results of the committee's investigation and work, the factors bearing on its substantive decisions not to prosecute the derivative actions, and the factual aspects of the underlying activities of the board. These are all matters falling within the ambit of the business judgment doctrine and thus excluded from judicial scrutiny. The decision of the trial court in dismissing the complaint was proper. Reversed.

DISSENT: (Cooke, J.) In the first place, the business judgment rule is only conditionally applicable in this case, which is so different from the typical situation in which that rule would be invoked. Second, the directors and members of the litigation committee have the sole knowledge of the facts upon which its applicability turn. The majority rule fosters a classic "Catch-22 situation." One cannot obtain disclosure because he has not come forward with facts, which by their very nature are discernible only after disclosure. The result is to render corporate directors largely unaccountable to the shareholders whose business they are elected to govern.

Continued on next page.

EDITOR'S ANALYSIS: Although the current trend tends toward accepting the rationale of this case, there are recent decisions taking a contrary approach. In Moldonado v. Flynn, - A.2d -, (Del.Ch. 1980), the court found that nothing in the business judgment rule gives a board the power to terminate a derivative suit. Rather, it concluded, the business judgment rule simply provides a shield with which directors may oppose stockholders' attacks on decisions made by them. Thus, once a corporation's board refuses to proceed with litigation, the stockholder has an independent right to redress the wrong by bringing a derivative action, so that the board cannot compel dismissal.

[For more information on Special Litigation Committees, see Casenote Law Outline on Corporations, Chapter 9, § I, Derivative Suits.]

QUICKNOTES

BUSINESS JUDGMENT RULE - Doctrine relieving corporate directors and/or officers from liability for decisions honestly and rationally made in the corporation's best interests.

PROXY STATEMENT - A statement, containing specified information by the Securities and Exchange Commission, in order to provide shareholders with adequate information upon which to make an informed decision regarding the solicitation of their proxies.

SHAREHOLDER'S DERIVATIVE ACTION - Action asserted by a shareholder in order to enforce a cause of action on behalf of the corporation.

NOTES:

ZAPATA CORP. v. MALDONADO
Corporation (D) v. Shareholder (P)
Del. Sup. Ct., 430 A.2d 779 (1981).

NATURE OF CASE: Interlocutory appeal in a stockholder's derivative suit.

FACT SUMMARY: Maldonado (P) had initiated a derivative suit charging officers and directors of Zapata (D) with breaches of fiduciary duty, but four years later an "Independent Investigation Committee" of two disinterested directors recommended dismissing the action.

CONCISE RULE OF LAW: Where the making of a prior demand upon the directors of a corporation to sue is excused and a stockholder initiates a derivative suit on behalf of the corporation, the board of directors or an independent committee appointed by the board can move to dismiss the derivative suit as detrimental to the corporation's best interests and the court should apply a two-step test to the motion: (1) has the corporation proved independence, good faith, and a reasonable investigation?; and (2) does the court feel, applying its own independent business judgment, that the motion should be granted?

FACTS: At the time Maldonado (P) instituted a derivative suit against Zapata (D), he was excused from making a prior demand on the board of directors because they were all defendants (Maldonado [P] asserting a breach of fiduciary duty on the part of officers and directors of Zapata [D]). The board had changed membership when, four years later, it appointed an "Independent Investigation Committee," composed of two new directors, to investigate the litigation. The committee recommended dismissing the action, calling its continued maintenance "inimical to the Company's best interests . . . ." In an interlocutory appeal before the Supreme Court of Delaware, the primary focus was on whether or not the aforementioned committee had the power to dismiss the action.

ISSUE: In a case in which a stockholder acted properly in instituting a derivative suit on behalf of the corporation without first making a demand on the board of directors to sue, can the board of directors or an independent committee they appoint move to dismiss the suit as detrimental to the best interests of the corporation?

HOLDING AND DECISION: (Quillen, J.) Yes. Where, as in this case, a stockholder acted properly in bringing a derivative suit without first demanding the directors file suit (i.e., where such a demand is "excused"), the board of directors or an independent committee they appoint has the power to choose not to pursue the litigation because such would not be in the best interests of the corporation. The fact that a majority of the board may have been

tainted by self-interest is not per se a legal bar to the delegation of the board's power to an independent committee composed of disinterested board members. Thus, a committee, such as that involved in this case, can properly act for the corporation to move to dismiss derivative litigation that is believed to be detrimental to the corporation's best interests. When faced with such a motion, the court should give each side an opportunity to make a record on the motion. The moving party should be prepared to meet the normal burden of showing that there is no genuine issue as to any material fact and that it is entitled to dismiss as a matter of law. The court should apply a two-step test to the motion. First, it should inquire into the independence and good faith of the committee and the bases supporting its conclusions. To aid in such inquiries, limited discovery may be ordered. If the court determines either that the committee is not independent or has not shown reasonable bases for its conclusions, or if the court is not satisfied for other reasons relating to the process, including but not limited to the good faith of the committee, the court shall deny the corporation's motion. It must be remembered that the corporation has the burden of proving independence, good faith, and reasonableness. It the court is satisfied that the committee was independent and showed reasonable bases for good-faith findings and recommendations, the court may proceed, in its discretion, to the second step. This second step provides the essential key in striking the balance between legitimate corporate claims as expressed in a derivative stockholder suit and a corporation's best interests as expressed by an independent investigating committee. The court should determine, applying its own independent business judgment, whether the motion should be granted. This second step is intended to thwart instances where corporation actions meet the criteria of stop one, but the result does not appear to satisfy the spirit, or where corporate actions would simply prematurely terminate a stockholder grievance deserving of further consideration in the corporation's interest. Of course, the court must carefully consider and weigh how compelling the corporate interest in dismissal is when faced with a non-frivolous lawsuit. It should, when appropriate, give special consideration to matters of law and public policy in addition to the corporation's best interests. If, after all of this, the court's independent business judgment is satisfied, it may proceed to grant the motion, subject, of course, to any equitable terms or conditions it finds necessary or desirable. Reversed and remanded for further proceedings.

Continued on next page.

EDITOR'S ANALYSIS: Other courts have chosen to treat this type of situation as one where the "business judgment" rule is applicable. They look to see if the committee to whom the board of directors delegated the responsibility of determining if the litigation at issue should be continued was composed of independent and disinterested members and if it conducted a proper review of the matters before it to reach a good-faith business judgment concerning whether or not to continue the litigation. If it did, the committee's decision stands. This court found that approach too one-sided, as tending to wrest bona fide derivative actions away from well-meaning derivative plaintiffs and robbing the shareholders of an effective intracorporate means of policing boards of directors.

[For more information on Demand on Directors, see Casenote Law Outline on Corporations, Chapter 9, § I, Derivative Suits.]

QUICKNOTES

8 DEL. C. § 141(a) - Businesses shall be managed by a board of directors.

BUSINESS JUDGMENT RULE - Doctrine relieving corporate directors and/or officers from liability for decisions honestly and rationally made in the corporation's best interests.

NOTES:

SUGARLAND INDUSTRIES, INC. v. THOMAS

Corporation (D) v. Controlling shareholder (P)

Del. Sup. Ct., 420 A.2d 142 (1980).

NATURE OF CASE: Appeal from an order awarding attorney fees in a shareholder derivative suit to enjoin a proposed sale of land owned by a corporation.

FACT SUMMARY: When the Thomases (P), members of the family controlling Sugarland Industries, Inc. (D), thought the price offered for land owned by the corporation was too low, they consulted counsel, who later sought an award of fees for their efforts, which had resulted in a much higher sale price for the land.

CONCISE RULE OF LAW: Attorneys for shareholder plaintiffs are entitled to a fair percentage of the benefit inuring to the corporation and its stockholders as a result of their efforts.

FACTS: Sugarland Industries (D), a family-controlled corporation, was attempting to sell land owned by the corporation. Concerned that the offering price was too low, the Thomases (P), members of Sugarland's (D) controlling family, sought legal advice, later filing suit to enjoin the sale. As a result of the Thomases' (P) attorneys' efforts, a higher second bid was made. The land was finally sold for a much higher price than the original offer. A second action then ensued to determine the damage phase of the controversy. Although the first action was resolved quickly, the second action took three years. The Thomases' (P) attorneys sought about $6,000,000 for their services in both phases of the litigation. The court awarded them $3,500,000. Both Sugarland (D) and the intervenor trustee bank, which owned about 23% of Sugarland (D) stock, appealed. The Thomases (P) cross-appealed the interest on the awards.

ISSUE: Are attorneys for shareholder plaintiffs entitled to a fair percentage of the benefit inuring to the corporation and its stockholders as a result of their efforts?

HOLDING AND DECISION: (Duffy, J.) Yes. Attorneys for shareholder plaintiffs are entitled to a fair percentage of the benefit inuring to the corporation and its stockholders as a result of their efforts. In this case, the record reveals that the services of the Thomases' (P) attorneys benefitted Sugarland (D) to the extent of the $3,200,000 difference between the original offer and the second bid. However, how one should view the additional $11 million plus received in the final sale price is not so clear. The 20% factor applied by the chancellor is valid as to the $3 million dollar sale price increase. However, 5% of the additional $11 million increase is fair and reasonable compensation for the skills and expertise of the attorneys. Affirmed in part and reversed in part.

EDITOR'S ANALYSIS: The chancellor listed the pertinent factors to be considered in the award of attorney fees as the amount of time and effort applied by counsel, the complexities of the litigation, and the skills applied to their resolution. Under Delaware law, the standard of review of an award of attorney fees in chancery is abuse of discretion. The supreme court agreed with the chancellor's findings but disagreed with his crediting the attorneys with the entire amount received over the original offer.

[For more information on recovery of counsel fees, see Casenote Law Outline on Corporations, Chapter 9, § I, Derivative Suits.]

QUICKNOTES

ABUSE OF DISCRETION - A determination by an appellate court that a lower court's decision was based on an error of law.

NOTES:

KAPLAN v. RAND
Shareholders (P) v. Lawyer (D)
192 F.3d (1999).

NATURE OF THE CASE: Appeal from a judgment in favor of plaintiffs based on a breach of duty in shareholders' derivative suit.

FACT SUMMARY: After obtaining a settlement in a shareholders' derivative suit, the shareholders dispute the awarding of attorney's fees based on the disproportionately large amount charged by counsel in comparison to the slight benefit obtained by the settlement.

CONCISE RULE OF LAW: Attorney's fees may not be awarded where the settlement of a derivative action provides no substantial benefit to a corporation or its shareholders.

FACTS: Kaplan (P) and other plaintiffs brought a derivative action in the right of and for the benefit of Texaco to remedy injuries suffered by the company and its corporate assets as the result of mismanagement and alleged discriminatory employment practices. Both sides moved to dismiss and commenced settlement discussion pending disposition of the motions. As an agreement for settlement was reached, the district court denied the pending motions to dismiss without prejudice and with leave to renew if the settlement agreement was never realized. However, the district court ultimately approved the agreement and appointed a Special Master to inquire into the awarding of legal fees pursuant to the terms of the agreement. The settlement terms governing counsel fees were held in dispute by the shareholders (P), based on their method of calculation and proportion of benefit achieved on behalf of the company. Rand (D) objected to the reduction in his fee as a representative of Kaplan (P) and the other plaintiffs in the derivative suit.

ISSUE: May attorney's fees be awarded where the settlement of a derivative action provides no substantial benefit to a corporation or its shareholders?

HOLDING: (Miner, J.) No. Attorney's fees may not be awarded where the settlement of a derivative action provides no substantial benefit to a corporation or its shareholders. The plaintiffs in a derivative action may recover attorney's fees out of any common fund created by the successful efforts of the suit against the corporation. However, it is also well–established that counsel fees are justified where the derivative action results in a significant non-monetary benefit to the corporation. The relevant case law shows that plaintiffs in a derivative action are entitled to counsel fees upon settlement of an action only where the non-monetary benefits secured are substantial in nature. Rand (D) asserts that counsel encountered substantial obstacles while bringing the derivative action to a successful conclusion, but this contention does not address the issue of counsel's providing only superficial benefit to the parties in question. The settlement of the derivative action provided no substantial benefit to the corporation or its shareholders (P) and attorney's fees are not justified under the circumstances. This court therefore reverses the judgment of the district court. Remanded for the entry of judgment denying counsel fees.

EDITOR'S ANALYSIS: In drafting its opinion, the court does not expressly define what constitutes "substantial benefits" when evaluating a completed settlement in a derivative suit. However, the court cites several cases where prior courts established comparable standards. In Seinfeld v. Robinson, 246 A.D.2d 291, 1998, the court found no substantial benefits where the settlement secured a stipulation preventing acquisition of more than fifty percent of any banking business without the approval of a majority of shareholders. However, in Mills v. Electric Auto-Lite Co., 396 U.S. 375, 1970, substantial benefit existed where the settlement vindicated a statutory policy against unregistered offerings in favor of the corporation. The court noted in the present case that such benefit was substantial because it had a "therapeutic" effect on the well-being of the corporation and furnished a broad benefit to all shareholders.

QUICKNOTES

SHAREHOLDER'S DERIVATIVE ACTION - Action asserted by a shareholder in order to enforce a cause of action on behalf of the corporation.

ALCOTT v. M.E.V. CORP.

Shareholder (P) v. Corporation (D)

Cal. Ct. App., 193 Cal. App. 3d 797 (6th Dist. 1987).

NATURE OF CASE: Appeal from an award of defendants' attorney fees in a derivative action for which the defendants were awarded summary judgment.

FACT SUMMARY: After M.E.V. Corp. (D) and the other defendants in this stockholder derivative action prevailed in pretrial motions, Alcott (P) challenged the attorney fees awarded to M.E.V. (D) by the court, arguing that no security had been sought or posted.

CONCISE RULE OF LAW: California state law contains no provision for an award of attorney fees where security is not sought or posted.

FACTS: This stockholder derivative action collapsed after M.E.V. Corp. (D) and all other defendants prevailed in pretrial skirmishes. Thereafter, M.E.V. Corp. (D) and the other defendants won their demands for attorney fees, even though no security had been sought by M.E.V. (D) or posted by Alcott (P). Alcott (P) appealed the award of attorney fees, arguing that § 800 of the California Corporation Code rendered such fees recoverable only out of a posted security bond. M.E.V. (D) responded that, under § 800, prevailing defendants were entitled to their attorney fees.

ISSUE: Does California state law contain a provision for an award of attorney fees where security is not sought or posted?

HOLDING AND DECISION: (Brauer, J.) No. California state law contains no provision for an award of attorney fees where security is not sought or posted. Here, no security was either sought by M.E.V. (D) or posted by Alcott (P). In the 1982 amendment to § 800, no language was added from which a legislative intention could be inferred to transmute a "security" statute into a "liability" one. Furthermore, Civil Code § 1717, cited by M.E.V. Corp. (D) and the other defendants as standing for a right of reciprocity, by its terms applies only to contracts and not to fee-shifting statutes or court-imposed public policies. Thus, the fact that Alcott (P) and the other plaintiffs might have been entitled to attorney fees had they prevailed in their derivative action has no relevance here. No attorney fees are recoverable here. Reversed.

EDITOR'S ANALYSIS: The rule applied here was enunciated in *Freeman v. Goldberg*, 55 Cal.2d 622 (1961). The court of appeals here declared that there are good reasons why a broadening of § 1717 to allow the prevailing defendants here the right to recover attorney fees, a right the plaintiffs would have if they had prevailed, ought not to be undertaken, even aside from the fact that it would constitute an improper judicial intrusion into the legislative sphere. The reciprocity feature of § 1717 was designed to further the aim of remedying an inequality in bargaining power. But one-sided statutory and judicially mandated fee-shifting provisions serve a specific public policy which would be vitiated by the grant of reciprocity.

[For more information on security for expenses statutes, see Casenote Law Outline on Corporations, Chapter 9, § I, Derivative Suits.]

QUICKNOTES

SHAREHOLDER'S DERIVATIVE ACTION - Action asserted by a shareholder in order to enforce a cause of action on behalf of the corporation.

CAL. CIVIL CODE § 717 - In contract actions, if the contract provides for one side to receive attorney fees then the prevailing party shall be entitled to the fees.

NOTES:

WALTUCH v. CONTICOMMODITY SERVICES, INC.

Officer/Employee (P) v. Corporation (D)

88 F.3d 87 (2nd Cir. 1996).

NATURE OF CASE: Appeal of denied indemnification.

FACT SUMMARY: After incurring legal expenses in defending himself, Waltuch (P) was denied indemnification by his employer, ContiCommodity Services (D), due to a negotiated settlement by Conti (D) of all claims against him.

CONCISE RULE OF LAW: Delaware's mandate that a corporation indemnify directors or officers for the successful defense of certain claims includes those cases where a third- party settlement induced dismissal of those claims.

FACTS: Famed silver trader Norton Waltuch (P) was an employee of ContiCommodity Services (D). Several suits naming Waltuch (P) were settled by Conti (D). The suits were based upon fraudulent silver trading activities allegedly performed by Waltuch (P). In settling the claims against Waltuch (P), Conti (D) negotiated a settlement of $35 million dollars. The settlement also included a provision that dismissed all claims against Waltuch (P) with prejudice. In his own defense activities, Waltuch (P) incurred $2,228,586 in legal expenses and costs, with $1.2 million of that for the defense of private civil actions. Waltuch (P) then sought indemnification from Conti (D). An independent legal counsel concluded that Waltuch (P) was not entitled to indemnification. Although Article Nine of Conti's (D) Certificate of Incorporation provided for indemnification unless the individual concerned was held liable for negligence or misconduct in the performance of his duties, the court denied his indemnification request based upon public policy limitations in § 145 of the Delaware General Corporation Law. Waltuch (P) appealed the trial court's refusal to grant indemnification.

ISSUE: Does Delaware's mandate that a corporation indemnify directors or officers for the successful defense of certain claims include those cases where a third party induced dismissal of those claims?

HOLDING AND DECISION: (Jacobs, J.) Yes. The Delaware's mandate that a corporation indemnify directors or officers for the successful defense of certain claims includes those cases where a third-party settlement induced dismissal of those claims. The language of § 145 of the Delaware General Corporation Law in this case requires only that the officer or the director prevail in the defense of their claims. It is widely accepted that a dismissal of claims with prejudice constitutes a successful outcome. Whether a third party settled the claims for the director or officer is irrelevant under the statute; success is all that is required. Here, Waltuch (P) prevailed in his defense of the private civil claims. That Conti (D) settled the claims for him does not relieve the obligation to indemnify Waltuch (P) for $1.2 million. Conti (D) could have settled its claims without settling Waltuch's (P), but that was not the outcome. Reversed on the issue of indemnification for the private lawsuits.

EDITOR'S ANALYSIS: Delaware is typically known for its pro-corporate posture. However, the reading of Delaware law in this case is somewhat less than desirable to the corporation. There is very little in the Delaware corporation laws that is mandatory, but indemnification of directors and officers who successfully defend themselves against certain claims is mandatory. The mandatory indemnification is primarily a choice made in the law to encourage successful individuals to serve as corporate directors and officers without fear that their high profile will subject them to needless liability.

[For more information on mandatory indemnification, see Casenote Law Outline on Corporations, Chapter 9, § II, Mandatory or Permissive Indemnification.]

QUICKNOTES

INDEMNIFICATION: Reimbursement for losses sustained or security against anticipated loss or damages.

NOTES:

CLARKE v. GREENBERG
Clarke not identified (P) v. Shareholder (D)
296 N.Y. 146, 71 N.E.2d 443 (1947).

NATURE OF CASE: Appeal from lower court's dismissal of plaintiff's case upon demurrer by defendant.

FACT SUMMARY: Greenberg (D) had settled a stockholder's derivative action out of court to his personal benefit. Clarke (P) sought to have proceeds of settlement paid over to corporation.

CONCISE RULE OF LAW: A derivative action by a stockholder plaintiff suing on behalf of the corporation belongs primarily to the corporation and any recovery, whether by judgment or by settlement, belongs to the corporation.

FACTS: Greenberg (D) initiated a stockholder's derivative action on behalf of Associated Gas and Electric Co. against the directors of the corporation for mismanagement. Before the case came to trial, a settlement agreement was reached. The terms of the agreement were that Greenberg (D) would stipulate to a discontinuance of the lawsuit and in return the corporation would purchase his shares, having a market value of $51.88, for $9,000. The agreement itself was not presented to the court for approval. Only the stipulation for discontinuance was received and the action dismissed. Clarke (P) brought suit against Greenberg (D) alleging the settlement recovery in excess of the market value of the shares belonged to the corporation and not to Greenberg (D) individually.

ISSUE: When a shareholder institutes a derivative suit an behalf of a corporation, do the proceeds of a private outside-of-court settlement belong to the individual shareholder?

HOLDING AND DECISION: (Dye, J.) No. When a stockholder sues on behalf of the corporation in a derivative action his relationship to the corporation is one of a fiduciary. The corporation is the real party in interest on the plaintiff's side and any recovery belongs to the corporation. This is very clear where the action proceeds through trial to judgment. Any recovery resulting from that judgment would clearly belong to the corporation. The same result would occur where a settlement proposal is submitted to the court for approval. The approval by the court would result in a judgment. Where the settlement is made outside the court, the same principle would still apply. The shareholder's cause of action is not founded in his own right to sue but upon the corporation's cause of action. It follows, therefore, that to allow that individual shareholder to profit from the suit would be to unjustly enrich him at the expense of the corporation. Any recovery is impressed with a constructive trust for the benefit of the corporation. The lower court's dismissal of Clarke's (P) suit for failure to state facts sufficient to constitute a cause of action was error. Clarke (P) has indeed stated sufficient facts to entitle him to a hearing on the merits.

EDITOR'S ANALYSIS: While this case appears to correct the inequity of the previous case, Manufacturers Mutual, it still does not provide a satisfactory protection for the corporation and the other shareholders.

QUICKNOTES
DERIVATIVE SUIT - Action asserted by a shareholder in order to enforce a cause of action on behalf of the corporation.

NOTES:

CHAPTER 12
STRUCTURAL CHANGES

QUICK REFERENCE RULES OF LAW

1. **Sale of Substantially all assets.** Under Delaware law the decision of a corporation to sell all or substantially all of its property and assets requires not only the approval of the corporation's board of directors, but also a resolution adopted by a majority of the outstanding stockholders of the corporation entitled to vote. (Katz v. Bregman)

   [For more information on Acts of Board Directors, see Casenote Law Outline on Corporations, Chapter 2, § II, Viewing the Corporation from Within.]

2. **The Stock Modes and the De Facto Merger Theory.** A corporation may sell its assets to another corporation even if the result is the same as a merger without following the statutory merger requirements. (Hariton v. Arco Electronics,Inc.)

   [For more information on Asset Sales, see Casenote Law Outline on Corporations, Chapter 8, § I, State Corporation Law.]

3. **The Stock Modes and the De Facto Merger Theory.** A transaction which is in the form of a sale of corporate assets but which is in effect a de facto merger of two corporations must meet the statutory merger requirements in order to protect the rights of minority shareholders. (Farris v. Glen Alden Corp.)

   [For more information on De Facto Merger Doctrine, see Casenote Law Outline on Corporations, Chapter 8, § I, State Corporation Laws.]

4. **Triangular Mergers and Share Exchanges.** Pennsylvania corporate law provides voting and dissenter's rights for shareholders of parties to a merger and the de facto merger doctrine does not apply to extend those rights to shareholders of entities that are not parties to the merger. (Terry v. Penn Central Corp.)

   [For more information on Dissenters' Rights, see Casenote Law Outline on Corporations, Chapter 8, § I, State Corporation Laws.]

5. **Substantive Fairness.** When the terms of a proposed merger are, in the light of all relevant factors of valuation, fair to the minority shareholders, and there is no evidence of fraud or bad faith, the proposed merger will not be enjoined. (Sterling v. Mayflower Hotel Corp.)

   [For more information on Dissenters' Rights, see Casenote Law Outline on Corporations, Chapter 8, § I, State Corporation Laws.]

6. **Tender Offers.** Unless it is shown that the directors' decision in fighting a takeover was primarily based on perpetuating themselves in office, or some other breach of fiduciary duty, a court will not substitute its judgment for that of the board. (Unocal Corp v.Mesa Petroleum Co.)

   [For more information on directors' fiduciary duties in a takeover, see Casenote Law Outline on Corporations, Chapter 8, § IV, Fiduciary Duties of Care and Loyalty.]

7. **Corporation Combination.** When seeking to secure minority shareholder approval for a proposed cashout merger, the corporations involved must comply with the fairness test which has two basic interrelated aspects: (1) fair dealings — which imposes a duty on the corporations to completely disclose to the shareholders all

information germane to the merger; and (2) fair price — which requires that the price being offered for the outstanding stock be equivalent to a price determined by an appraisal where "all relevant nonspeculative factors" were considered. (Weinberger v. UOP, Inc.)

[For more information on Dissenters' Rights, see Casenote Law Outline on Corporations, Chapter 8, § I, State Corporation Laws.]

8. **Tender Offers.** Boards of directors may, under the business judgment rule, validly protect the corporation from hostile takeovers through the use of a Preferred Share Purchase Rights Program.(Moran v. Household International, Inc.)

[For more information on Business Judgment Rule, see Casenote Law Outline on Corporations, Chapter 4, § I, State Corporation Codes and the Business Judgment Rule.]

9. **Tender Offers.** While directors may have regard for various constituencies in discharging their responsibilities vis-a-vis an attempted takeover, there must be rationally related benefits accruing to the stockholders and once the corporate dissolution becomes inevitable the directors must allow market forces to operate freely to bring the shareholders of the target corporation the best price available for their equity. (Revlon, Inc. v. MacAndrews & Forbes Holdings, Inc.)

[For more information on Directors' Adoption of a Merger Plan, see Casenote Law Outline on Corporations, Chapter 8, § IV, Fiduciary Duties of Care and Loyalty.]

10. **Tender Offers.** The business judgment rule will be applied to a board's adoption of a defensive measure where the board proves reasonable grounds for believing that a danger to corporate policy and effectiveness existed, and that the defensive measure was reasonable in relation to the threat posed. (Paramount Communications, Inc. v. Time Inc.)

[For more information on strategy to repel hostile takeovers, see Casenote Law Outline on Corporations, Chapter 8, § IV, Fiduciary Duties of Care and Loyalty.]

11. **Tender Offers.** The conduct of corporate directors will be subjected to enhanced scrutiny for reasonableness where it involves the approval of a transaction resulting in a sale of control and the adoption of defensive measures in response to a threat to corporate control. (Paramount Communications, Inc. v. QVC Network)

[For more information on fiduciary duties of target companies, see Casenote Law Outline on Corporations, Chapter 8, § IV, Fiduciary Duties of Care and Loyalty.]

12. **Tender Offers.** To the extent that a contract, or provision thereof, purports to require a board to act or not act in such a fashion as to limit the exercise of fiduciary duties, it is invalid and unenforceable. (Quickturn Design Systems, Inc. v. Shapiro)

KATZ v. BREGMAN
Shareholder (P) v. Chief executive officer (P)
Del. Ct. of Chancery, 431 A.2d 1274 (1981).

NATURE OF CASE: Action to enjoin proposed sale of corporate assets.

FACT SUMMARY: In Katz's (P) action against Bregman (D), the chief executive officer of Plant Industries, to enjoin the proposed sale of the Canadian assets of Plant, Katz (P), a Plant shareholder, contended that a sale of substantially all the assets of a corporation required the unanimous vote of the stockholders.

CONCISE RULE OF LAW: Under Delaware law the decision of a corporation to sell all or substantially all of its property and assets requires not only the approval of the corporation's board of directors, but also a resolution adopted by a majority of the outstanding stockholders of the corporation entitled to vote.

FACTS: Katz (P) was the owner of approximately 170,000 shares of common stock of Plant Industries. Bregman (D), the chief executive officer of Plant, embarked on a course of action designed to dispose of Plant's Canadian assets. Katz (P) then brought an action to enjoin the sale of the Canadian assets, contending that a sale of all or substantially all the assets of a corporation required the unanimous vote of the shareholders.

ISSUE: Under Delaware law, does the decision of a corporation to sell all or substantially all of its property and assets require the approval not only of the corporation's board of directors, but also a resolution adopted by a majority of the outstanding shareholders of the corporation entitled to vote?

HOLDING AND DECISION: (Marvel, J.) Yes. Under Delaware law, the decision of a corporation to sell all or substantially all of its property and assets requires not only the approval of the corporation's board of directors, but also a resolution adopted by a majority of the outstanding stockholders of the corporation entitled to vote. Katz (P), in his bid for relief sought, relied on the fact that the board studiously refused to consider a potentially higher bid for the assets in question. Here, the proposed sale of Plant's Canadian operations would, if consummated, constitute a sale of substantially all of the assets of Plant Industries as presently constituted. Thus, under the law of the State of Delaware, an injunction should issue preventing the consummation of such sale at least until it has been approved by a majority of the outstanding stockholders of Plant, entitled to vote at a meeting duly called on at least 20 days' notice. A preliminary injunction against the consummation of such transaction, at least until stockholder approval is obtained, will be granted.

EDITOR'S ANALYSIS: At common law, it is generally accepted that a sale of substantially all assets of a corporation required unanimous shareholder approval. This is based on the theory that such a sale breached an implied contract among the shareholders to further the corporate enterprise. The case law has held that a sale of substantially all assets in the ordinary course of business does not require shareholder approval on the theory that such a sale does not prevent furtherance of the corporate enterprise.

[For more information on Acts of Board Directors, see Casenote Law Outline on Corporations, Chapter 2, § II, Viewing the Corporation from Within.]

QUICKNOTES

SUBSIDIARY - A company a majority of whose shares are owned by another corporation and which is subject to that corporation's control.

8 DEL. C., § 271 - Governs mergers where purchasing corporation buys with their own shares.

NOTES:

HARITON v. ARCO ELECTRONICS, INC.
Shareholder (P) v. Corporation (D)
182 A.2d 22; aff'd, 188 A.2d 123 (1963).

NATURE OF CASE: Action to declare sale of corporate assets void.

FACT SUMMARY: Arco (D) sold all of its assets to Loral Corporation in exchange for Loral common stock. Hariton (P), a shareholder in Arco (D), challenged the transaction as a de facto merger.

CONCISE RULE OF LAW: A corporation may sell its assets to another corporation even if the result is the same as a merger without following the statutory merger requirements.

FACTS: Arco (D) was an electronics distributor and Loral an electronics producer. The two corporations entered into an agreement under which Arco's assets would be sold to Loral in exchange for Loral stock, after which the Loral stock would be distributed to Arco (D) shareholders and Arco would dissolve. Arco (D) called a special meeting at which the shareholders present voted unanimously in favor of the sale. After the transaction was carried out, Hariton (P), an Arco (D) shareholder, challenged the action as a de facto merger and sued to have it set aside since the statutory merger provisions were not complied with. Arco (D) argued that it had engaged in a legal sale of corporate assets and had complied with all the applicable provisions.

ISSUE: If a transaction is in the form of a sale of corporate assets, but has the same effect as if a merger had been undertaken, must the formalities of a merger be followed?

HOLDING AND DECISION: (Southerland, C.J.) No. The statutes dealing with merger and sale of corporate assets may be overlapping in the sense that they may be used to achieve similar results, but the two procedures are subject to equal dignity. If all of the applicable provisions are complied with, a corporation may achieve a result in a manner which would be illegal under another statute. In other words, there is no interaction between these statutes, and since the sale of corporate assets statute was followed correctly, the provisions of the merger statute are of no relevance. The theory of de facto merger can only be introduced by the legislature, not the courts. Also, it is impossible to differentiate this transaction from one in which no dissolution of the selling corporation is required by the agreement since Arco (D) continued in existence after the sale, even though only to distribute the Loral stock to its shareholders. Therefore, Arco (D) didn't immediately cease to exist as it would have in an actual merger. Finally, the rationale of de facto merger which is based upon the theory that a shareholder shouldn't be forced to accept a new investment in a different corporation fails in this case. In Delaware, there is no right of appraisal for a sale of corporate assets, so Hariton (P) knew when he purchased the Arco (D) stock that Arco (D) might at any time sell all of its assets for stock in another corporation.

EDITOR'S ANALYSIS: The Hariton decision rejects the de facto merger doctrine set forth in Farris. The reason for the Hariton holding is a desire to give corporations greater freedom of reorganization than is given under the restrictive merger statutes. The court mentions that the fact that no appraisal right is given for a sale of corporate assets is a possible indication of legislative sympathy for corporate freedom. The Hariton result is the minority rule and has been criticized for its emphasis on the form rather than the substance of the transaction in question. Since the merger procedure is authorized to achieve the result sought by Arco (D), it seems unfair to allow the use of another device to obtain the same result indirectly in order to deny the protections given to minority shareholders under the more direct approach.

[For more information on Asset Sales, see Casenote Law Outline on Corporations, Chapter 8, § I, State Corporation Law.]

QUICKNOTES

MERGER - The acquisition of one company by another, after which the acquired company ceases to exist as an independent entity.

8 DEL. C., § 271 - Governs mergers where purchasing corporation buys with their own shares.

DE FACTO MERGER - The acquisition of one company by another without compliance with the requirements of a statutory merger but treated by the courts as such.

NOTES:

FARRIS v. GLEN ALDEN CORPORATION
Shareholder (P) v. Corporation (D)
Pa. Sup. Ct., 393 Pa. 440, 143 A.2d 25 (1958).

NATURE OF CASE: Action to enjoin performance of a corporate reorganization agreement.

FACT SUMMARY: Glen Alden (D) and List Corporation entered into a reorganization agreement under which Glen Alden (D) was to acquire List's assets. Farris (P), a stockholder in Glen Alden (D), sued to enjoin performance of this agreement.

CONCISE RULE OF LAW: A transaction which is in the form of a sale of corporate assets but which is in effect a de facto merger of two corporations must meet the statutory merger requirements in order to protect the rights of minority shareholders.

FACTS: List, a holding company, purchased 38.5% of the outstanding stock of Glen Alden (D), a corporation engaged in mining and manufacture, and placed three of its directors on the Glen Alden (D) board. The two corporations entered into a "reorganization agreement" under which Glen Alden (D) was to purchase the assets of List and take over List's liabilities; List shareholders would receive stock in Glen Alden; and List would be dissolved. Notice of this agreement was sent to the shareholders of Glen Alden (D), who approved the agreement at their annual meeting. Farris (P), a shareholder of Glen Alden (D), filed this suit to enjoin performance of the agreement on the ground that the notice to the shareholders of the proposed agreement did not conform to the statutory requirements for a proposed merger. Glen Alden (D) defended on the basis that the form of the transaction was a sale of assets rather than a merger so the merger statute was inapplicable.

ISSUE: Is the "reorganization agreement" a plan for a de facto merger, requiring conformance by the corporations to the merger statutes?

HOLDING AND DECISION: (Cohen, J.) Yes. To decide whether a transaction is in fact a merger or only a sale of assets, a court must look not to the formalities of the agreement but to its practical effect. Under Pennsylvania law, a shareholder of a corporation which is planning to merge has a right to dissent and get paid fair value for his shares, but has no such rights if his corporation is merely purchasing the assets of another corporation. A transaction is a de facto merger, and these rights must be granted to dissenting shareholders, if the agreement will so change the corporate character that to refuse to allow the shareholder to dissent will, in effect, force him to give up his shares in one corporation and accept shares in an entirely different corporation. If this agreement is performed, Farris (P) will become a shareholder in a larger corporation which is engaged in an entirely different type of business; the new corporation will have a majority of directors appointed by List; Farris (P) will have a smaller percentage of ownership because of the shares issued to the List shareholders; and the market value of his shares will decrease. This, then, is a de facto merger and Glen Alden (D) must follow the statutory merger requirements even though the transaction is in the form of a purchase of List's assets. Also, even if this were a purchase of assets, the reality of the agreement is that List is acquiring Glen Alden, despite the form which states that Glen Alden (D) is acquiring List, and under Pennsylvania law shareholders of a purchased corporation also have a statutory right to dissent. Therefore, even if this were not a de facto merger, Farris (P) still has a right to dissent.

EDITOR'S ANALYSIS: Because of the statutory merger requirements, corporations will try to achieve the effect of a merger by alternative methods, such as a sale of assets or a sale of stock. The formal merger requirements are consent by the shareholders of both corporations and majority approval by the directors. Glen Alden illustrates the resulting rights of a dissenting shareholder to demand appraisal — requiring the corporation to purchase his shares before the merger can take place. The rationale of the appraisal right is that the shareholder purchased the shares of a specific corporation, and to force him to exchange his stock in the corporation he chose for stock in an entirely different corporation is to deprive him of his property. Compare this with the rationale in Applestein v. United Board & Carton Corp.

[For more information on De Facto Merger Doctrine, see Casenote Law Outline on Corporations, Chapter 8, § I, State Corporation Laws.]

QUICKNOTES
DE FACTO MERGER - The acquisition of one company by another without compliance with the requirements of a statutory merger but treated by the courts as such.

PENN. CORP. LAW § 311(f) - Shareholders of a corporation that acquires another corporation by issuance of stock shall not be entitled to rights and remedies of dissenting shareholders.

TERRY v. PENN CENTRAL CORP.
Shareholder (P) v. Corporation (D)
668 F.2d 188 (3d Cir. 1981).

NATURE OF CASE: Diversity action to enforce voting and dissenters' rights.

FACT SUMMARY: Terry (P) and other shareholders in Penn Central (D) sought judicial enforcement of voting and dissenters' rights to which they maintained they were entitled even though the underlying transaction that they complained of was a merger of Colt Industries Inc. into PCC Holdings, Inc., a wholly-owned subsidiary of Penn Central (D).

CONCISE RULE OF LAW: Pennsylvania corporate law provides voting and dissenter's rights for shareholders of parties to a merger and the de facto merger doctrine does not apply to extend those rights to shareholders of entities that are not parties to the merger.

FACTS: Some of the shareholders in Penn Central (D), including Terry (P), brought an action to enforce voting and dissenters' rights in relation to a proposed merger between PCC Holdings, Inc., a wholly-owned subsidiary of Penn Central (D), and Colt Industries Inc. Pennsylvania law provides for such rights for shareholders of parties to a merger. Terry (P) maintained that the merger was a de facto merger between Colt and Penn Central (D), and that the Penn Central (D) shareholders were thus entitled to the voting and dissenters' rights provided for by Pennsylvania law. Relief was denied, and an appeal followed.

ISSUE: Does the de facto merger doctrine apply to extend to shareholders of entities that are not parties to the merger those voting and dissenters' rights given by state statute to the shareholders of parties to a merger?

HOLDING AND DECISION: (Adams, C.J.) No. Under Pennsylvania law, shareholders of corporations that are parties to a plan of merger are entitled to dissent and appraisal rights. The law also dictates that for acquisitions other than by merger the only rights are those based upon the statutory provision that grants dissent and appraisal rights in those limited instances in which an acquisition is accompanied by "the issuance of voting shares of such corporation to be outstanding immediately after the acquisition sufficient to elect a majority of the directors of the corporation." The merger at issue does not put Penn Central (D) shareholders under the latter statutory provision. Nor does the de facto merger doctrine provide a mechanism for the Penn Central (D) stockholders to claim rights under the first-mentioned statutory provision as parties to the merger. Affirmed.

EDITOR'S ANALYSIS: Historically, there was a period in which the courts favored the de facto merger doctrine and applied it widely. In a number of states, the legislature responded by rewording statutes or adding provisions designed to constrict the de facto merger doctrine. Since then, the courts have applied it very sparingly.

[For more information on Dissenters' Rights, see Casenote Law Outline on Corporations, Chapter 8, § I, State Corporation Laws.]

QUICKNOTES

DE FACTO MERGER - The acquisition of one company by another without compliance with the requirements of a statutory merger but treated by the courts as such.

PENNSYLVANIA BUS. CORP. LAW, § 908 - Shareholders objecting to a merger are entitled to sell at market value.

NOTES:

STERLING v. MAYFLOWER HOTEL CORP.
Shareholder (P) v. Corporation (D)
33 Del. Ch. 293, 93 A.2d 107, 38 A.L.R. 2d 425 (1952).

NATURE OF CASE: Suit to enjoin proposed merger of two corporations.

FACT SUMMARY: Mayflower Corp. (D) and Hilton Hotels Corp. entered into a merger agreement under which one share of Mayflower (D) would be exchanged for one share of Hilton. Sterling (P), a Mayflower (D) shareholder, attacked the transaction as unfair to minority shareholders.

CONCISE RULE OF LAW: When the terms of a proposed merger are, in the light of all relevant factors of valuation, fair to the minority shareholders, and there is no evidence of fraud or bad faith, the proposed merger will not be enjoined.

FACTS: Mayflower (D) owned and operated one hotel. Hilton Hotels purchased a majority of the outstanding Mayflower (D) shares at $19.10 a share in contemplation of a merger. After obtaining majority control, Hilton Hotels replaced the entire Mayflower (D) board of directors with its own nominees. To determine the proper basis of exchange of Mayflower (D) stock for Hilton stock under the merger, the board of directors hired a financial analyst to make an independent study. The original result of the study was that the proper basis of exchange should be three-fourths of a share of Hilton for one share of Mayflower, but, after a delay, an updated report found the proper basis of exchange to be one for one. The board relied on this report in drawing up the proposed merger, and the plan was approved by the Mayflower (D) shareholders. Sterling (P), a minority Mayflower (D) shareholder, brought suit to enjoin the approved merger because a quorum of Mayflower directors was not present when the merger plan was approved and on the additional ground that the terms were unfair to minority shareholders.

ISSUE: Is the proposed merger with its parent corporation so unfair to minority shareholders that the merger must be enjoined?

HOLDING AND DECISION: (Southerland, C.J.) No. After considering all relevant factors, the basis of exchange of Mayflower (D) stock for Hilton stock is found fair to minority shareholders. The basic question in determining the fairness of terms of the proposed merger is whether, after the conversion of stock, a shareholder will have the substantial equivalent of the value of the shares he had before conversion. Since Hilton is a majority shareholder and has appointed all of the directors, Hilton stands in a fiduciary position in relation to the minority shareholders in dealing with their property. Since Hilton is on both sides of the transaction, Hilton has the burden of establishing the fairness of the proposed exchange, and is subject to close judicial scrutiny. Since Hilton and Mayflower (D) decided to merge, they can use that procedure, but they have a duty to give the minority

fair and equitable terms of conversion. Sterling's (D) position is that, despite the fact that the transaction is termed a merger, in reality it is a sale of assets by a fiduciary to himself. If this argument were accepted, the court could determine fairness only by comparing the value of the assets given up by Mayflower (the value of the hotel property itself) with the value of the Hilton shares given in exchange. The value of the assets of the corporation is called the liquidity value (as contrasted to the market value) of the shares. This proposed test must be rejected. In a sale of corporate assets, the corporation is liquidated and the corporation gets the value of the assets sold. In a merger, the business continues and the shareholder's investment continues, and the shareholder is to recover shares substantially equal to those he had before the merger. Since there is an exchange of stock in two going concerns, the liquidity value is only one factor to be considered in arriving at a fair value for comparison purposes. Since this is a hotel business and the assets are fixed (not to be sold), the value of the shares is also to be determined by the earning power of the stock. Taking all of these factors into consideration, the report of the financial analyst shows that the conversion rate was fair, and the merger will not be enjoined. The fact that Hilton purchased shares at $19.10 is not proof that the shares are worth that for conversion purposes because Hilton paid greater than real value in order to get a large enough block of stock to assure majority control. Sterling (P) also challenges the action of the board of directors on the ground that a quorum of disinterested (unconnected with Hilton) directors was not present. However, the certificate of incorporation of Mayflower (D) permits the counting of interested directors for quorum purposes, and this provision is valid. Of course, this does not affect the remaining question of the fairness of the action taken, which was discussed above.

EDITOR'S ANALYSIS: In this case, rather than claiming his appraisal rights, Sterling (P) challenged the fairness of the proposed merger. Unlike the Ziebarth case, the court here allows a challenge on the ground of unfairness rather than requiring proof of fraud. The Sterling discussion of valuation is also relevant to the right of appraisal. Rather than stating that market value is to be paid to a dissenting shareholder, most statutes only state that "fair value" must be paid, and the same factors as discussed in Sterling determine what is fair value. The basis is generally the investment value which turns on the future prospects of earnings and opportunities. As Sterling points out, the present value of the assets of the corporation is not controlling except in businesses such as a corporation involved in selling real estate. Instead, the test is the future earning power of the stock being valued.

[For more information on Dissenters' Rights, see Casenote Law Outline on Corporations, Chapter 8, § I, State Corporation Laws.]

UNOCAL CORP. v. MESA PETROLEUM CO.
Target corporation (D) v. Takeover corporation (P)
Del. Sup. Ct., 493 A.2d. 946 (1985).

NATURE OF CASE: Interlocutory appeal from a temporary restraining order.

FACT SUMMARY: Mesa (P), which was a stockholder in Unocal (D), was attempting a takeover that Unocal's (D) directors tried to fight by making an exchange offer from which Mesa (P) was excluded.

CONCISE RULE OF LAW: Unless it is shown that the directors' decision in fighting a takeover was primarily based on perpetuating themselves in office, or some other breach of fiduciary duty, a court will not substitute its judgment for that of the board.

FACTS: In response to a takeover attempt by Mesa (P), one of the shareholders in Unocal (D), the Board of Directors of Unocal (D) determined that the takeover was not in the best interests of the corporation and should be fought. To do so, Unocal (D) made its own exchange offer, from which Mesa (P) was excluded. Mesa (P) sought and obtained a preliminary injunction from proceeding with the exchange offer unless it included Mesa (P). One of the main issues when the matter was heard via an interlocutory appeal was whether or not the action taken by the board was covered by the business judgment rule.

ISSUE: Will a Court substitute its own judgment for that of the board unless it is shown by a preponderance of the evidence that the directors' decision in fighting a takeover by one of the shareholders was primarily based on perpetuating themselves in office, or some other breach of fiduciary duty?

HOLDING AND DECISION: (Moore, J.) No. Unless it is shown by a preponderance of the evidence that the directors' decision in fighting a takeover by one of the shareholders in the corporation was primarily based on perpetuating themselves in office, or some other breach of fiduciary duty, a Court will not substitute its judgment for that of the board. There is no duty owed to a stockholder in a corporation that would preclude the directors from fighting a takeover bid by the stockholder if the board determines that the takeover is not in the best interests of the corporation. If such a decision is made, the court will not substitute its judgment for that of the board unless it is shown by a preponderance of the evidence that the directors' decision was primarily based on perpetuating themselves in office, or some other breach of fiduciary duty such as fraud, overreaching, lack of good faith, or being uninformed. No such showing was made here. Reversed.

EDITOR'S ANALYSIS: The business judgment rule protects only those actions by directors that are reasonable in relation to the threat posed. Among the considerations the courts have held are appropriate concerns of the board of directors in taking "defensive" actions is the impact on "constituencies" other than shareholders (such as creditors, customers, employees, and maybe even the community generally) and, also, the risk of nonconsummation.

[For more information on directors' fiduciary duties in a takeover, see Casenote Law Outline on Corporations, Chapter 8, § IV, Fiduciary Duties of Care and Loyalty.]

QUICKNOTES

TENDER OFFER - An offer made by one corporation to the shareholders of a target corporation to purchase their shares subject to number, time, and price specifications.

PROXY STATEMENT - A statement, containing specified information by the Securities and Exchange Commission, in order to provide shareholders with adequate information upon which to make an informed decision regarding the solicitation of their proxies.

8 DEL. C. § 141(a) - Businesses shall be managed by a board of directors.

INTERLOCUTORY APPEAL - The appeal of an issue that does not resolve the disposition of the case, but is essential to a determination of the parties' legal rights.

NOTES:

WEINBERGER v. UOP, INC.
Former minority shareholder (P) v. Corporation (D)
Del. Sup. Ct., 457 A.2d 701 (1983).

NATURE OF CASE: Class action to rescind a merger.

FACT SUMMARY: Claiming that a cash-out merger between UOP (D) and Signal (D) was unfair, Weinberger (P), a former minority shareholder of UOP, brought a class action to have the merger rescinded.

CONCISE RULE OF LAW: When seeking to secure minority shareholder approval for a proposed cashout merger, the corporations involved must comply with the fairness test which has two basic interrelated aspects: (1) fair dealings — which imposes a duty on the corporations to completely disclose to the shareholders all information germane to the merger; and (2) fair price — which requires that the price being offered for the outstanding stock be equivalent to a price determined by an appraisal where "all relevant nonspeculative factors" were considered.

FACTS: Signal, Inc. (D) owned 50.5% of UOP (D) stock. Seven of UOP's (D) 13 directors, including the President, were also directors or employees of Signal (D). Arledge and Chitiea, who were directors of UOP (D) and Signal (D), prepared a feasibility study for Signal (D). The study reported that it would be a good investment for Signal (D) to acquire the remaining 49.5% of UOP shares through a cashout merger at any price up to $24 per share. The study was given to all the Signal (D) directors including those who also served as directors on UOP's (D) Board. However, the evidence indicates that the study was never disclosed to UOP's (D) six non-Signal, i.e., outside, directors. Nor was it disclosed to the minority shareholders who owned the remaining 49.5% of UOP stock. On February 28, Signal (D) offered UOP (D) a cash-out merger price of $21 per share. Four business days later on March 6, the six non-Signal UOP directors (the seven common Signal-UOP directors abstained from the voting) voted to approve the merger at $21 per share. The vote was largely due to the fact that at the time, UOP's (D) market price was only $14.50 per share and also there was a "fairness opinion letter" from UOP's (D) investment banker stating that the $21 per share was a fair price. The merger was then approved by a majority (51.9%) of the minority, i.e., the remaining 49.5%, of UOP (D) shareholders. Weinberger (P), a former minority shareholder of UOP (D) then brought a class action to have the merger rescinded, claiming it was unfair to UOP's (D) former shareholders. The Court of Chancery held for UOP (D) and Signal (D). Weinberger (P) appealed.

ISSUE: May a minority shareholder successfully challenge the approval of a cash-out merger that was approved by the majority of the minority shareholders?

HOLDING AND DECISION: (En banc) Yes. A minority shareholder may successfully challenge the approval of a cash-out merger that was approved by the majority of the minority shareholders if he can demonstrate that the corporations involved failed to comply with the fairness test in securing the approval. The fairness test consists of two basic interrelated aspects. The first aspect is "fair dealings," which imposes a duty on the corporations involved to completely disclose to the minority shareholders all information germane to the merger. Here Signal (D) failed to disclose, to the non-Signal UOP (D) directors and the minority shareholders of UOP (D), the Arledge-Chitiea feasibility study that reported it would be a "good investment" for Signal (D) to acquire the minority shares up to a price of $24 per share. In addition, UOP's minority was given the impression that the "fairness opinion letter" from UOP's investment banker had been drafted only after the banker had made a careful study, when, in fact, the investment banker had drafted the letter in three days with the price left blank. Consequently, Signal (D) did not meet the "fair dealing" aspect of the test. The second aspect of the fairness test is "fair price," which requires that the price being offered for the outstanding stock be equivalent to an appraisal where "all relevant nonspeculative factors" were considered. In this case, the Court of Chancery tested the fairness of Signal's (D) $21 per share price against the Delaware weighted average method of valuation. That method shall no longer exclusively control the determination of "fair price." Rather, a new method which considers "all relevant nonspeculative factors" shall now be used for determining fair price. This new method is consistent with the method used in determining a shareholder's appraisal remedy. Here, the Court of Chancery did not consider the $24 per share price determined by the Arledge-Chitiea study. Nor did the Court consider Weinberger's (P) discounted cash flow analysis, which concluded that the UOP (D) stock was worth $26 per share on the date of merger. Therefore, since these factors were not considered, it cannot be said that the $21 per share price paid by Signal (D) meets the new method of determining fair price. Finally, in view of the new, more liberal test for determining fair price, together with the Chancery Court's broad remedial discretion, it is concluded that the business purpose requirement for mergers, as required by the trilogy of Singer, Tanzer, and Najjar, 407 A.2d 1032 (Del. Sup. Ct. 1979), adds no further protection to minority shareholders. Accordingly, the business purpose requirement is no longer law. Reversed and remanded.

Continued on next page.

EDITOR'S ANALYSIS: This case demonstrates the use of a cash-out merger to eliminate or "freeze out" the minority interest. A footnote in the case suggests that Signal's (D) freeze out of UOP's (D) minority interest would have met the Court's fairness test if UOP (D) had appointed an independent negotiating committee of its non-Signal directors to deal with Signal (D) at arm's length.

[For more information on Dissenters' Rights, see Casenote Law Outline on Corporations, Chapter 8, § I, State Corporation Laws.]

QUICKNOTES

FREEZE-OUT - Merger whereby the majority shareholder forces minority shareholders into the sale of their securities.

BUSINESS PURPOSE RULE - Doctrine relieving corporate directors and/or officers from liability for decisions honestly and rationally made in the corporation's best interests.

INTERESTED DIRECTOR - A director of a corporation who has a personal interest in the subject matter of a transaction between the corporation and another party.

NOTES:

MORAN v. HOUSEHOLD INTERNATIONAL, INC.
Shareholder (P) v. Corporation (D)
Del. Sup. Ct., 500 A.2d 1346 (1985).

NATURE OF CASE: Appeal from enforcement of a Preferred Share Purchase Rights Plan.

FACT SUMMARY: Moran (P) contended the Household (D) board of directors lacked authority to thwart takeover bids through the use of a "Preferred Share Purchase Rights Plan."

CONCISE RULE OF LAW: Boards of directors may, under the business judgment rule, validly protect the corporation from hostile takeovers through the use of a Preferred Share Purchase Rights Program.

FACTS: In an attempt to thwart hostile takeover attempts, the board of directors of Household (D) adopted an amendment to its bylaws which provided that if a tender offer for 30% of the corporation's shares were announced, or if any one entity obtained 20% or more of the outstanding stock, common stockholders were entitled to the issuance of one Right per common share. Each Right then was entitled to purchase a fractional amount of a new preferred stock. If the Right was not redeemed, following a takeover, the holder could purchase $200 worth of the common stock of the tender offer, and a shareholder of Household (D) sued, contending such a plan was beyond the power of the board of directors. The trial court upheld the plan, and Moran (P) appealed.

ISSUE: May boards of directors validly protect the corporation from hostile takeovers through the use of a Preferred Share Purchase Rights Program?

HOLDING AND DECISION: (McNeilly, J.) Yes. Boards of directors may, under the business judgment rule, validly protect the corporation from hostile takeovers through the use of a Preferred Share Purchase Rights Program. The Rights were intended to and will be exercised upon the occurrence of the triggering events. Thus the plan cannot be considered a sham and was implemented with the best interests of the corporation in mind. This use of such a plan does not alter the structure by which the corporation is controlled, and, therefore, it was a valid defensive mechanism. Affirmed.

EDITOR'S ANALYSIS: Hostile takeovers have prompted many potential target corporations to adopt defensive tactics such as that illustrated in the present case. Such mechanisms are aimed at making the target less attractive by making the takeover more expensive. Differing levels of voting power triggered by a threshold level of concentrated ownership is a typical defensive device.

[For more information on Business Judgment Rule, see Casenote Law Outline on Corporations, Chapter 4, § I, State Corporation Codes and the Business Judgment Rule.]

QUICKNOTES
TENDER OFFER - An offer made by one corporation to the shareholders of a target corporation to purchase their shares subject to number, time, and price specifications.

BUSINESS JUDGMENT RULE - Doctrine relieving corporate directors and/or officers from liability for decisions honestly and rationally made in the corporation's best interests.

HOSTILE TENDER OFFER - Refers to a situation in which an outside group attempts to seize control of a target corporation against the will of the targeted company's officers, directors or shareholders.

8 DEL. C. § 151(g) - Governs rules on creating a new class of stock.

8 DEL. C. § 157 - Corporations may create different classes of stock with different rights.

NOTES:

REVLON, INC. v. MacANDREWS & FORBES HOLDINGS, INC.

Target corporation (D) v. Takeover corporation (P)

Del. Sup. Ct., 506 A.2d 173 (1986).

NATURE OF CASE: Interlocutory appeal from order enjoining certain corporate actions.

FACT SUMMARY: In seeking a preliminary injunction, MacAndrews (P) challenged the validity of certain actions taken by the directors of Revlon (D) in the face of what they considered to be a hostile takeover bid.

CONCISE RULE OF LAW: While directors may have regard for various constituencies in discharging their responsibilities vis-a-vis an attempted takeover, there must be rationally related benefits accruing to the stockholders and once the corporate dissolution becomes inevitable the directors must allow market forces to operate freely to bring the shareholders of the target corporation the best price available for their equity.

FACTS: Revlon's (D) board of directors took a number of actions designed to thwart what it considered to be a hostile takeover attempt by Pantry Pride. MacAndrews (P) was the controlling stockholder of Pantry Pride. A preliminary injunction was sought by MacAndrews (P) to enjoin certain actions Revlon's (D) directors had taken to thwart the takeover efforts. Specifically, challenge was made to the lock-up option and no-shop agreements made with Forstmann Little & Co., designed to enhance Forstmann's efforts at a friendly takeover. In addition to other evidence, the trial court heard evidence that the lock-up option allowing a favorable purchase of certain Revlon (D) assets by Forstmann were improper because the dissolution of Revlon (D) had become inevitable and that it rested on consideration of constituencies other than the stockholders (specifically, holders of certain Notes issued by Revlon as one of the measures to thwart the takeover by Pantry Pride). Revlon (D) appealed the decision granting the temporary injunction.

ISSUE: Once the dissolution of a corporation has become inevitable, must the directors allow market forces to operate freely to bring the shareholders of the target corporation the best price available for their equity?

HOLDING AND DECISION: (Yes. As long as directors of a target corporation legitimately conclude that a takeover bid is not in the corporation's best interests, they are free to take defensive action to prevent the takeover as long as they act with due care in so doing. They can consider other constituencies, as long as there are rationally related benefits accruing to the stockholders. However, once the corporate dissolution becomes inevitable, they must allow market forces to operate freely to bring the shareholders of the target corporation the best price available for

their equity. The evidence here indicates a strong possibility that once that point of inevitable dissolution was reached, Revlon's (D) directors continued to take action favoring one competitive bidder over another. In this context, such action is not entitled to the deference accorded it by the business judgment rule. Affirmed.

EDITOR'S ANALYSIS: One of the common mechanisms used to defend against a hostile takeover is the "poison pill." It is a plan by which shareholders in the target corporation are given the right to be bought out by the corporation at a substantial premium on the occurrence of a stated triggering event. Such a plan resulted in the Notes Revlon (D) issued in this case.

[For more information on Directors' Adoption of a Merger Plan, see Casenote Law Outline on Corporations, Chapter 8, § IV, Fiduciary Duties of Care and Loyalty.]

QUICKNOTES

LEVERAGED BUY OUT - A transaction whereby corporate outsiders purchase the outstanding shares of a publicly held corporation mostly with borrowed funds.

8 DEL. C. § 141(a) - Businesses shall be managed by a board of directors.

BUSINESS JUDGMENT RULE - Doctrine relieving corporate directors and/or officers from liability for decisions honestly and rationally made in the corporation's best interests.

POISON PILL - A tactic employed by a company, which is the target of a takeover attempt, to make the purchase of its shares less attractive to a potential buyer by requiring the issuance of a new series of shares to be redeemed at a substantial premium over their stated value if a party purchases a specified percentage of voting shares of the corporation.

NOTES:

PARAMOUNT COMMUNICATIONS, INC. v. TIME, INC.
Takeover corporation (P) v. Target corporation (D)
Del. Sup. Ct., 571 A.2d. 1140 (1989).

NATURE OF CASE: Appeal from denial of a motion to enjoin a tender offer.

FACT SUMMARY: After Time (D) and Warner Communications had finalized Time's (D) acquisition of Warner, Paramount Communications (P) made a tender offer for Time (D), which Time's (D) board rejected in the belief that the merger with Warner was in the shareholders' best interests in the long-term.

CONCISE RULE OF LAW: The business judgment rule will be applied to a board's adoption of a defensive measure where the board proves reasonable grounds for believing that a danger to corporate policy and effectiveness existed, and that the defensive measure was reasonable in relation to the threat posed.

FACTS: After extensive negotiations with Warner Communications, Time's (D) board approved a stock-for-stock merger with Warner. Time (D) publicized the lack of debt in the transaction as being one of its chief benefits. Paramount Communications (P) then announced a $175 per share offer for Time (D), which Time (D) formally rejected. Believing that Paramount's (P) offer presented a threat to Time's (D) control of its own destiny and the "Time Culture," the board decided to fund the acquisition of Warner by incurring $7–10 billion of debt, despite its original assertion that the debt-free nature of the combination was one of its principal benefits. Time's (D) board also rejected Paramount's (P) later offer of $200 per share, on the grounds that it was still inadequate and that Time's (D) acquisition of Warner offered a greater long-term value for the stockholders without threatening Time's (D) survival and its culture. Paramount (P), along with two groups of Time (D) shareholders, sought to enjoin Time's (D) tender offer. When the court of chancery denied the motions, this appeal followed.

ISSUE: Will the business judgment rule be applied to a board's adoption of a defensive measure where the board proves reasonable grounds for believing that a danger to corporate policy and effectiveness existed and that the defensive measure was reasonable in relation to the threat posed?

HOLDING AND DECISION: (Horsey, J.) Yes. The business judgment rule will be applied to a board's adoption of a defensive measure where the board proves reasonable grounds for believing that a danger to corporate policy and effectiveness existed and that the defensive measure was reasonable in relation to the threat posed. Where a board's reaction to a hostile tender offer is found to constitute only a defensive response and not an abandonment of the corporation's continued existence,

the duties established by Revlon, Inc. v. MacAndrews & Forbes Holdings, Inc., 506 A.d. 173, 182 (Del. Sup. 1986) are not triggered. However, the duties established by Unocal Corp. v. Mesa Petroleum Co., 493 A.d. 946, 955 (Del. Sup.. 1985) do attach. There was ample evidence in the record to support the Chancellor's conclusion that the Time (D) board's original decision to expand the business of the company through its merger with Warner was entitled to the protection of the business judgment rule. However, the revised agreement was defense-motivated and designed to avoid the potentially disruptive effect that Paramount's (P) offer would have had on consummation of the proposed merger were it put to a shareholder vote. Thus, the Unocal two-tiered test must be applied. Although the Chancellor blurred somewhat the discrete analyses required under Unocal, he did conclude that Time's (D) board reasonably perceived Paramount's (P) offer to be a significant threat to the planned Time-Warner merger and that Time's (D) response was not overly broad. The revised agreement and its accompanying safety devices did not preclude Paramount (P) from making an offer for the combined Time-Warner company or from changing the conditions of its offer so as not to make the offer dependent upon the nullification of the Time-Warner agreement. Affirmed.

EDITOR'S ANALYSIS: Although Time (D) was required, as a result of Paramount's (P) hostile offer, to incur a heavy debt to finance its acquisition of Warner, that fact alone did not render the board's decision unreasonable so long as the directors reasonably perceived the debt load not to be so injurious to the corporation as to jeopardize its well being. The fiduciary duty to manage a corporate enterprise includes the selection of a time frame for achievement of corporate goals. That duty may not be delegated to the stockholders. Directors are not obliged to abandon a deliberately conceived long-term corporate plan for a short-term shareholder profit unless there is clearly no basis to sustain the corporate strategy.

[For more information on strategy to repel hostile takeovers, see Casenote Law Outline on Corporations, Chapter 8, § IV, Fiduciary Duties of Care and Loyalty.]

QUICKNOTES

TENDER OFFER - An offer made by one corporation to the shareholders of a target corporation to purchase their shares subject to number, time, and price specifications.

PARAMOUNT COMMUNICATIONS, INC. v.
QVC NETWORK, INC.

Corporation/Board of Director (D) v.
Corporation/Shareholders (P)

Del. Sup. Ct., 637 A.d. 34 (1993).

NATURE OF CASE: Appeal from a preliminary injunction against defensive measures employed to thwart an unsolicited tender offer.

FACT SUMMARY: When the Paramount (D) directors chose a merger with Viacom (D) over the more valuable, unsolicited, hostile offer of QVC (P), the Court of Chancery granted a preliminary injunction, finding that the Paramount (D) directors violated their fiduciary duties.

CONCISE RULE OF LAW: The conduct of corporate directors will be subjected to enhanced scrutiny for reasonableness where it involves the approval of a transaction resulting in a sale of control and the adoption of defensive measures in response to a threat to corporate control.

FACTS: After extensive negotiations, Paramount (D) entered into an agreement with Viacom (D), whereby Paramount (D) would merge with and into Viacom (D). The merger agreement contained several defensive provisions designed to make it more difficult for a potential competing bid to succeed. Nevertheless, QVC (P) proposed a merger in which it would acquire Paramount (D). Viacom (D) and QVC (P) then entered into a bidding war for Paramount (D), with QVC (P) finally offering the highest amount for a proposed merger. The Paramount Board (D) turned down the more lucrative QVC (P) offer in favor of Viacom (D), in the stated belief that the Viacom (D) transaction would be more advantageous to Paramount's (D) future business prospects than a QVC (P) transaction. QVC (P) and certain stockholders of Paramount (D) commenced separate actions (later consolidated), seeking preliminary and permanent injunctive relief against Paramount (D), certain members of the Paramount Board (D), and Viacom (D). The Court of Chancery granted a preliminary injunction, finding that the Paramount (D) directors violated their fiduciary duties by favoring the Paramount-Viacom (D) transaction over the more valuable, unsolicited offer of QVC (P). Paramount (D) appealed.

ISSUE: Will the conduct of corporate directors be subjected to enhanced scrutiny for reasonableness where it involves the approval of a transaction resulting in a sale of control and the adoption of defensive measures in response to a threat to corporate control?

HOLDING AND DECISION: (Veasey, J.) Yes. The conduct of corporate directors will be subjected to enhanced scrutiny for reasonableness where it involves the approval of a transaction

resulting in a sale of control and the adoption of defensive measures in response to a threat to corporate control. In the sale of control context, the directors must focus on one primary objective — to secure the transaction offering the best value reasonably available for the stockholders — and they must exercise their fiduciary duties to further that end. Furthermore, when entering into the agreement with Viacom (D), and thereafter, the Paramount Board (D) clearly gave insufficient attention to the potential consequences of the defensive measures demanded by Viacom (D). The Stock Option Agreement, for example, was not "capped" to limit its maximum dollar value and had the potential to reach, and in this case did reach, unreasonable levels. Further, the No-Shop Provision inhibited the Paramount Board's (D) ability to negotiate with other potential bidders, particularly QVC (P). QVC's (P) unsolicited bid presented the opportunity for significantly greater value for the stockholders and enhanced negotiating leverage for the directors. Rather than seizing those opportunities, the Paramount (D) directors chose to wall themselves off from material information which was reasonably available and to hide behind the defensive measures as a rationalization for refusing to negotiate with QVC (P) or seeking other alternatives. Affirmed and remanded.

EDITOR'S ANALYSIS: The Paramount-Viacom (D) transaction had economic consequences of considerable significance to the Paramount (D) stockholders. Once control shifted, the current Paramount (D) stockholders would have no leverage in the future to demand another control premium, since they would then be minority stockholders. As a result, they were entitled to receive a control premium and/or protective devices of significant value. There were no such protective provisions in the Viacom-Paramount (D) transaction.

[For more information on fiduciary duties of target companies, see Casenote Law Outline on Corporations, Chapter 8, § IV, Fiduciary Duties of Care and Loyalty.]

QUICKNOTES

VESTED RIGHT - Rights in pension or other retirement benefits that are attained when the employee satisfies the minimum requirements necessary in order to be entitled to the receipt of such benefits in the future.

QUICKTURN DESIGN SYSTEMS INC. v. SHAPIRO
Target company (D) v. Hostile takeover bidder (P)
Del. Sup. Ct., 721 A.2d 1281 (1998).

NATURE OF CASE: Appeal from an order holding that a target company's directors had breached their fiduciary duties.

FACT SUMMARY: When Mentor Graphics Company (P), a hostile bidder, sought to acquire Quickturn (D), Quickturn's (D) board amended its bylaws to delay the ability of a newly-appointed, Mentor (P)-elected board to redeem the shareholders rights plan

CONCISE RULE OF LAW: To the extent that a contract, or provision thereof, purports to require a board to act or not act in such a fashion as to limit the exercise of fiduciary duties, it is invalid and unenforceable.

FACTS: In response to a tender offer and proxy contest initiated by Mentor (P), the Quickturn (D) board of directors had adopted a Delayed Redemption Provision (DRP) to its shareholders rights plan, and an amendment to the corporate bylaws delaying the holding of any special shareholders meetings. Mentor (P), the hostile bidder, and Shapiro (P), a shareholder, filed actions for declaratory and injunctive relief in the Court of Chancery, challenging the legality of both defensive responses. The Court of Chancery concluded that the by-law amendment was valid but the DRP was invalid. Quickturn (D) appealed.

ISSUE: Is a contract, or provision thereof, that purports to require a board to act or not act in such a fashion as to limit the exercise of fiduciary duties, invalid and unenforceable?

HOLDING AND DECISION: (Holland, J.) Yes. To the extent that a contract, or provision thereof, purports to require a board to act or not act in such a fashion as to limit the exercise of fiduciary duties, it is invalid and unenforceable. Under state law, the board of directors has the ultimate responsibility for managing the business and affairs of a corporation. Any limitation on the board's authority must be set out in the certificate of incorporation. Quickturn's (D) DRP tends to limit in a substantial way the freedom of newly elected directors' decisions on matters of management policy. Therefore it violates the duty of each director to exercise his own best judgment on matters coming before the board. Affirmed.

EDITOR'S ANALYSIS: When the board of a Delaware corporation takes action to resist a hostile takeover, the board of directors' defensive actions are subjected to enhanced judicial scrutiny. For a target board's actions to be entitled to business judgment rule protection, the target board must first establish that it had reasonable grounds to believe that the hostile bid constituted a threat to corporate policy and effectiveness. The defensive measures must also be proportionate, that is, reasonable in relation to the threat that the board reasonably perceived. The court found that the DRP could not pass this proportionality test.

13

CHAPTER 13
DISTRIBUTIONS TO SHAREHOLDERS

QUICK REFERENCE RULES OF LAW

1. **Traditional Statutes.** A corporation's balance sheets are not conclusive of whether the Delaware statute forbidding impairment of capital has been violated. (Klang v. Smith's Food and Drug Centers, Inc.)

2. **Purchase by a Corporation of it's own Stock.** Corporate purchase of its shares is permitted under Wisconsin law if, at the time of such acquisition, the corporation is not and would not thereby be rendered insolvent. (Neimark v. Mel Kramer Sales, Inc.)

[For more information on Acquisition, see Casenote Law Outline on Corporations, Chapter 8, § I, State Corporation Laws.]

KLANG v. SMITH'S FOOD & DRUG CENTERS, INC.

Shareholder (P) v. Corporation (D)

Del. Sup. Ct., 702 A.2d 150 (1997).

NATURE OF CASE: Appeal from dismissal of a purported class action to have certain transactions in a corporate merger and repurchase rescinded.

FACT SUMMARY: Klang (P) filed a class action complaint against Smith's Food & Drug (D) to rescind a merger transaction, arguing that repurchase of shares resulted in impairment of capital and the methodology used in its solvency opinion was inappropriate.

CONCISE RULE OF LAW: A corporation's balance sheets are not conclusive of whether the Delaware statute forbidding impairment of capital has been violated.

FACTS: Smith's Food & Drug Centers, Inc. (SFD) (D) entered into an agreement with Yucaipa Companies for a merger under which SFD (D) was to repurchase up to 50% of its shares. SFD (D) hired an investment firm to examine these transactions and issue a report with a solvency opinion. The firm determined that the merger could occur without risking SFD's (D) solvency or impairing SFD's (D) capital. Accordingly, the transactions closed, and SFD (D) repurchased 50% of its shares. Klang (P) filed a class action complaint with a motion to rescind the transactions, arguing that the stock repurchase violated 8 Del. C ss 160 by impairing SFD's (D) capital, as evidenced by SFD's (D) books showing a negative net worth following its transactions with Yucaipa. The lower court dismissed Klang's (P) claims in full, and he appealed.

ISSUE: Is the balance sheet method of determining surplus conclusive in finding whether the Delaware statute forbidding impairment of capital has been violated?

HOLDING AND DECISION: (Veasey, J.) The balance sheet method is not conclusive in determining whether the Delaware statute forbidding impairment of capital has been violated. Section 160 provides that a corporation may not repurchase its shares if doing so would result in an impairment of capital; a corporation may only repurchase shares if using "surplus." In showing surplus, a corporation may revalue its assets and liabilities to thereby comply with the statute. The statute defining surplus through "net assets" does not set forth a particular method in determining surplus; as long as the evaluation is based on good faith, acceptable data, and reasonable methods to render a surplus that is not so unrealistic that is would constitute actual or constructive fraud, a board may deviate from the balance sheet method. Affirmed.

EDITOR'S ANALYSIS: Balance sheet tests have been used to determine if a dividend would impair capital. This case allows a board to reasonably diverge from the balance sheet method if calculations are completed in good faith and with reasonable techniques. The court noted that restricting the calculation of surplus to a balance sheet method would not only be unrealistic (in that elements such as unrealized appreciation and depreciation might not be reflected on the sheet, but also potentially frustrate the purpose of statutes against impairment of capital (namely, to prevent draining of corporate assets and to maintain healthy corporations).

QUICKNOTES

CLASS ACTION - A suit commenced by a representative on behalf of an ascertainable group that is too large to appear in court, who shares a commonality of interests and who will benefit from a successful result.

NOTES:

NEIMARK v. MEL KRAMER SALES, INC.
Director (P) v. Corporation (D)
Wis. Ct. of App., 102 Wis.2d 282 (1981).

NATURE OF CASE: Appeal from order of specific performance of a stock redemption agreement.

FACT SUMMARY: In Neimark's (P) action against Mel Kramer Sales, Inc. (D) for specific performance of a stock redemption agreement, Neimark (P) contended that Kramer's (D) failure to perform the agreement constituted injury to Kramer (D) because such conduct neglected to take advantage of a $60,000 credit upon the purchase price of the stock and hazarded the acquisition of the stock by outsiders.

CONCISE RULE OF LAW: Corporate purchase of its shares is permitted under Wisconsin law if, at the time of such acquisition, the corporation is not and would not thereby be rendered insolvent.

FACTS: Neimark (P) was vice president and a director of Mel Kramer Sales, Inc. (D). Neimark (P) sought, after the death of Mel Kramer, founder and majority shareholder of Kramer (D), specific performance of an agreement for the redemption of stock owned by the late Mel Kramer. The agreement, executed several months before Mel Kramer's death, required Kramer (D) to purchase, and a deceased shareholder's estate to sell, all of the deceased shareholder's stock in Kramer at $400 per share. The redemption price of Mel Kramer's stock would have been $408,000, less a specifically provided credit of $50,000. At Mel Kramer's death, his widow was reluctant to have Kramer (D) redeem the shares owned by her husband's estate. Neimark (P) insisted that Kramer (D) redeem the estate's shares, arguing that Kramer's (D) failure to do so constituted injury to Kramer (D) because such conduct neglected to take advantage of the $50,000 credit upon the purchase price of the stock and hazarded the acquisition of the stock by outsiders. The trial court ordered specific performance of the stock redemption agreement, concluding that failure to perform would result in injury to Kramer (D). Kramer (D) appealed.

ISSUE: Is corporate purchase of its shares permitted, under Wisconsin law, if, at the time of such acquisition, the corporation is not and would not thereby be rendered insolvent?

HOLDING AND DECISION: (Decker, C.J.) Yes. Corporate purchase of its shares is permitted, under Wisconsin law, if, at the time of such acquisition, the corporation is not and would not thereby be rendered insolvent. Here, the trial court's finding was that performance of the stock redemption agreement would not render the corporation insolvent. This conclusion is not contrary to the great weight and clear preponderance of the evidence. In fact, the evidence establishes the fact that the corporation had the ability to pay its debts as they became due. Upon Mel Kramer's death, it became the obligation of Kramer (D) to redeem his stock according to the redemption agreement, provided the corporation could remain solvent in doing so. This court agrees with the trial court's finding of fact that it could. Affirmed.

EDITOR'S ANALYSIS: Often, agreements concerning a repurchase of corporate stock contemplate a future rather than a present transfer of stock. For example, it is not unusual for a corporation to issue stock and at the same time enter an agreement that either gives the corporation an option to repurchase the stock or gives the shareholder an option to resell it. Such agreements are most often used to facilitate the original marketing of stock.

[For more information on Acquisition, see Casenote Law Outline on Corporations, Chapter 8, § I, State Corporation Laws.]

QUICKNOTES

DERIVATIVE SUIT - Action asserted by a shareholder in order to enforce a cause of action on behalf of the corporation.

REDEMPTION - The repurchase of a security by the issuing corporation according to the terms specified in the security agreement specifying the procedure for the repurchase.

§ 180.385(1) - Prohibits acquisition by a corporation of its own stock if the corporation would be rendered insolvent.

NOTES:

14

CHAPTER 14
THE PUBLIC DISTRIBUTION OF SECURITIES

QUICK REFERENCE RULES OF LAW

1. **What Constitutes a "Securities".** Demand notes offered by an organization to support its general operations are securities. (Reves v. Ernst & Young)

2. **The Requirement of Registration.** The exemption in § 4(1) of the Securities Act of 1933, which exempts transactions by an issuer not involving any public offering from the registration requirement, applies only when all the offerees have access to the same kind of information that the act would make available if registration were required. (S.E.C. v. Ralston Purina Co.)

   [For more information on Federal Securities, § 4, see Casenote Law Outline on Corporations, Chapter 5, § III, Federal Securities Act, §§ 3 and 4.]

3. **Liabilities Under the Securities Act.** In a suit to recover damages under § 11 of the Securities Act of 1933 for the filing of a registration statement with material omissions and false statements, defendants other than the issuer can avoid liability by proving a "due diligence" defense. (Escott v. BarChris Constr. Corp.)

   [For more information on Federal Securities Act, § 11, see Casenote Law Outline on Corporations, Chapter 5, § IV, Federal Securities Act, §§ 11, 12 and 17.]

REVES v. ERNST & YOUNG
Parties not identified
494 U.S. 56 (1990).

NATURE OF CASE: Appeal of reversal of award of damages for violations of federal securities laws.

FACT SUMMARY: A controversy arose as to whether demand notes offered by an organization to support its general operations were securities.

CONCISE RULE OF LAW: Demand notes offered by an organization to support its general operations are securities.

FACTS: The Farmer's Cooperative of Arkansas and Oklahoma offered promissory notes, payable on demand, as part of an "Investment Program." The notes paid an adjustable interest rate. The notes were unsecured and used to fund the Cooperative's general operations. The Cooperative became insolvent, and its notes were worthless. Various plaintiffs filed an action against Ernst & Young (D), the auditor of the Cooperative's financial statements, alleging violations of state and federal securities laws. The district court found the notes to be securities, and the plaintiffs received $6.1 million in damages. The Eighth Circuit reversed, holding the notes not to be securities. The Supreme Court granted review.

ISSUE: Are demand notes offered by an organization to support its general operation securities.

HOLDING AND DECISION: (Marshall, J.) Yes. Demand notes offered by an organization to support its general operations are securities. "Notes" come within the statutory definition of a security. However, recognizing that not all notes come within the commonly understood notion of what a security is, this being an investment of money in a common enterprise managed by others in the expectation of receiving a profit, some judicially created exceptions exist. If the note is given to facilitate the purchase of a particular asset, it will not be considered a security. A home mortgage is a good example of this. Also fitting into this analysis is the reasonable expectation of the note holder. In light of this standard, there can be little question but that the instruments involved here are securities. They reflect investments in the general operations of the business in question, the principal and interest to be repaid out of the business' general profits. This, despite the absence of equity participation, is not dissimilar from common stock, the paradigm of a security. For these reasons, the Eight Circuit was incorrect. Reversed.

CONCURRENCE: (Stevens, J.) The statute excludes notes of less than nine months' maturity, which demand notes are. However, clear precedent limits this exclusion to commercial paper, not investment instruments.

CONCURRENCE AND DISSENT: (Rehnquist, C.J.) Demand notes should come within the less-than-nine-month maturity exclusion of § 3(a)(10) of the 1934 Securities Exchange Act.

EDITOR'S ANALYSIS: The human mind is infinitely ingenious with respect to devising investment strategies, and for that reason it was long ago recognized that a detailed list of what is and what is not security would be impossible to compile. Consequently, the statutory definition found in § 3(a)(10) is both lengthy and broad. The Supreme Court distilled the rather verbose language of the section in SEC v. W.J. Howey Co., 328 U.S. 293 (1946), to define as a security an interest in a common enterprise, managed by individuals other than the investor, with reasonable expectation of profit.

QUICKNOTES
SECURITIES EXCHANGE ACT, § 3(a)(10) - Defines security as any note, stock, debenture, etc.

NOTES:

SEC v. RALSTON PURINA CO.
Government agency (P) v. Stock issuer (D)
346 U.S. 119 (1953).

NATURE OF CASE: Action to enjoin the unregistered offerings of stock under the Securities Act of 1933.

FACT SUMMARY: Ralston Purina (D) offered treasury stock to their key employees which the SEC (P) attempted to enjoin.

CONCISE RULE OF LAW: The exemption in § 4(1) of the Securities Act of 1933, which exempts transactions by an issuer not involving any public offering from the registration requirement, applies only when all the offerees have access to the same kind of information that the act would make available if registration were required.

FACTS: Since 1911, Ralston Purina (D) had a policy of encouraging stock ownership among its employees and, since 1942, had made unissued common shares available to some of them. Ralston Purina (D) had sold nearly $2,000,000 of stock to employees between the years of 1947 and 1951. They had attempted to avoid the registration requirements of the Securities Act of 1933, under the exemption contained in § 4(1) of the Act which exempted transactions by an issuer not involving any public offering. Each year between 1947 and 1951, Ralston Purina (D) authorized the sale of common stock to employees who, without any solicitation by the Company or its officers or employees, inquired as to how to purchase common stock of Ralston Purina (D). The branch and store managers were advised that only the employees who took the initiative and were interested in buying stock at the present market prices would be able to purchase the stock. Among those taking advantage of the offer were employees with the duties of artist, bakeshop foreman, chow-loading foreman, clerical assistant, copywriter, electrician, stock clerk, mill office clerk, order credit trainee, production trainee, stenographer, and veterinarian. The buyers resided in fifty widely separated communities scattered throughout the United States. The record showed that in 1947, 243 employees bought stock, 20 in 1948, 414 in 1949, 411 in 1950, and, in 1951, 165 made applications to purchase the stock. No actual records were kept showing how many employees were offered the stock, but it was estimated that, in 1951, at least 500 employees were offered the stock. Ralston Purina (D) had approximately 7,000 employees during the years in question. Ralston Purina (D) based its exemption claim on the classification that all the offerees were key employees in its organization. Its position at trial was that a key employee included an individual who was eligible for promotion; an individual who especially influenced others or who advised others; a person whom the employees looked to in some special way; one who carried some special responsibility and who was sympathetic to management, and one who was ambitious and who the management felt was likely to be promoted to a greater responsibility. They admitted, however, that an offering to all of its employees would be a public offering. The district court held that the exemption applied and dismissed the suit and the court of appeals affirmed the decision.

ISSUE: Does an offer of stock by a company to a limited number of its employees automatically qualify for the exemption for transactions not involving any public offering?

HOLDING AND DECISION: (Clark, J.) No. The Securities Act does not define what is a private offering and what is a public offering. It is clear that an offer need not be open to the whole world to qualify as a public offering. If Ralston Purina (D) had made the stock offer to all of its employees, it would have been a public offering. The court looked at the intent of the Securities Act, which is to protect investors by promoting full disclosure of information thought to be necessary for informed investment decisions. When the Act grants an exemption, the class of people involved were not considered as needing the disclosure that the Act normally requires. Therefore, when an offering is made to people who can fend for themselves, the transaction is considered to be one not involving a public offering. Most of the employees purchasing the stock from Ralston Purina (D) were not in a position to know or have access to the kind of information which registration under the Act would disclose, and, therefore, were in need of the protection of the Act. Stock offers made to employees may qualify for the exemption if the employees are executive personnel who, because of their position, have access to the same kind of information that the Act would make available in the form of a registration statement. Absent such a showing of special circumstances, employees are just as much members of the investing public as any of their neighbors in the community. The burden of proof is on the issuer of the stock, who is claiming an exemption to show that he qualifies for the exemption. Also, since the right to an exemption depends on the knowledge of the offerees, the issuer's motives are irrelevant. It didn't matter that Ralston Purina's (D) motives may have been good, because they didn't show that their employees had the requisite information. Therefore, judgment reversed.

Continued on next page.

EDITOR'S ANALYSIS: The exemption discussed above is now found in § 4(2) instead of § 4(1). This case is considered to be the leading case in this area. The test established in this case is still used in determining whether an offering qualifies for the non-public offering exemption of § 4(2). Some of the factors used in determining whether the offerees have sufficient access to information concerning the stock is the number of offerees, the size of the offering, the relationship of the offerees, the manner of the solicitation of the offerees, and the amount of investment experience of the offerees.

[For more information on Federal Securities, § 4, see Casenote Law Outline on Corporations, Chapter 5, § III, Federal Securities Act, §§ 3 and 4.]

QUICKNOTES

BLUE SKY LAW - State law regulating the sale of securities in order to protect investors from fraudulent companies and/or offerings.

SECURITIES EXCHANGE ACT § 4(2) - Exempts transactions by an issuer not involving any public offering from registration requirements.

NOTES:

ESCOTT v. BARCHRIS CONSTR. CORP.
Debenture purchaser (P) v. Issuer (D)
283 F.Supp. 643 (S.D. N.Y. 1968).

NATURE OF CASE: Action under § 11 of the Securities Act of 1933 to recover damages for the filing of a registration statement with material omissions and false statements.

FACT SUMMARY: Escott (P), a purchaser of BarChris (D) debentures, brought a suit for damages claiming that its registration statement had material omissions and false statements.

CONCISE RULE OF LAW: In a suit to recover damages under § 11 of the Securities Act of 1933 for the filing of a registration statement with material omissions and false statements, defendants other than the issuer can avoid liability by proving a "due diligence" defense.

FACTS: On behalf of himself and all other purchasers of BarChris (D) debentures, Escott (P) brought suit under § 11 of the Securities Act of 1933 to recover damages for the alleged filing of a registration statement with material omissions and false statements. The defendants included the underwriters, BarChris's (D) auditors, and those persons who signed the registration statement. In addition to simply denying the registration statement was false, the defendants each claimed to have individually exercised "due diligence" in connection with the registration statement so as to be free from liability under the defense permitted in § 11.

ISSUE: Does § 11 of the Securities Act of 1933 provide a "due diligence" defense to defendants, other than the issuer, who are sued for damages in connection with the filing of a registration statement with material omissions and false statements?

HOLDING AND DECISION: (McLean, J.) Yes. When suit is brought under § 11 of the Securities Act of 1933 to recover damages for the filing of a registration statement with material omissions and false statements, any defendant other than the issuer can avoid liability by proving that he acted with "due diligence" in relation to the statement. A non-expert defendant is liable for material misstatements or omissions in these parts of the statement not based on experts' reports (the "non-expertised" portions) absent proof that he made a reasonable investigation as a result of which he had reasonable ground to believe and did believe that the registration statement was true and that no material fact was omitted. As to the non-expertised portions of the statement, a non-expert defendant can avoid liability only by proving that he had no reasonable ground to believe, and did not believe, there were any untrue statements or material omissions. A director must use the reasonable care to investigate the facts which a prudent man would employ in the management of his own property. In this case, all of the inside directors and officers have failed to prove they acted with "due diligence" as to either the non-expertised portions or the expert portions of the registration statement. As the outside directors, their "due diligence" defense failed with regard to the non-expertised portions because they failed to familiarize themselves with the registration statement and to make at least some inquiry into its major points. However, as to the expert portions of the statement, wherein the outside directors relied on audited figures, the "due diligence" defense rises to preclude liability. It was proven that the outside directors relied on the expertise of the auditors and their confidence in them. Under the circumstances, this constituted "due diligence." As to the underwriters, a "reasonable investigation" by them must be construed to require more effort on their part than the mere accurate reporting in the prospectus of "data presented" to them by the company. The underwriters must make some reasonable attempt to verify the data submitted to them, which simply was not done in this case. Underwriters may not rely solely on the company's officers or on the company's counsel because a prudent man in the management of his own property would not rely on them, as that is the applicable standard. In this case, however, the underwriter did act with "due diligence" in relying on the expertise of the auditors as to the 1960 audited figures, and liability as to that expert portion of the statement is thus precluded. Turning to the expert defendant, namely the auditors, such a defendant is liable only for material misstatements or omissions in those parts of the registration statement based on his reports. Liability is precluded, however, where he can prove that a reasonable investigation gave him reasonable ground to believe that part of the registration statement made upon his authority as an expert contained no material misstatements or omissions. Here, the auditors simply failed to make a reasonable investigation to ascertain the truth of the facts upon which they developed the statements they made in the registration statement. Thus, the auditors have failed to establish a "due diligence" defense.

EDITOR'S ANALYSIS: Section 11 makes the issuer strictly liable for material misstatements or omissions in the registration statement, meaning he cannot utilize a "due diligence" defense. However, he and every other defendant is entitled to offer proof that some portion or all of the depreciation in value of the securities that resulted in the plaintiff's loss was due to something other than the material misstatements or omissions for which he is liable. If he is successful, he is not liable for that part of the plaintiff's loss attributable to some other cause. A further cap on damages exists in that the plaintiff has an upper limit on recovery equal to the price at which the security was originally offered to the public.

Continued on next page.

[For more information on Federal Securities Act, § 11, see Casenote Law Outline on Corporations, Chapter 5, § IV, Federal Securities Act, §§ 11, 12 and 17.]

QUICKNOTES

DEBENTURES - Long-term unsecured debt securities issued by a corporation.

SECURITIES ACT § 11 - Prohibits registration statements with false information or material emissions.

MATERIALITY - Importance; the degree of relevance or necessity to the particular matter.

DUE DILIGENCE - The standard of care as would be taken by a reasonable person in accordance with the attendant facts and circumstances.

NOTES:

GLOSSARY
COMMON LATIN WORDS AND PHRASES ENCOUNTERED IN THE LAW

A FORTIORI: Because one fact exists or has been proven, therefore a second fact that is related to the first fact must also exist.

A PRIORI: From the cause to the effect. A term of logic used to denote that when one generally accepted truth is shown to be a cause, another particular effect must necessarily follow.

AB INITIO: From the beginning; a condition which has existed throughout, as in a marriage which was void ab initio.

ACTUS REUS: The wrongful act; in criminal law, such action sufficient to trigger criminal liability.

AD VALOREM: According to value; an ad valorem tax is imposed upon an item located within the taxing jurisdiction calculated by the value of such item.

AMICUS CURIAE: Friend of the court. Its most common usage takes the form of an amicus curiae brief, filed by a person who is not a party to an action but is nonetheless allowed to offer an argument supporting his legal interests.

ARGUENDO: In arguing. A statement, possibly hypothetical, made for the purpose of argument, is one made arguendo.

BILL QUIA TIMET: A bill to quiet title (establish ownership) to real property.

BONA FIDE: True, honest, or genuine. May refer to a person's legal position based on good faith or lacking notice of fraud (such as a bona fide purchaser for value) or to the authenticity of a particular document (such as a bona fide last will and testament).

CAUSA MORTIS: With approaching death in mind. A gift causa mortis is a gift given by a party who feels certain that death is imminent.

CAVEAT EMPTOR: Let the buyer beware. This maxim is reflected in the rule of law that a buyer purchases at his own risk because it is his responsibility to examine, judge, test, and otherwise inspect what he is buying.

CERTIORARI: A writ of review. Petitions for review of a case by the United States Supreme Court are most often done by means of a writ of certiorari.

CONTRA: On the other hand. Opposite. Contrary to.

CORAM NOBIS: Before us; writs of error directed to the court that originally rendered the judgment.

CORAM VOBIS: Before you; writs of error directed by an appellate court to a lower court to correct a factual error.

CORPUS DELICTI: The body of the crime; the requisite elements of a crime amounting to objective proof that a crime has been committed.

CUM TESTAMENTO ANNEXO, ADMINISTRATOR (ADMINISTRATOR C.T.A.): With will annexed; an administrator c.t.a. settles an estate pursuant to a will in which he is not appointed.

DE BONIS NON, ADMINISTRATOR (ADMINISTRATOR D.B.N.): Of goods not administered; an administrator d.b.n. settles a partially settled estate.

DE FACTO: In fact; in reality; actually. Existing in fact but not officially approved or engendered.

DE JURE: By right; lawful. Describes a condition that is legitimate "as a matter of law," in contrast to the term "de facto," which connotes something existing in fact but not legally sanctioned or authorized. For example, de facto segregation refers to segregation brought about by housing patterns, etc., whereas de jure segregation refers to segregation created by law.

DE MINIMUS: Of minimal importance; insignificant; a trifle; not worth bothering about.

DE NOVO: Anew; a second time; afresh. A trial de novo is a new trial held at the appellate level as if the case originated there and the trial at a lower level had not taken place.

DICTA: Generally used as an abbreviated form of obiter dicta, a term describing those portions of a judicial opinion incidental or not necessary to resolution of the specific question before the court. Such nonessential statements and remarks are not considered to be binding precedent.

DUCES TECUM: Refers to a particular type of writ or subpoena requesting a party or organization to produce certain documents in their possession.

EN BANC: Full bench. Where a court sits with all justices present rather than the usual quorum.

EX PARTE: For one side or one party only. An ex parte proceeding is one undertaken for the benefit of only one party, without notice to, or an appearance by, an adverse party.

EX POST FACTO: After the fact. An ex post facto law is a law that retroactively changes the consequences of a prior act.

EX REL.: Abbreviated form of the term ex relatione, meaning, upon relation or information. When the state brings an action in which it has no interest against an individual at the instigation of one who has a private interest in the matter.

FORUM NON CONVENIENS: Inconvenient forum. Although a court may have jurisdiction over the case, the action should be tried in a more conveniently located court, one to which parties and witnesses may more easily travel, for example.

GUARDIAN AD LITEM: A guardian of an infant as to litigation, appointed to represent the infant and pursue his/her rights.

HABEAS CORPUS: You have the body. The modern writ of habeas corpus is a writ directing that a person (body) being detained (such as a prisoner) be brought before the court so that the legality of his detention can be judicially ascertained.

IN CAMERA: In private, in chambers. When a hearing is held before a judge in his chambers or when all spectators are excluded from the courtroom.

IN FORMA PAUPERIS: In the manner of a pauper. A party who proceeds in forma pauperis because of his poverty is one who is allowed to bring suit without liability for costs.

INFRA: Below, under. A word referring the reader to a later part of a book. (The opposite of supra.)

IN LOCO PARENTIS: In the place of a parent.

IN PARI DELICTO: Equally wrong; a court of equity will not grant requested relief to an applicant who is in pari delicto, or as much at fault in the transactions giving rise to the controversy as is the opponent of the applicant.

IN PARI MATERIA: On like subject matter or upon the same matter. Statutes relating to the same person or things are said to be in pari materia. It is a general rule of statutory construction that such statutes should be construed together, i.e., looked at as if they together constituted one law.

IN PERSONAM: Against the person. Jurisdiction over the person of an individual.

IN RE: In the matter of. Used to designate a proceeding involving an estate or other property.

IN REM: A term that signifies an action against the res, or thing. An action in rem is basically one that is taken directly against property, as distinguished from an action in personam, i.e., against the person.

INTER ALIA: Among other things. Used to show that the whole of a statement, pleading, list, statute, etc., has not been set forth in its entirety.

INTER PARTES: Between the parties. May refer to contracts, conveyances or other transactions having legal significance.

INTER VIVOS: Between the living. An inter vivos gift is a gift made by a living grantor, as distinguished from bequests contained in a will, which pass upon the death of the testator.

IPSO FACTO: By the mere fact itself.

JUS: Law or the entire body of law.

LEX LOCI: The law of the place; the notion that the rights of parties to a legal proceeding are governed by the law of the place where those rights arose.

MALUM IN SE: Evil or wrong in and of itself; inherently wrong. This term describes an act that is wrong by its very nature, as opposed to one which would not be wrong but for the fact that there is a specific legal prohibition against it (malum prohibitum).

MALUM PROHIBITUM: Wrong because prohibited, but not inherently evil. Used to describe something that is wrong because it is expressly forbidden by law but that is not in and of itself evil, e.g., speeding.

MANDAMUS: We command. A writ directing an official to take a certain action.

MENS REA: A guilty mind; a criminal intent. A term used to signify the mental state that accompanies a crime or other prohibited act. Some crimes require only a general mens rea (general intent to do the prohibited act), but others, like assault with intent to murder, require the existence of a specific mens rea.

MODUS OPERANDI: Method of operating; generally refers to the manner or style of a criminal in committing crimes, admissible in appropriate cases as evidence of the identity of a defendant.

NEXUS: A connection to.

NISI PRIUS: A court of first impression. A nisi prius court is one where issues of fact are tried before a judge or jury.

N.O.V. (NON OBSTANTE VEREDICTO): Notwithstanding the verdict. A judgment n.o.v. is a judgment given in favor of one party despite the fact that a verdict was returned in favor of the other party, the justification being that the verdict either had no reasonable support in fact or was contrary to law.

NUNC PRO TUNC: Now for then. This phrase refers to actions that may be taken and will then have full retroactive effect.

PENDENTE LITE: Pending the suit; pending litigation underway.

PER CAPITA: By head; beneficiaries of an estate, if they take in equal shares, take per capita.

PER CURIAM: By the court; signifies an opinion ostensibly written "by the whole court" and with no identified author.

PER SE: By itself, in itself; inherently.

PER STIRPES: By representation. Used primarily in the law of wills to describe the method of distribution where a person, generally because of death, is unable to take that which is left to him by the will of another, and therefore his heirs divide such property between them rather than take under the will individually.

PRIMA FACIE: On its face, at first sight. A prima facie case is one that is sufficient on its face, meaning that the evidence supporting it is adequate to establish the case until contradicted or overcome by other evidence.

PRO TANTO: For so much; as far as it goes. Often used in eminent domain cases when a property owner receives partial payment for his land without prejudice to his right to bring suit for the full amount he claims his land to be worth.

QUANTUM MERUIT: As much as he deserves. Refers to recovery based on the doctrine of unjust enrichment in those cases in which a party has rendered valuable services or furnished materials that were accepted and enjoyed by another under circumstances that would reasonably notify the recipient that the rendering party expected to be paid. In essence, the law implies a contract to pay the reasonable value of the services or materials furnished.

QUASI: Almost like; as if; nearly. This term is essentially used to signify that one subject or thing is almost analogous to another but that material differences between them do exist. For example, a quasi-criminal proceeding is one that is not strictly criminal but shares enough of the same characteristics to require some of the same safeguards (e.g., procedural due process must be followed in a parol hearing).

QUID PRO QUO: Something for something. In contract law, the consideration, something of value, passed between the parties to render the contract binding.

RES GESTAE: Things done; in evidence law, this principle justifies the admission of a statement that would otherwise be hearsay when it is made so closely to the event in question as to be said to be a part of it, or with such spontaneity as not to have the possibility of falsehood.

RES IPSA LOQUITUR: The thing speaks for itself. This doctrine gives rise to a rebuttable presumption of negligence when the instrumentality causing the injury was within the exclusive control of the defendant, and the injury was one that does not normally occur unless a person has been negligent.

RES JUDICATA: A matter adjudged. Doctrine which provides that once a court of competent jurisdiction has rendered a final judgment or decree on the merits, that judgment or decree is conclusive upon the parties to the case and prevents them from engaging in any other litigation on the points and issues determined therein.

RESPONDEAT SUPERIOR: Let the master reply. This doctrine holds the master liable for the wrongful acts of his servant (or the principal for his agent) in those cases in which the servant (or agent) was acting within the scope of his authority at the time of the injury.

STARE DECISIS: To stand by or adhere to that which has been decided. The common law doctrine of stare decisis attempts to give security and certainty to the law by following the policy that once a principle of law as applicable to a certain set of facts has been set forth in a decision, it forms a precedent which will subsequently be followed, even though a different decision might be made were it the first time the question had arisen. Of course, stare decisis is not an inviolable principle and is departed from in instances where there is good cause (e.g., considerations of public policy led the Supreme Court to disregard prior decisions sanctioning segregation).

SUPRA: Above. A word referring a reader to an earlier part of a book.

ULTRA VIRES: Beyond the power. This phrase is most commonly used to refer to actions taken by a corporation that are beyond the power or legal authority of the corporation.

ADDENDUM OF FRENCH DERIVATIVES

IN PAIS: Not pursuant to legal proceedings.

CHATTEL: Tangible personal property.

CY PRES: Doctrine permitting courts to apply trust funds to purposes not expressed in the trust but necessary to carry out the settlor's intent.

PER AUTRE VIE: For another's life; in property law, an estate may be granted that will terminate upon the death of someone other than the grantee.

PROFIT A PRENDRE: A license to remove minerals or other produce from land.

VOIR DIRE: Process of questioning jurors as to their predispositions about the case or parties to a proceeding in order to identify those jurors displaying bias or prejudice.

REV 1-95

CASENOTE LEGAL BRIEFS